MATRICENTRIC

Theory, Activism, Practice

Andrea O'Reilly

DEMETER

Matricentric Feminism
Theory, Activism, Practice
Andrea O'Reilly

Copyright © 2021 Demeter Press

Individual copyright to their work is retained by the authors. All rights reserved. No part of this book may be reproduced or transmitted in any form by any means without permission in writing from the publisher.

Demeter Press
140 Holland Street West
P. O. Box 13022
Bradford, ON L3Z 2Y5
Tel: (905) 775-9089
Email: info@demeterpress.org
Website: www.demeterpress.org

Demeter Press logo based on the sculpture "Demeter" by Maria-Luise Bodirsky www.keramik-atelier.bodirsky.de

First edition published in 2016
This second edition published 2021

Printed and Bound in Canada

Front cover image: "A Gem in a Sea of Fire", Stephanie Jonsson.
Typesetting: Michelle Pirovich

Library and Archives Canada Cataloguing in Publication
Title: Matricentric feminism : theory, activism, practice / by Andrea O'Reilly.
Names: O'Reilly, Andrea, 1961- author.
Description: 2nd edition. | Includes bibliographical references.
Identifiers: Canadiana 2021015280X | ISBN 9781772583762 (softcover)
Subjects: LCSH: Feminist theory. | LCSH: Feminism. | LCSH: Mothers. | LCSH: Motherhood.
Classification: LCC HQ1190 .O74 2021 | DDC 305.4201,Äîdc23

For Terry Conlin,
My most avid supporter, my toughest critic, my closest friend,
and my partner in life.

Contents

Acknowledgements
7

Preface
Matricentric Feminism: Beyond Gender and towards
Resistant and Inclusive Mothering
Andrea O'Reilly
9

Foreword
Matricentric Feminism is a Gift to the World
Petra Bueskens
35

Introduction
41

Chapter One
Matricentric Feminism as Scholarship:
Maternal Theory
49

Chapter Two
Matricentric Feminism as Activism:
The Twenty-First-Century Motherhood Movement
135

Chapter Three
Matricentric Feminism as Practice:
Feminist Mothering
165

Chapter Four
Matricentric Feminism and its Relationship
to Academic Feminism
213

Works Cited
251

Appendices
267

About the Author
283

About the Cover Artist
285

Acknowledgements

I opened the acknowledgements to my book *Toni Morrison and Motherhood: A Politics of the Heart* (2004) citing a quotation from Morrison's *Song of Solomon*. The narrator, commenting upon the importance of othermothering, says this about Hagar Dead: "She needed what most colored girls needed: a chorus of mamas, grandmamas, aunts, cousins, sisters, neighbors, Sunday school teachers, best girlfriends, and what all to give her the strength life demanded of her—and the humor with which to live it" (311). I believe that scholars, likewise, need a "chorus of mamas" to think and write well. Fortunately, I have been blessed with a symphony in my life. Over the past twenty-five years as I have thought and written about mothers, mothering, and feminism, my chorus of mamas bestowed upon me the strength a scholarly life demands and the humour with which to live it.

I am deeply grateful to the late Sara Ruddick for giving us a vision of empowered mothering in her book *Maternal Thinking,* and for championing me as I struggled to create my own. Thank you to the members of the Motherhood Initiative for Research and Community Involvement (MIRCI), in particular Petra Bueskens, Rebecca Bromwich, Deborah Byrd, Regina Edmonds, Linda Ennis, May Friedman, Jenny Jones, Linda Hunter, Laure Kruk, Memee Lavell-Harvard, Caroline McDonald-Harker, Lynn O'Brien Hallstein, Liz Podnieks, and Marie Porter. My thinking on mothering was enhanced and sustained by this wonderful community of scholars. Thank you as well to my graduate students whose scholarship has enriched my own; in particular Vanessa Reimer, Gary Lee Pelletier, Melinda Vandenbeld Giles, Sarah Sahagian, Florence Pasche Guignard, Terri Hawkes, Paula John, Kaley Ames, Lisa Sandlos and Maria Collier de Medonca. I am deeply indebted to Nicole Doro for her proficient proofreading under impossible deadlines. A huge thank you to Angie Deveau for her brilliant and tenacious research on the place of motherhood scholarship in academic feminism and to Lisa Brouckxon for her beautiful art on the book's cover. Special thanks to Petra Bueskens for her careful reading of the manuscript and for writing the splendid Foreword. And deepest thanks to Jesse O'Reilly-Conlin who, through his accomplished copy-editing, not only created order from chaos but did so with good cheer and generous support.

Deepest appreciation to Stephanie Jonsson for her stunning artwork for the book's cover and to Fiona Green for her illuminating review of the preface and our smart email/phone conversations. Thanks as always to my son Jesse for once again doing his magic with copy-editing, and to my daughter Casey for listening as I worked through the hard questions of inclusion without exclusion and for showing me the forest within the trees. Deep gratitude as well to Demeter's type setter and designer Michelle Pirovich who once again created order from the chaos and to Jena Woodhouse for her impeccable proofing of the manuscript.

My deepest gratitude goes to my children Casey, Erin and Jesse, and to my spouse Terry Conlin. Thank you, to paraphrase Emma Bombeck, "for loving me the most, when I deserved it the least."

Preface

Matricentric Feminism: Beyond Gender and towards Resistant and Inclusive Mothering

In this book, I seek to define matricentric feminism, examine its enactments in theory, activism, and practice, and then consider matricentric feminism in relation to feminist theory and women's studies, or what may be termed "academic feminism." Since the publication of the first edition of *Matricentric Feminism* in late 2016, numerous scholars, writers, and activists across diverse perspectives and disciplines have taken up matricentric feminism to explore topics as varied as literature, film, art, photography, public policy, politics, incarceration, critical disability, health, violence against women, and activism, to name but a few. Two journals have published special double issues on matricentric feminism: the Australian journal *Hecate* (2019) and *The Journal of the Motherhood Initiative* (2019). Indeed, a Google search of the term "matricentric feminism" reveals eleven thousand entries. This scholarship recognizes the need for a distinctive feminism for and about mothers, and it explores mothers' particular needs, experiences, and desires, which continue to be marginalized as compared to nonmothers. Moreover, this research, as Tatjana Takseva notes, takes up matricentric feminism's emphasis on "the performativity embedded in the maternal role to highlight the socially constructed nature of expectations and ideas associated with maternity and to reveal the often-neglected agency involved in taking on and performing the role of mother" (27). In this preface, I will focus on four central concerns of matricentric feminism: the specific political import and intent of racialized women's motherwork, the radical queering of empowered mothering, the real and prevalent oppressions of motherwork, and, finally, the foregrounding of mothers and mothering in feminism. This discussion takes up these concerns with attention to the use of the words "mothers" and "mothering" in matricentric feminism. Overall, I argue that matricentric feminism affords a gender-neutral understanding of motherwork in its positioning of mothering as a verb and allows for an appreciation of how mother-work is deeply gendered and how this may be challenged and changed through empowered mothering. Thus, matricentric feminism, I argue, moves beyond gender towards resistant and inclusive mothering.

Why Mothers and Mothering?

A central aim of matricentric feminism as theory, as discussed in chapter one of the book, is to examine and theorize normative motherhood. Where does it come from? And why? What are its defining features and demands? How does it work as a regulatory discourse and practice? The opening section of the book's first chapter surveys the emergence of motherhood as a normative and patriarchal institution and then considers how and why normative motherhood becomes the only legitimate discourse and practice of motherhood to oppress and regulate mothers and their mothering. I introduce here what I have termed the ten dictates of normative motherhood: essentialization, privatization, individualization, naturalization, normalization, idealization, biologicalization, expertization, intensification, and depoliticalization. Essentialization positions maternity as the basis of female identity, whereas privatization locates motherwork solely in the reproductive realm of the home. Similarly, individualization causes such mothering to be the work and responsibility of one person, and naturalization assumes that maternity is natural to women—that is, all women naturally know how to mother—and that the work of mothering is driven by instinct rather than intelligence and developed by habit rather than skill. In turn, normalization limits and restricts maternal identity and practice to one specific mode: the nuclear family. Wherein, the mother is a wife to a husband, and she assumes the role of the nurturer, and the husband assumes that of the provider. The expertization and intensification of motherhood—particularly as they are conveyed in what Sharon Hays has termed "intensive mothering" and what Susan Douglas and Meredith Michaels call "the new momism"—cause childrearing to be all consuming and expert driven. Idealization sets unattainable expectations of and for mothers, and depoliticalization characterizes child-rearing solely as a private and nonpolitical undertaking, with no social or political import. Finally, biologicalization, in its emphasis on blood ties, positions the cisgender birthmother as the "real" and authentic mother. Normative motherhood is only available to mothers who can enact and fulfill these ten dictates: mothers who cannot, or will not, do so because they are young, queer, single, racialized, trans, or nonbinary are defined and positioned as de facto bad mothers.

Non-normative mothers—whether they are defined and categorized as such by age, race, sexuality, or biology—can never be the so-called good mothers of normative motherhood. In the second part of the first chapter, I examine the maternal identities and practices of these mother outlaws and explore how they counter and correct as well as destabilize and disrupt normative motherhood. Each identity is positioned and discussed as a mode of empowered mothering that seeks to challenge and change normative motherhood through what I term the five A's of empowered mothering: agency, autonomy, authenticity, authority, and advocacy/activism. In this section of chapter one I consider the counter practices of feminist, Black, queer, and Indigenous mothers. With each, I continue to use the words "mothers" and "mothering" to describe resistant identities and practices. However, as I note in the introduction and emphasize throughout the book, the term "mother" refers to any individual who engages in motherwork; it is not limited to cisgender women but it includes anyone who takes upon the work of mothering as a central part of their life. Building upon Sara Ruddick's concept of maternal practice, matricentric feminism positions the word "mother" as a verb, as something one does—a practice. For Ruddick, as Sarah LaChance Adams notes, "it is the practice of mothering that makes one a mother, not a biological or social imperative [and] therefore, the title of 'mother' is not strictly limited to biological mothers, or even women" (727). She continues: "Maternal commitment is voluntary and conscious; it is not inevitable, nor is it dictated by nature" (727). Repositioning mother from a noun to a verb degenders mothering and divests care of biology to dislodge the gender essentialism that grounds and structures normative motherhood.

However, despite this degendering of mothering in matricentric feminism, some have argued that the term still excludes trans and nonbinary folks and have called for more inclusive language to replace the words "mothers" and "mothering" with "parents" and "parenting." Indeed, as Sarah Ratchford comments: "As a gender-nonconforming person, I feel left out of the parenting discussion. It's time we became more inclusive in our language." In the introduction to their forthcoming book *The Liminal Chrysalis: Imagining Reproduction and Parenting Futures beyond the Binary,* H. Kori Doty and A.J. Lowik argue that "Trans and non-binary people, of all identities and expressions, are framed as the exception, even as aberrational." With this preface of the second edition of *Matricentric Feminism,* I want to take up in these concerns to consider how to navigate and negotiate creating inclusive language while simultaneously recognizing that for many mothers and in particular contexts, mothering is a culturally and politically determined concept that still has significance and consequence. In this discussion, I argue that replacing the word "mothering" with "parenting" is particularly problematic for racialized women because it dilutes the specific political import and intention of their motherwork and denies the significance of maternal identity for reproductive justice. Furthermore, the word "parenting" does not effectively convey the radical queering of empowered mothering. Using the term "parents"—that is, conflating mothers with fathers—is often also disingenuous if not dangerous because it deflects, disguises, and denies the very real and prevalent gendered oppressions of motherwork. Moreover, switching to the term "parenting" makes mothering invisible, both as it is practiced and researched. However, as I make these arguments, I also recognize how problematic the terms "mothers" and "mothering" are for trans and nonbinary individuals. Overall, I seek to explore how to achieve inclusion without exclusion by positioning mothering as a verb while simultaneously acknowledging the gendered oppressions of motherwork. In the words of Ratchford: "I am here for women's stories being heard and centred. If anything, mothers should receive more care, love and attention. But I also want to see the same visibility and welcome extended to trans and gender-nonconforming parents. Almost all of the issues that affect mothers affect trans and non-binary parents, too."

"Deeply Political": The Specific Meanings and Practices of Racialized Women's Motherwork

Black motherhood, in the words of Dani McClain, is "deeply political" (4). In *We Live for the We: The Political Power of Black Motherhood*, McClain writes the following: "Our job as Black mothers is to keep pushing the liberation ball down the course. Our obligation is to leave the world better for [our children] and to ensure that they are equipped with the tools that they need to fight.... Black mothering is a political project, and our mission—should we choose to accept it—is nothing short of revolutionary" (4, 201). Chapter one of this book explores how the Black maternal practices of other/community mothering, social activism, and nurturance as resistance render Black mothering profoundly political and public in contrast to the dictates of normative motherhood discussed above. Patricia Hill Collins uses the term "motherwork" to refer to what is usually meant by nurturance, love, or mothering generally ("Shifting the Center"). Hill Collins's word choice is significant because it foregrounds mothering as labour and calls attention to the ways in which mothering is socially and politically motivated and experienced in African American culture. Her emphasis is on the ways in which the concerns of what she calls "racial ethnic mothers" differ from those in the dominant culture. She identifies the goals of "racial ethnic" mothers as the following: keeping the children born to you; supporting the physical survival of those children; teaching the children resistance and how to survive in a racist world; providing those children their racial-cultural history and identity; and practicing a social activism and communal mothering on behalf of all the community's children. Hill Collins argues that this construction of mothering as social activism empowers Black women because motherhood operates, in her words, as "a symbol of power" ("The Meaning of Motherhood" 51). "A substantial portion of Black women's status in African American communities," writes Hill Collins, "stems not only from their roles as mothers in their own families but from their contributions as community othermothers to Black community development as well" (51). As Wanda Thomas Bernard and Candace Bernard emphasize: "More than a personal act, Black motherhood is very political. Black mothers and grandmothers are considered the guardians of the generations [and] Black mothers have historically been charged with the responsibility of providing education, social, and political awareness, in addition to unconditional love, nurturance, socialization, and values to their children, and the children in their communities" (47). Black motherhood, as Nina Jenkins concludes, "is a site where [Black women] can develop a belief in their own empowerment [and] Black women can see motherhood as providing a base for self-actualization, for acquiring status in the Black community and as a catalyst for social activism" (206).

Moreover, as discussed in chapter one of *Matricentric Feminism*, mothers and motherhood are valued by and central to African American culture; mothering is what makes possible the physical and psychological wellbeing and empowerment of African American people and the larger African American culture. The focus of Black motherhood in both practice and thought is how to preserve, protect, and, more generally, empower Black children so that they may resist racist practices that seek to harm them and grow into adulthood whole and complete. African American mothering differs from the dominant model and serves to empower mothers because the nurturance of family is defined and experienced specifically as an act of resistance. Theorist bell hooks has observed that the Black family, or what she terms as the "homeplace," operates as a site of resistance and that African American culture has "long recognized the subversive value of homeplace and homeplace has always been central to the liberation struggle" (42). Like hooks, Hill Collins maintains that children learn at home how to identify and challenge racist practices, and it is at home that children learn about their heritage and community. In their motherwork and in their homeplace, Black mothers create empowering safe spaces for their children to immunize them from the harms of racist ideology. Black mothering, thus, differs radically from normative motherhood, which configures home as a politically neutral space and views nurturance as no more than the natural calling of mothers. Black mothers achieve power and worth precisely in and through their politically and socially determined motherwork—to quote Cecelie S. Berry, "Home is where the Revolution is."

Motherhood is likewise a site of empowerment and resistance for Indigenous mothers. Indigenous scholar Jennifer Brant argues that Indigenous cultures hold a matriarchal worldview, which holds women in high esteem and honours them as powerful for their ability to give life to the community both in a physical and spiritual sense (112). Indigenous scholars and activists Dawn Memee Lavell-Harvard and Jeanette

Corbiere Lavell emphasize the following: "The historical persistence of our cultural difference generation after generation (despite the best assimilative efforts of both Church and State) is a sign of our strength and our resistance. That we have historically and continually mothered in a way that is 'different' from the dominant culture, is not only empowering for our women, but is potentially empowering for all women" (3). Indeed, as explored by Indigenous scholar Kim Anderson, Indigenous women have maintained and revived their own distinct ideology of motherhood. "Through collectivism, spirituality, and the application of sovereignty," Anderson explains, "Native mothers have shaped empowered mothering experiences in spite of the capitalist, Christian, and colonial frameworks that have worked together to support patriarchal western motherhood in Native communities" (762). In contrast to the gendered spheres of patriarchy wherein women are assigned to the private, reproductive sphere and men to the public, productive realm—Indigenous economies "are not characterized by a public/private dichotomy, nor are they hierarchical or inherently oppressive to one gender.... [Rather] they were understood to be interdependent, equally valuable and flexible" (Anderson 762). And because, as Anderson goes on to explain, "these economies were upheld through kinship systems, mothers lived and worked in extended families, precluding the possibility of an isolated and subordinate mother as family servant" (763). Indeed, as Amber Kinser comments, "In Indigenous cultures, women's traditional roles have long been recognized and celebrated as powerful" (6). Moreover, as Anderson explains, family in Indigenous culture, "can be a site of resistance and renewal," (762) as with hooks's theory of homeplace. Lavell-Harvard and Corbiere Lavell emphasize that "For most members of the Aboriginal community, everyday survival is still dependent on extensive networks of family and friends who support and reinforce each other" (189). Indigenous ideologies of mothering "provide strategies of resistance, reclamation and recovery" and "show the resiliency of Indigenous women in their ability to hold on to and practice traditional customs despite colonial influences and the role that reclaiming those practices has in the healing and recovery of Indigenous families" (Anderson 762). Thus, similar to Black mothers, Indigenous mothers achieve power and worth precisely through their politically and socially valued motherwork.

In Indigenous culture, the maternal body is also often experienced and positioned as a site of resistance and empowerment. Indigenous scholar Renee Mazinegilzihigo-Kwe Bedard in her recent article "A Manifesto on the Sacredness of Anishinaabe Mothers' Breasts" emphasizes the importance of a mother's breast within the Anishinaabe cultural traditions and worldviews. In her article, she develops a theory and practice of empowered mothering for Indigenous women based on and specific to "the mother's breasts, which honours the breasts of women as sacred embodiments of female gifts bestowed on women" (109). She continues: "These are gifts of life giving through our womb and the gift to sustain life with our breasts" (109). Significantly, she includes with this statement the following endnote:

> I understand this language may appear to exclude those individuals who identify on or with the feminine gender spectrum in the LGBTQ2S community; however, the language I use embodies the cultural legacy of Anishinaabe women's bodies that can give birth and breastfeed. Furthermore, I also recognize that some women may not be able to conceive, give birth naturally, or breastfeed. Regardless of our physical differences or challenges with fertility as Anishinaabe women, we are still the descendants of Aki, and her gifts extend to a complex array of mothering practices that are not solely grounded in the physical ability to conceive, birth, or breastfeed. (119)

With resistance and empowerment achieved and enacted in both the cultural practices of mothering and the physical embodiment of the maternal, Indigenous mothers must claim and hold the language of mothers and mothering for their resistance and empowerment. Thus, for Indigenous and Black mothers, the words "parenting" and "parents" do not reflect their culturally specific mode of mothering and serve to erase the power and value these mothers attain in and through their maternal identities and practices.

I also argue that Indigenous and Black mothers must also assert and retain a maternal identity for reproductive justice. Reproductive justice, as Natalie Fixmer-Oraiz explains, "is widely understood to mean the right to determine whether, when, and with whom one creates a family in safety and in dignity" (513). She goes on to say that reproductive justice "centers on three values: the right *not* to have a child; the right to *have* a child; and the right to *parent* children in safe and healthy environments" (512). Black and Indigenous mothers have long been denied the right to have a child and to parent that child. "The histories of marginalized women," as Fixmer-Oraiz notes, "reveal institutionalized efforts to punish or deny motherhood to women who desire it: these same women are also more vulnerable to state refusal to ensure the social conditions and resources necessary for self-determination and autonomous decision making" (511). Brant elaborates: "Justified by deeply entrenched settler ideologies that deemed Indigenous women uncivilized and uncivilizing, legally sanctioned initiatives such as the Indian Act of 1876, the eugenics movement, the pass system, residential schools, and child welfare interventions directly impeded the birthing and parenting rights of Indigenous women" (112).

Dorothy Roberts's book *Killing the Black Body: Race, Reproduction, and the Meaning of Liberty* explores "the long experience of dehumanizing attempts to control Black women's reproductive lives" (11). She elaborates on the history of racism and reproductive freedom in the United States:

> This history—from slave masters' economic stake in bonded women's fertility to the racist strains of early birth control policy to sterilization abuse of Black women during the 1960s and 1970s to the current campaign to inject Norplant and Depo-Provera in the arms of Black teenagers and welfare mothers—paints a powerful picture of the link between race and reproductive freedom in America (11).

Moreover, in her memoir *I Am Not Your Baby Mother: What It's Like to Be a Black British Mother,* Candice Brathwaite cites a 2018 report from the United Kingdom which reveals that Black British women are five times more likely to die in childbirth than any other race and that Black babies have a 121 per cent increased risk of being stillborn (123, 125). The Center for Disease Control and Prevention in the United States (US) similarly reports that between 2007 and 2016, Black mothers died at a rate of 3.2 times that of white mothers, whereas the 2018 US National Center for Statistics shows that Black women died of maternal causes 2.5 times more often than white women (Chuck). And although the more recent report indicates a decrease in Black maternal morbidity, the report cautions that the focus should not be the exact numbers but rather "what is important is that Black women have a much higher maternal mortality rate than white women" (Chuck). These realities of past sterilization as well as higher maternal mortality rates for racialized women show that they often cannot even become mothers; moreover, the histories of slavery for Black women and residential schooling for Indigenous women, along with the disproportionate numbers of their children in foster care, mean that these mothers often cannot mother the children born to them.

To become and be a mother as a Black and Indigenous woman is, thus, a radical act of defiance and resistance, as it defies and disrupts the cultural denial and disparagement of racialized women's motherwork and motherlove. Commenting on the enslaved mother Sethe in her novel *Beloved*, Toni Morrison asserts as follows: "Sethe's claim is an unheard-of outrageous claim for a slave woman to make; for what Sethe is claiming is the right and responsibility to say something about what happens to [her children]" (qtd. in Danille Taylor-Guthrie 252) I suggest that similar to the character of Sethe, racialized women, in claiming the identity of mother, assert the rights and responsibilities accorded to white mothers: They demand that they, not others, will determine the fate of their children. Thus, for racialized women, the words "mother" and "mothering" must be retained and preserved; to replace them with "parents" and "parenting" erases the specific and radical political intent and import of racialized women's motherwork and disregards, if not discounts, how claiming and holding a maternal identity is a necessary act of survival and resistance for Black and Indigenous women. As Fiona Green comments, "The grounding of intersectionality and how it plays out in the lives of those bearing and rearing children is so crucial to acknowledging and accepting various and multiple experiences and ways of doing the work of raising children—including non-binary and trans—without excluding, erasing those BIPOC [Black, Indigenous, and people of colour]." Indeed, the challenge is to determine how to include the meanings and practices of parenting for trans and nonbinary folks without excluding those of racialized women.

Queering Motherhood: Enactments of Empowered Mothering

Earlier, I explained that I use the term "empowering mothering" in matricentric feminism because it is overwhelmingly women who are oppressed by normative motherhood and who engage in various strategies to challenge and change normative motherhood. In enacting empowered mothering, these outlaw mothers, I argue, queer motherhood. In her chapter "Queer Mothering and the Question of Normalcy," Margaret Gibson asks, "Who are queer mothers?":

> Are all queer mothers women? Or might 'queer mothers' also include intersex, transgender or genderqueer people—or even some cisgender (non-transgender) men? Can queer mothers be partnered and parenting with men? Could queer mothers include all mothers who have sexually stigmatized relationships, including those from polyamorous or kink communities? Or is queer mother a moniker reserved for women with non-heterosexual identities such as lesbian, bisexual or queer? To complicate things further, how do we categorize queer mothers who are not legally (or sometimes socially) recognized as their children's kin? And where do we put queer-identified women who parent but don't identify with the word "mother"? (347)

Such questions trouble the presumed gender, family, and sexual scripts of the dominant relations and make "mother" a contested and unstable social category. Indeed, queering, as Gibson explains in the introduction to her book *Queering Motherhood: Narrative and Theoretical Approaches*, "makes the things we otherwise take for granted suddenly unpredictable, uncooperative, and unexpected" (1). Thus, the concept of queering motherhood extends beyond the experiences of queer or trans parents—although they are central to this endeavour and start, in Gibson's words, "where any of the central gendered, sexual, relational, political and/or symbolic components of 'expected' motherhood are challenged" (6). To queer motherhood, "is to re-think, re-shape, re-establish notions and practices of [normative] motherhood" (12). To queer motherhood, thus, is to destabilize normative motherhood, particularly its ideological mandates of essentialization, normalization, naturalization, and biologicalization.

Black families in their practices of other/communal mothering and extended kin "challenge heteronormative ideas of family," and, thus, we must "name the specific ways that the queerness of family can benefit those involved" (McClain 60). Feminist mothers likewise queer mothering in their practices of coparenting and political activism as do lesbian mothers through same-sex parenting. Trans and nonbinary parents, as Doty and Lowik argue, challenge the

> constructedness of sex, on which the gender binary is built; as a challenge to the constructedness of compulsory heterosexuality, which is itself reliant on the sex/gender binaries; as a challenge to the transnormative assumptions which limit trans reproductive and parenting possibilities; as a challenge to the repronormative way that sexed bodies are affixed to gender identities are tethered to reproductive experiences are tied to parenting roles.

The authors also emphasize that trans and nonbinary parenting allow us to "imagine a future for reproduction and parenting beyond the binary." Each counter-practice, I argue, resists normative motherhood.

What I am suggesting here is that the social location of the mother or parent determines what strategy they will use in their resistance to normative motherhood; their modes of resistances will never be complete or include all mothers, nor can they. Young mothers may challenge the agism of normative motherhood, which limits the age parameters of when a woman should become a mother, whereas feminist mothers may insist upon the political dimension in their childrearing and through public activism. Racialized mothers may resist normative family configurations through communal-othermothering, fictive kin, and extended families, whereas queer mothers may do so through comothering or nonconforming gender identities and relationships. Ultimately, the strategies chosen by any marginalized group of mothers and parents—whether they be Indigenous, trans, young, or racialized—need to be acknowledged, allowed, and respected while remembering their inherent limitations for other marginalized mothers. I also argue that they all queer motherhood and, in so doing, show that not all parents are women or that there is one right or correct way to create family. Queering motherhood means as well that the desire and ability to mother is not innate to one sex and that kinship is not only defined by blood. Queering motherhood, thus, makes possible the very identities and practices needed for empowered modes of mothering—a multitude of maternal identities, diverse family formations, and a variety of motherhood practices. To queer motherhood is, thus, to empower mothers and parents.

Gendered Oppressions of Motherwork

As we must retain the words "mothers" and "mothering" to respect the specific political import and intent of racialized women's motherwork and to acknowledge the diverse resistant practices that queer normative motherhood, we must also do so to emphasize the lived gendered oppressions of motherwork. To conflate mothers with fathers in the word "parents" disguises, deflects, and denies how carework is emphatically and unequivocally gendered in patriarchal societies. Michelle Hughes Miller elaborates:

> Neutral language is often used to erase gendered, racialized, classed differences among individuals. The goal is often purportedly equality or inclusion, but that is rarely the outcome we see. Instead, that erasure of specificity is important and dangerous. In the case of the use of parenting versus mothering, while the actions of mothering could be performed by anyone (Ruddick), they are overwhelmingly performed by women. Parenting and caregiving as neutral concepts both presume that anyone **can** do and everyone **does** do these tasks, when data are clear: everyone does not do these tasks, and certainly not to the extent that those who identify as women do. Thus, the problem with neutral language is its negation of the motherwork that women actually engage in, often to the detriment of their other labor, such as paid work, and their leisure time, and sometimes their physical and mental well-being.

Indeed, fathers are not oppressed by an institution of fatherhood as mothers are by the institution of motherhood.

In contemporary patriarchal culture, normative motherhood defines mothering as natural to women and essential to their being, positions mothers as the central caregivers of their biological children, and assumes that children require full-time mothering. Good mothers are nurturing, altruistic, patient, devoted, loving, and selfless; they always put the needs of their children before their own and are available to them whenever needed. And should mothers work outside the home, their children rather than their employment should be at the centre of their life. Good mothers are the primary caregivers of their children, and the care potentially provided by others is viewed as inferior and deficient. Feminist scholars rightly argue that normative motherhood is disempowering if not oppressive for a multitude of reasons, including the individualization and devaluation of motherwork, the endless tasks of privatized mothering, the incompatibility of wage work and motherwork, and the impossible standards of idealized motherhood. Moreover, all statistics and studies confirm that mothers do the bulk of motherwork and often, as Hughes Miller notes above, to the detriment of their employment, leisure, and wellbeing. Hence, it is mothers not fathers who are restrained and regulated by normative discourses and practices of care labour. To imply otherwise through the term "parents" is not only disingenuous and specious but potentially injurious.

In fall 2020, I was asked to review an article on academic parents that aimed to understand the complexity of academic work and parenthood and contribute to the conversation about the relations between them. The article explored how academics' experiences of being both a parent and an academic vary and that this variation relates to the different ways in which academics understand the meaning of each of these two roles and what they are trying to achieve within them. The article emphasized that achieving gender equality in higher education is "partly dependent on supporting academics' roles as *parents*." Although the article yielded original and astute insights into the meaning of parenting and academe for parent academics and did briefly attend to gender as one of the complexities, it still largely took up its analysis from a gender-neutral lens. In its revised form, the authors paid more attention to how gender is crucially a key variable in the meanings and experiences of being a parent academic. I mention this article here because it shows how through a gender-neutral lens the concept of parenting can lead to partial understanding and misguided recommendations. Academic parenting is not the same for mothers and fathers. It is mothers as parents who encounter the motherhood penalty: the systemic disadvantages in pay, perceived competence, and benefits relative to fathers.

Academic mothers also have more responsibility for childcare and family-life management. Joan Williams argues that mothers face a "maternal wall" because they are unable to meet these ideal-worker norms. In fact, Williams defines the maternal wall as "bias and stereotyping that affect mothers in particular as opposed to women in general" (97). The maternal wall manifests itself in both obvious and subtle ways, including the following: negative competence assumptions (e.g., once they become mothers, women are regarded as less committed to their careers); negative prescriptive stereotyping, both benevolent and hostile (e.g., it is assumed that mothers should be more feminine and devoted to family, lest they be viewed as too masculine); and attribution bias (e.g., the assumption that if mothers are away from or late to work, then, it is because of their children) (97). The maternal wall, Williams continues, is made up of three interconnected practices that compel mothers out of the workforce: "the executive schedule (extensive overtime), the marginalization of part-time workers, and the expectation that workers who are 'executive material' will relocate their families to take a better job" (70).

Studies of both academic women and mothers (Mason and Goulden, "Do Babies Matter?"; Mason and Goulden, "Do Babies Matter [Part II]?"; Wolfinger et al.) reveal that gender discrimination against academic mothers continues to be widespread in academe, primarily because of women's ongoing caregiving responsibilities. Indeed, even though more and more women are completing PhDs and are entering the academic pipeline, academic mothers do not have gender equity with male academics, including male academics who also have children. Mary Ann Mason and Marc Goulden, for example, argue that "Even though women make up nearly half of the PhD population, they are not advancing at the same rate as men to the upper ranks of the professoriate; many are dropping out of the race" ("Do Babies [Part II]" 11). The primary reason women are dropping out of the pipeline is because having children penalizes academic mothers far more than it does academic fathers; indeed, sometimes having children even benefits academic fathers. Mason and Goulden wryly argue that "'Married with children' is the success formula for men, but the opposite is true for women, for whom there is a serious 'baby gap'" ("Do Babies [Part II]" 11). More pointedly, in their earlier essay, Mason and Goulden also note the following: "There is a consistent and large gap in achieving tenure between women who have early babies and men who have early babies [having a baby prior to five years after a parent completes his or her PhD], and this gap is surprisingly uniform across the disciplines and across types of institutions" ("Do Babies Matter?" 24). They also highlight how having babies earlier seems to help men: "Men who have early babies achieve tenure at slightly higher rates than people who do not have early babies" (24). The opposite is the case for women who have babies earlier. Consequently, Mason and Goulden find that women with early babies often "do not get as far as ladder-rank jobs," and they often make family-work choices that "force them to leave the academy or put them into the second tier of faculty: the lecturers, adjuncts, and part-time faculty" ("Do Babies Matter" 24). Even though more women are earning their doctorates, Alice Fothergill and Kathryn Felty also note that "the structure of tenure-track jobs has not changed in any real way to accommodate them" (17). Perhaps this is why "the number of women in tenure-track jobs has declined: from 46 percent in 1977 to 32 percent in 1995" (Fothergill and Felty 17). Angela Simeone argues that the research on motherhood in academe confirms the following:

> Marriage and family, while having a positive effect on the [academic] careers of men, has a negative effect on the progress of women's careers. Married women, particularly with children are more likely to have dropped out of graduate school, have interrupted or abandoned their careers, be unemployed or employed in a job unrelated to their training, or to hold lower academic rank. (12)

The research is clear: Academic norms have harmful effects on academic women's careers once they become mothers. And, thus, to use the words "parents" and "parenting" dilutes and obscures the real discrimination mothers face.

The current pandemic has likewise revealed and confirmed the necessity of using the words "mothers" and "mothering" so that the very real and prevalent gendered affects of COVID-19 do not disappear through the concept of parenting. Recently Fiona Green and I published *Mothers, Mothering, and Covid-19: Dispatches from a Pandemic*. Arguably, we could have used "parents" and "parenting" in the title, but to do so would have been disingenuous and erroneous because it is mothers, not fathers, who have been most affected by the pandemic;

mothers, not fathers, have been forced to do the necessary and arduous carework to sustain their families and communities. Mothers, not fathers, do the bulk of domestic labour, childcare, and elder care. And with the implementation of social isolation and pandemic protocols, the burden of their carework has increased exponentially in both time and concern, as mothers are running households with little or no support, under close to impossible conditions, while also often engaged in wage labour. One Canadian study reports that men spent an average of thirty-three hours of caregiving per week before the pandemic and forty-six hours during the pandemic. Women spent an average of sixty-eight hours before the pandemic and ninety-five hours during it (Gregory). The pandemic has particularly compounded the "third shift"—the emotional and intellectual labour of motherwork. Such labour also mirrors what philosopher Sara Ruddick has termed "maternal thinking": the organizing, remembering, anticipating, worrying, and planning that mothers take on for their family. Moreover, with COVID-19, many mothers are working in what may be termed the "fourth shift"—that is, the homeschooling of their children. A *New York Times* survey found that 80 per cent of mothers said they were picking up most of the responsibility for homeschooling, whereas only 3 per cent of women said that men were doing more (Daniel). Indeed, as Sara Petersen notes in her July 2020 *YahooStyle,* article: "The burden of unpaid labor in the home has always fallen disproportionally on mothers, but the pandemic has shone a glaring neon light into a situation that has always been impossible." Despite the cataclysmic upheavals of the pandemic, one fact remains unchanged: Motherwork remains invisible, devalued, and taken for granted. Indeed, as Andrea Flynn observes: "The coronavirus has laid bare many divisions in our society. And, like any serious crisis does, it has elevated the extent to which structural sexism permeates our lives: impacting the gendered division of labor within the home and also shaping what is possible for women, and particularly mothers, in the public sphere." We conclude the introduction to the Mothers, Mothering and COVID-19 book writing: "Many feminist and social justice researchers and activists see the COVID-19 crisis as opening space for a coalition movement for workplace justice and for the re-evaluation of carework as an essential part of an economic agenda. This collection dispatches the maternal visions and voices for this necessary and long-overdue conversation on, and action towards, empowered social change" (29). However, I emphasize here that these necessary conversations and actions towards empowered social change are only possible with the words "mothers" and "mothering" as well as a matricentric focus, which recognizes and supports the crucial work mothers are doing as frontline workers to keep families functioning throughout this pandemic.

Foregrounding Mothers and Mothering in Feminism

Finally, I argue that as the words "parents" and "parent" disguise the real and prevalent gendered oppressions of carework, they also render invisible motherhood as it is experienced and studied. When words are eliminated, so too are the concepts they refer to. In chapter four of *Matricentric Feminism,* I explore matricentric feminism in relation to feminist theory and women's studies, or what may be termed "academic feminism." More specifically, this chapter argues that matricentric feminism has largely been ignored by feminist scholars and has yet to be incorporated into the field of academic feminism. As this field has grown and developed as a scholarly field, it has incorporated various theoretical models and diverse perspectives to represent the specific concerns and experiences of particular groups of women, such as global feminism, queer feminism, third-wave feminism, and womanism. In contrast, academic feminism has not recognized or embraced a feminism developed from and for the specific experiences and concerns of mothers, or what I have termed "matricentric feminism." The chapter considers both the disavowal of motherhood in twentieth-century academic feminism and the disappearance of motherhood in twenty-first-century academic feminism and then ruminates on possible reasons for the exclusion of matricentric feminism in academic feminism, including confusing mothering with motherhood, the conflation of matricentric feminism with maternalism and gender essentialism, and the cultural ascendancy of postmaternal thinking. Matricentric feminism, as noted above and emphasized throughout the book, understands motherhood to be socially and historically constructed by imperialist, white supremacist, and capitalist patriarchy; it positions mothering as a practice and not as a fixed, stable, and essentialist identity. Thus, as Fiona Green emphasizes: "To move forward to a decolonial and gender inclusive, non-biological essentialist way and understanding of the work (motherwork) of raising human beings, the complexities of people's identities and their relationship with colonial/imperialist, white supremacist, capitalist patriarchy and the carework necessary in rearing children are crucial." This is indeed the aim of matricentric feminism, as it challenges the assumption that maternity is natural to women—all women naturally know how to mother—and that the work of mothering is driven by instinct rather than intelligence and developed by habit rather than skill. Although matricentric feminism does hold a matrifocal perspective and insists that mothering does matter, it does not advance a maternalist argument or agenda.

However, matricentric feminism—in its focus on the gendered experience of mothering (and the related ones of pregnancy, childbirth, and breastfeeding)—does force us to address the thorny issue of gender differences. Feminist theory, with the notable exception of cultural-difference feminism, positions gender difference as central to, if not the cause of, women's oppression. Liberal feminists advocate what has been called "sameness feminism," wherein women become more like men. Radical-libertarian feminists promote androgyny, and poststructuralist feminists seek to destabilize and deconstruct gender difference altogether. Indeed, as Niamh Moore notes, "Challenging biological determinism and other essentialisms has been a crucial policy strategy for feminists" (qtd. in Stephens 141). Thus, because feminists are uncomfortable with anything that underscores gender differences and suggests essentialism (i.e., cisgender men are naturally this way, and cisgender women are naturally this way), motherhood becomes problematic, as it more than anything else marks binary gender differences. And because gender differences are seen as structuring and maintaining male dominance, many feminists seek to downplay and disavow anything that marks these differences—the main one, of course, being motherhood. For many feminists, to call attention to women's specific gendered subjectivity as a mother is to subscribe to an essentialist viewpoint—acknowledging and affirming what is seen as marking and maintaining gender differences and, hence, the oppression of women. As Julie Stephens writes in *Confronting Postmaternal Thinking*: "The primary focus of the second-wave feminist movement has been one long struggle against essentialism, whether this be biological, cultural or ideological. This makes any discussion linking women and care, or mothering and nurture, particularly troubling" (10). Consequently, as Stephens goes on to argue, "Any activism done in the name of the maternal will be unsettling, particularly for those who perceive feminism as primarily a struggle against essentialism" (141). Indeed, as Tatjana Takseva emphasizes, "Within the mainstream feminist paradigm, the absence of the maternal bespeaks the perspective that the feminist empowerment project is essentially incompatible with the social and personal entanglements arising out of the maternal role" (29).

I agree that gender is constructed in the West by colonial and imperialist white supremacist capitalist patriarchy—sex does not equal gender or as Simone de Beauvoir said, "one is not born a woman but made one"—and, thus, people cannot define themselves or limit their lives to what is socially constructed by gender. However, I likewise believe that feminists should not disavow motherhood or erase it through parenting language to facilitate this destabilizing of gender. I believe it is possible to simultaneously argue that both gender and motherhood are constructed and that motherhood matters and is often integral to a mother's sense of self and her experience of the world. In my view, the apprehension over gender differences, identities, and expressions is the elephant in the room of academic feminism; it has shut down necessary and needed conversations about important—and, yes, gendered—dimensions of women's lives: menstruation, pregnancy, childbirth, breastfeeding, and mothering. Some mothers are finding that they can no longer talk about their reproductive identities and experiences without being called essentialist. But maternal scholars do not reduce women's sense of self to motherhood, nor do they say that this is what makes a woman or that motherhood is more important than other variables that constitute the self. They say only that motherhood matters and that it is central and integral to understanding the lives of anyone who identifies as a mother. Indeed, while matricentric feminism does create a space for women to talk about and theorize mothering, as it is both embodied and practiced, it does not limit discussions of mothering to embodiment or to the maternal practices of cisgender women. Rather, the terms "mother" and "mothering" in matricentric feminism refer to any individual who engages in motherwork and includes anyone who takes upon the work of mothering as a central part of their life. However, without these terms, the concept of motherhood may be completely erased through the word "parenting." Indeed, as the research on both academic mothers and COVID-19 shows and confirms, mothers and mothering must be foregrounded to understand maternal oppressions and to reach appropriate responses.

Inclusion Without Exclusion

Nonetheless, I understand that words do matter and that many trans and nonbinary individuals regard the words "mothers" and "mothering" as exclusionary. So, the challenge is how do we include trans and nonbinary practices of parenting without excluding those of mothers. How can we use the terms "parenting" and "parents" without erasing the specific meanings of motherwork for racialized women, minimizing the radical queering of empowered mothering, deflecting the very real gendered oppressions of motherwork, and making invisible mothering both as it is practiced and researched? I suggest that in everyday conversations and circumstances, the words "parenting" and "parents" should be used as well as in in most legal, educational, and medical contexts. However, in the specific context of racialized women, empowered mothering, gendered resistance, and the oppressions of motherwork (as lived and studied), the words "mothers" and "mothering" must be retained. Gemma Bath argues the following: "Removing the entirety of gendered language is a long road because it's so entrenched. But creating a more inclusive, non-binary and respectful dialogue with what we *do* have available to us doesn't have to be." She continues: "There's always going to be a level of push back from those who don't think the way we speak should change. But we're always inventing new words: think 'clickbait,' 'selfies' and 'podcasts.'" Although I agree with Bath that we should be inventing new words for inclusivity, I also suggest that normative words can be reclaimed and reconstituted to become resistant and potentially inclusive. Words such as "queer," "slut," and "breeder" have been reclaimed and have become transgressive, and so too can the words "mothers" and "mothering." Matricentric feminism recuperates the word "mothering" by positioning it as a verb and divesting it of biology, thus making it not only resistant but inclusive. Speaking about inclusive language, Bath writes, "The more we see gender-neutral terms front and centre, the more they will become normalized." And I would add that that the more we position mothering as a transgressive verb, the more it will include all parents. And to borrow from Bath's words, that is why both strategies "are important because we have a responsibility in 2021 to make everyone in our society feel seen, heard and understood."

Conclusion

Through positioning mothering as a verb, matricentric feminism allows for gender neutrality, and in its understanding of maternal oppression and resistance, the term likewise provides needed gendered analyses. Matricentric feminism ultimately moves beyond gender. In its explicit and emphatic matrifocal perspective, matricentric feminism is concerned with anyone who identifies as a mother and/or practices mothering. In this, matricentric feminism is certainly a feminism for trans and nonbinary individuals who take up nongendered practices of mothering. Although matricentric feminism may not be of interest to nonmothers, this is not their feminism; it is for and about mothers. There are other feminisms for those who do not identify as mothers or practice mothering, whether they are cisgender, trans, or nonbinary. Even though matricentric feminism certainly invites all to use its theory, activism, and practice, in its focus on mothers and mothering, it does exclude those disinterested in mothering, but as I argue in this book, this exclusion is necessary, as mothers need a feminism of their own. Moving beyond gender, matricentric feminism delivers resistant and inclusive maternal identities and practices for all who seek empowered social change. As a result, matricentric feminism must be finally and fully recognized as necessary for, and integral to, feminist theory as well as its disciplines of gender and women's studies.

Works Cited

Anderson, Kim. "Giving Life to the People: An Indigenous Ideology of Motherhood." *Maternal Theory: Essential Readings*, edited by Andrea O'Reilly, Demeter Press, 2007, pp. 761-81.

Bath, Gemma. "An Australian University Has Offered New Words for 'Mother' and 'Father'; This Is Why It Matters." *MamaMia*, 16 Feb. 2021, www.mamamia.com.au/gender-neutral-terms-mother-father/. Accessed 20 Feb. 2021.

Bedard, Renee Mazinegilzihigo-Kwe. "A Manifesto on the Sacredness of Anishinaabe Mothers' Breasts." *Breasts Across Motherhood: Lived Experiences and Critical Examinations*, edited by Patricia Drew and Rossan Edwards, Demeter Press, 2020, pp. 109-22.

Bernard, Wanda Thomas, and Candace Bernard. "Passing the Torch: A Mother and Daughter Reflect on Their Experiences across

Generations." *Canadian Women's Studies Journal/cahier de la femme*, vol. 18, no. 2-3, 1998, pp. 46-50.

Berry, Cecelie S. "Home Is Where the Revolution Is." *Salon*, 1999, www.salon.com/1999/09/29/moms_at_home/. Accessed 10 Sept. 2016.

Brant, Jennifer. "Indigenous Mothering: Birthing the Nation from Resistance to Revolution." *Routledge Companion to Motherhood*, edited by Lynn Hallstein O'Brien, Andrea O'Reilly and Melinda Vandenbeld Giles, Routledge Press, 2019, pp. 11-121.

Brathwaite, Candice. *I Am Not Your Baby Mother: What's It Like to Be a Black British Mother*. Quercus Books, 2020.

Chuck, Elizabeth. "The U.S. Finally Has Better Maternal Mortality Data. Black Mothers Still Fare the Worst." *NBC News*, 20 Jan. 2020, www.nbcnews.com/health/womens-health/u-s-finally-has-better-maternal-mortality-data-black-mothers-n1125896. Accessed 18 Feb. 2021.

Daniel, Zoe. "How Coronavirus Has Changed the Roles in the Family Home." *ABC News*, 13 May 2020, www.abc.net.au/news/2020-05-13/coronavirus-has-changed-roles-in-family-home/12239542?fbclid=IwAR1PRqB8h_4M0XGbulzpGjUN5Zg89IXHavtHyRAC0trw4AVmckwG9DPyhVM. Accessed 5 June 2020.

Doty, H. Kori, and A. J. Lowik. *The Liminal Chrysalis: Imagining Reproduction and Parenting Futures Beyond the Binary*. Demeter Press, 2022.

Douglas, Susan J., and Meredith Michaels. *The Mommy Myth: The Idealization of Motherhood and How It Has Undermined Women*. Free Press, 2004

Fixmer-Oraiz, Natalie. "Motherhood and the Struggle for Reproductive Justice." *Routledge Companion to Motherhood*, edited by Lynn Hallstein O'Brien, Andrea O'Reilly and Melinda Vandenbeld Giles, Routledge Press, 2019, pp. 510-19.

Flynn, Andrea. "The 'All-Consuming' Emotional Labor Caused by Coronavirus—and Shouldered by Women." *Ms.*, 31 Mar. 2020, msmagazine.com/2020/03/31/op-ed-the-all-consuming-emotional-labor-caused-by-coronavirus-and-disproportionately-shouldered-by-women/. Accessed 5 June 2020.

Fothergill, Alice, and Kathryn Felty. "'Worked Very Hard and Slept Very Little:' Mothers on the Tenure Track in Academia." *Journal of* the *Association for Research on Mothering*, vol. 5, no. 2, 2003, pp. 7-19.

Gibson, Margaret, editor. *Queering Motherhood: Narrative and Theoretical Perspectives*. Demeter Press, 2014.

Gibson, Margaret. "Queer Mothering and the Question of Normalcy." *Mothers, Mothering, and Motherhood Across Cultural Difference*, edited by Andrea O'Reilly, Demeter Press, 2014, pp 269-284.

Greggory, Laurel. "Mothers Taking on 'Shocking' Number of Hours Caring for Children during Pandemic: Study." *Global News*, 20 Oct. 2020, globalnews.ca/news/7408226/mothers-hours-child-care-pandemic-study/. Accessed 4 Jan. 2021.

Green, Fiona. "Email correspondence." February 2021.

Hays, Sharon. *The Cultural Contradictions of Motherhood*. Yale University Press, 1996.

Hecate.45: 1&2 2019; Published 2020.

Hill Collins, Patricia. "Shifting the Center: Race, Class, and Feminist Theorizing about Motherhood." *Mothering: Ideology, Experience, and Agency*, edited by Evelyn Nakano Glenn et al., Routledge, 1994, pp. 45-65.

Hill Collins, Patricia. "The Meaning of Motherhood in Black Culture and Black Mother-Daughter Relationships." *Double Stitch: Black Women Write About Mothers and Daughters*, edited by Patricia Bell-Scott, et al., Harper Perennial, 1993, pp. 42-60.

hooks, bell. *Yearning: Race, Gender, and Cultural Politics*. South End, 1990.

Jenkins, Nina. "Black Women and the Meaning of Motherhood." *Redefining Motherhood: Changing Patterns and Identities*, edited by Sharon Abbey and Andrea O'Reilly, Second Story Press, 1998, pp. 201-213.

Journal of the Motherhood Initiative. 10; 1&2; 2019.

Kinser, Amber E, editor. *Mothering in the Third Wave*. Demeter Press, 2008.

LaChance, Sarah Adam. "Maternal Thinking." *The Encyclopedia of Motherhood*, edited by Andrea O'Reilly, Sage Press, 2010, pp. 726-727.

Lavell-Harvard, Dawn Memee, and Jeanette Corbiere Lavell, editors. *Until Our Hearts Are on the Ground: Aboriginal Mothering, Oppression, Resistance and Rebirth*. Demeter Press, 2006.

Mason, Mary Ann, and Marc Goulden. "Do Babies Matter?: The Effect of Family Formation on the Lifelong Careers of Academic Men and Women" *Academe*, vol. 88, no. 6, 2002, pp. 21-27.

Mason, Mary Ann, and Marc Goulden. "Do Babies Matter (Part II)?: Closing the Baby Gap." *Academe*, vol. 90, no. 6, 2004, pp. 10-15.

McClain, Dani. *We Live for the We: The Political Power of Black Motherhood.* Bold Type Books, 2019.

Miller Hughes, Michelle. "Email correspondence." February 2021.

O'Reilly, Andrea, and Fiona Green. *Mothers. Mothering, and COVID-19: Dispatches from a Pandemic.* Demeter Press, 2021.

Petersen, Sara. "After the Pandemic, We'll Finally Have to Address the Impossible State of Motherhood." *YahooStyle,* 24 June 2020, ca.style.yahoo.com/pandemic-ll-finally-address-impossible-193034205.html. Accessed 4 Jan. 2021.

Ratchford, Sarah. "The Way We Talk about Motherhood Is Deeply Alienating." *Today's Parent,* 2018, www.todaysparent.com/family/family-life/the-way-we-talk-about-motherhood-is-deeply-alienating/. Accessed 18 Feb. 2021.

Roberts, Dorothy. *Killing the Black Body: Race, Reproduction, and the Meaning of Liberty.* Pantheon Books, 1997.

Ruddick, Sara. *Maternal Thinking: Toward a Politics of Peace.* Beacon Press, 1989.

Stephens, Julie. *Confronting Postmaternal Thinking: Feminism, Memory, and Care.* Columbia University Press, 2011.

Takseva, Tatjana. "One Is Not Born but Rather Becomes a Mother: Claiming the Maternal in Women and Gender Studies." *Journal of the Motherhood Initiative*, vol. 10, no. 1-2, 2019, pp. 27-44.

Taylor-Guthrie, Danille. *Conversations with Toni Morrison.* Mississippi University Press, 1994.

Williams, Joan. *Unbending Gender: Why Family and Work Conflict and What to Do about It.* Oxford University Press, 2000.

Wolfinger, Nicholas, et al. "Alone in the Ivory Tower: How Birth Events Vary among Fast-Track Professionals." Paper presented at the *2008 Annual Meeting of the Population Association of America,* New Orleans, LA., 2008.

Foreword
Matricentric Feminism is a Gift to the World

Petra Bueskens

When I first met Andrea O'Reilly in 1999, she was not yet the famous professor of motherhood studies that she has become; she was an academic still struggling for tenure, mothering three children, working full time and publishing her first edited book. I saw her in a miniskirt by a vending machine with her characteristic bangled arms and had no sense that she was the professor I was here to meet. Over the course of that conference, we found deep common interests in our experience of becoming mothers in our early twenties and combining this with intensive graduate research. We also had a few too many wines and some adventures, which continue to animate our conversations to this day. Fast forward almost twenty years, and I am honoured to call her my friend, mentor, colleague, collaborator, and matricentric feminist conspirator.

Andrea's persona is the most curious and contagious mix of passionate politics with professorial acumen; she is of working-class origins but has "made it" in the male-stream academic system giving her a radical edge. This standpoint is enlarged by having to live and breathe the contradiction that is being a mother (of three) in academe. She has something of the 1970s feminist about her, something of the mum at the school gate and something of the literary professor. This combines to make her a force of nature and a fierce creator of matricentric feminist communities and spaces. O'Reilly is indefatigable with her journal, her association (its demise as arm and reinstatement as mirci), her press—the first feminist press devoted to the publication of books on motherhood, Demeter Press—her numerous conferences, publications, edited volumes, and last but not least, with her mentoring of matricentric feminist scholars and activists.

O'Reilly is one of those rare academics—rare under neoliberalism, and rare in disciplines like women's and gender studies, which are under-resourced and lack prestige—that she is not competing with anyone she meets above, below, or in parallel to her own career trajectory (which is itself defined by a much broader agenda than success in academe). She advances the careers of others by publishing graduate students—as she did me—and by supporting and promoting mother scholars, writers, artists, and activists. What O'Reilly is interested in is the creation of a *movement*; this enables her to hold together a multiplicity of diverse voices as is evidenced in this book, which is a veritable quilt of matricentric feminism.

Andrea has been a significant force in the creation of motherhood studies as an academic discipline and matricentric feminism as an intellectual and political force, and she does so in an uncharacteristically collectivist way. Many pay lip service to such an ethic, but Andrea puts it into practice in a way I have never quite seen before. This is because she is guided by her own matricentric ethic of care: the creation of a matricentric feminist community and culture. It is not an exaggeration to say this movement would not exist without her. Or, to put it another way, Andrea is at the centre of a movement that came together, as she recounts, at the cusp of the twenty-first century from key texts from the late second-wave feminism and onwards. In contrast to the women's movement more generally, O'Reilly insightfully points out that scholarship predates and underscores the development of the mothers' movement. In other words, the consciousness was raised, and then the groups were formed rather than the other way around.

In this book O'Reilly showcases this rich legacy—double entendre intended, given her strong foundations in Adrienne Rich's *Of Woman Born* (1976) and, in particular, her cardinal distinction between mother*hood* as institution and mother*ing* as practice. The legacy of Rich can be found in O'Reilly's *oeuvre* in many ways: her forensic analysis of the institution of motherhood; her dogged refusal to accept the strictures and oppressions of patriarchal motherhood; her critique of an essentialist conception of motherhood tying us to intensive and isolated self-sacrifice; and her commitment to intersectional perspectives. But it is perhaps best demonstrated in her commitment to identifying *empowered mothering* practices and politics.

Where Rich bequeathed the legacy of distinction, O'Reilly has picked up the gauntlet and fleshed out what it means to be an empowered mother—and there is a plethora of ways. Where Rich offered us one small, indeed whimsical biographical anecdote—referring to a summer holiday when her husband was away and she and her sons lived "as conspirators, outlaws from the institution of motherhood" —O'Reilly has made it her life's work to fill in the ellipses. What is an empowered mother? Let me count the ways: she is a mother with a community of allomothers or "other mothers"; she is a queer or lesbian mother; a feminist mother; a nonresident, a leaving or "revolving" mother (as I have explored in my own research); a single mother; a mother who integrates her maternal practice with her paid and/or creative work; and a mother who shares care, who works, or who does not work. For O'Reilly, as with Rich before her, empowered mothering can be mined from the archive of myth too. As she says, "[i]n patriarchal culture where there are so few examples, in either life or literature, of empowered mothering, Demeter's triumphant resistance serves as a powerful model."

An empowered mother is a category itself subject to critique insofar as there is not one single strategy that suffices over time or in different (sub)cultural contexts. The strategies that O'Reilly outlines are not available to all mothers as she says, nor are they strategies that we may necessarily want to practice—in the best interests of our child, family, community, or self. The point is through bringing together a rich tapestry of voices, O'Reilly opens the doors of possibility and through this, we can see the variegated landscapes of empowered mothering beyond the prevailing model of intensive motherhood or its polar opposite—the neoliberal model of self-sufficiency, which denies the centrality of care.

Importantly, different strategies may work at different times in our lives and in different social and cultural locales. Staying at home, for example, can be radical in a context that demands all women, including mothers of young dependent children, enter the paid labour force. On the other hand, extricating ourselves from the strictures of economic dependence in patriarchal marriages and providing for ourselves is also fundamentally empowering. More broadly, the inclusion of not just childless women but also mothers in senior office is critical to the reshaping of the world in socially just and sustainable terms. Working, not working, sharing, co-parenting, equality—may all be good at some stages but quite destructive or problematic at others.

We see this in prevailing mothering practices too. Most women wish to stay at home with newborn infants and those under a year (though not all are able to), whereas many begin to work again, albeit part-time, as their children get older. But even this varies with what mothers do and their socioeconomic location. As a writer, I started working again, albeit from home, when my last two babies were only weeks old. I kept writing while they slept. As a friend who is a nurse pointed out, this would not be possible for mothers like her who work outside the home. In this instance, paid leave is necessary and part of a matricentric feminist politics. For single mothers and mothers who wish to be at home, strong social welfare support and a universal basic income are essential to gender justice. For women with education and extant careers, funded childcare and flexible work are critical. For working-class mothers, both childcare and the campaign to raise wages, especially in female-dominated jobs (such as childcare), are imperative.

Whereas mothers of younger children need social support both to stay home and to work, mothers of older children often need support to undertake paid work, especially in the event of divorce. Again, however, some mothers of older children—think Ann Marie Slaughter's high-profile resignation from public office to be closer to her teenage son—seek to challenge the neoliberal culture of long work hours. Mothers of adult children face different issues again, as their accumulated wealth, including superannuation and home ownership, is typically far less than their male peers. This shows up for the increasing numbers of divorced women but is typically being concealed for those in intact marriages and/or high paying jobs (and often, of course, the two go together as privilege begets privilege). In many "advanced" capitalist nations like my own (Australia), older women are filling the ranks of the poor and homeless, primarily because they have been mothers. What an outrage that for years of dedicated service to society, older women are left in poverty and in a minority of cases, literally on the street. As we can see, empowered mothering and women's empowerment as mothers is a complex and varied landscape. Multiple differentiated strategies and perspectives are needed (and sometimes these are at cross purposes). This kaleidoscope of approaches makes mothering an art, a practice, and a politics that we must continually revise. As with our children, and indeed in unison with them, our mothering practices evolve and change and so must our maternal politics and our strategies for subversion. O'Reilly speaks to all these issues in her book and notes that *as a movement*, we do not need to choose between strategies—whether "strategic essentialist," liberal egalitarian, radical separatist, or an ethics of care—but to always keep a keen eye on context and social location and ask ourselves the relevance of any given strategy for the mothers at hand. The epistemic and political standpoint of all those mothering outside patriarchy, including in systems of race and class oppression, offers crucial resources for change. Indeed, *mothers offer a crucial standpoint* for social, political and economic change. Motherhood is an important category of analysis for understanding women's oppression.

Mothers are, O'Reilly contends, the unfinished business of feminism. Perhaps this is why there is still such ambivalence around the topic and why motherhood is so often conflated with "essentialism" and dismissed as the realm of the privileged. Sadly, as O'Reilly shows, such charges often come from within academic feminism itself. Could anything be further from the truth? Motherhood is itself an index of oppression as we can see in the career profiles and interrupted work histories, income, leisure (or lack thereof), and domestic inequality of mothers. Indeed, it is on this basis that a matricentric feminism is needed! It is needed precisely because being a mother continues to undermine women's equality and because that equality needs to be refracted through the lens of difference to accommodate the plethora of mothers' voices, in turn redefining the very meaning of equality. Perhaps, it is difference rather than equality we need, yet equality is a strategic step on this path. That is my own view. After all, we need formal equality before we can express our substantive differences. In this book, O'Reilly explores the theory, activism and practice of matricentric feminism, and she draws our attention to the neglected place of motherhood within academic feminism. This final chapter is fascinating, if depressing, as she marshals formidable evidence— course syllabi, conference presentations, journal articles and textbooks—to demonstrate the slow evisceration of motherhood from academic feminism. We have moved from what she terms the "disavowal" of motherhood as a legitimate category of analysis to its "disappearance" as fewer and fewer articles, chapters, papers and so forth are produced and accepted. Since the heyday of Rich and Chodorow (among many others) in the late seventies, such analysis has moved not just to the margins but right off the academic feminist page. Motherhood is ghettoized and ignored. As O'Reilly points out, "we're reading them [academic feminists] but they're not reading us." In other words, scholarly analysis of motherhood is now—contrary to its reality in the majority of women's lives—a marginal, if not nonexistent, interest in women's and gender studies! Talk of motherhood is embarrassingly mainstream, ostensibly apolitical, "essentialist" and a red rag to the intersectional, queer, trans-feminist bull. Of course, this is "bull" given the diversity of feminist mothers and feminist analyses of mothering—take a look at the last decade of Demeter Press publications for a marvellous showcase of diverse and intersectional work!

Mothers are the unspeakable of feminism, the "problem with no acceptable name." But it now has one: matricentric feminism. O'Reilly has bequeathed us with a term that is at once critical, political, avowedly feminist, and mother centred. This book is the culmination of a two-decade long project to find a theory and a practice of empowered mothering. O'Reilly has almost single-handedly crafted the discipline of motherhood studies, in which she has created an accessible corpus of work that other scholars, activists, and artist-practitioners may follow. This text serves as both a compendium of maternal theory—the philosophical cornerstone of matricentric feminism—and a call to both maternal activism and feminist mothering practice. It is also a clarion call to academic feminism to reposition and once again centre motherhood on the scholarly map of feminist analysis. Read deeply, this book is a connection to the motherline itself, which takes us all the way back to Demeter and her fight to preserve the mother-daughter relationship in the face of patriarchal conquest. Really, isn't it time we started listening to mothers?

Petra Bueskens
University of Melbourne
September 2016

Introduction

In *A Room of One's Own*, Virginia Woolf writes "a woman must have money and a room of her own if she is to write fiction" (1). For me, this quote serves to situate and frame what I explore in this book and what has been a passionate concern of mine over the past three decades as I have sought to do feminism as a mother and do mothering as a feminist: namely, that mothers need a feminism of their own. When I use the term "mothers," I refer to individuals who engage in motherwork or, as Sara Ruddick theorized, maternal practice. Such a term is not limited to biological mothers but to all people who do the work of mothering as a central part of their life. The aim of this book is to introduce this specific mode of feminism—what I have called "matricentric feminism"—and to document and detail how matricentric feminism is enacted in theory, activism, and practice. The book also, in its final chapter, examines the relationship between matricentric feminism and the larger field of academic feminism.

The book works from one particular assumption: mothering matters, and it is central to the lives of women who are mothers. In saying this, I am not suggesting that mothering is all that matters or that it matters the most; rather I am suggesting that any understanding of mothers' lives is incomplete without a consideration of how becoming and being a mother shape a woman's sense of self and how she sees the world. As a motherhood scholar, a director of a research centre on motherhood, an editor of a motherhood journal, and a publisher of a press on motherhood, I have talked to more mothers and read more motherhood scholarship than most, and I can say with confidence that for women who are mothers, mothering is a significant, if not a defining dimension of their lives, and that, arguably, maternity matters more than gender. I do not seek to substantiate these claims but rather take them as my starting point. Mothers need a feminism that puts motherhood at its centre.

Motherhood, it could be said, is the unfinished business of feminism. For example, a cursory review of recent scholarship on mothers and paid employment reveals that although women have made significant gains over the last three decades, mothers have not. Mothers in the paid labour force find themselves "mommy tracked," making sixty cents for every dollar earned by full-time fathers (Williams 2). Indeed, today the pay gap between mothers and non-mothers under thirty-five years of age is larger than the wage gap between young men and women (Crittenden 94). And although the "glass ceiling" and the "sticky floor" are still found in the workplace, most scholars argue that it is the "maternal wall" that impedes and hinders most women's progress in the workplace today. As Ann Crittenden writes: "Many childless women under the age of thirty-five believe that all the feminist battles have been won." But as Crittenden continues, "once a woman has a baby, the egalitarian office party is over" (88).

This book does not focus on why feminism has stalled for mothers; instead, the book positions mothers' needs and concerns as the starting point for a theory and politic on and for women's empowerment. This repositioning is not to suggest that a matricentric feminism should replace traditional feminist thought; rather, it is to emphasize that the category of mother is distinct from the category of woman and that many of the problems mothers face—social, economic, political, cultural, psychological, and so forth—are specific to women's role and identity as mothers. Indeed, mothers are oppressed under patriarchy as women and as mothers. Consequently, mothers need a matricentric mode of feminism organized from and for their particular identity and work as mothers. Indeed, a mother-centred feminism is needed because mothers—arguably more so than women in general—remain disempowered despite forty years of feminism. This book does not rationalize or defend the need for a mother-centred feminism, as it takes it as a given.

Instead, the book endeavours to describe and discuss this mode of mother-focused feminism—what I have termed matricentric feminism—which has emerged as a result of and in response to women's specific identities and work as mothers.

In this book, I use the term "matricentric" to define and describe a mother-centred mode of feminism. Feminist literary critic Elaine Showalter uses the term "gynocentric" to signify a woman-centred perspective ("Toward a Feminist Poetics"); similarly, I use matricentric to convey a mother-centred perspective. The choice to use the word matricentric over maternal and to use the term matricentric feminism instead of maternal feminism is done to distinguish a mother-focused feminism from the theory and politic of maternalism. Writer Judith Stadman Tucker argues that maternalism "conforms to the dominant ideology of motherhood and emphasizes the importance of maternal well-being to the health and safety of children." "Maternalism," she continues, "overlaps with what has been called 'difference feminism'—particularly the idea that women are 'naturally' or intuitively more empathic, less exploitive, and more closely attuned to relational ambience then men" ("Motherhood and its Discontents" 2). Likewise, Rachel V. Kutz-Flamenbaum, writing in the *Encyclopedia of Motherhood*, says:

> maternalism, like paternalism, is an ideology and philosophy. It asserts that "mother knows best" and that women, as a group, maintain a set of ideas, beliefs or experiences that reflect their motherly knowledge and motherly strengths. Maternalism suggests that women are (and should be) the moral conscience of humanity and asserts women's legitimate investment in political affairs through this emphasis. (2: 712)

Patrice DiQuinzio further elaborates that "Maternalist politics refers to political activism and political movements that invoke motherhood as the basis of women's agency" ("The Politics of the Mothers' Movement" 58).

A matricentric perspective, therefore, should not to be confused with a maternalist one. Although some perspectives in matricentric feminism may be considered maternalist, they are largely limited to the activism of certain motherhood organizations, as discussed in chapter two. Moreover, matricentric feminism, as argued in chapter one, understands motherhood to be socially and historically constructed, and positions mothering more as a practice than an identity. As well, as discussed in chapter one, central to matricentric feminist theory is a critique of the maternalist stance that positions maternity as basic to and the basis of female identity; as well, matricentric feminism challenges the assumption that maternity is natural to women (i.e., all women naturally know how to mother) and that the work of mothering is driven by instinct rather than intelligence and developed by habit rather than skill. Although matricentric feminism does hold a mother-centred perspective, it does not advance a maternalist argument or agenda. Thus, matricentric feminism marks the crucial difference between a focus on mothers from a politic of maternalism.

When discussing matricentric feminism, I draw on the concept of a matrifocal narrative, particularly as it has been developed in maternal literary theory. In her introduction to *The Mother/ Daughter Plot*, Marianne Hirsch queries why in Sophocles's *Oedipus Rex*, the voice of Jocasta, Oedipus' mother, is missing, and she connects this narrative silence to a larger literary lacuna: "In asking where the story of Jocasta is in the story of Oedipus, I am asking not only where the stories of women are in men's plots, but where the stories of mothers are in the plots of sons and daughters" (4). She concludes that "Clearly, to know Jocasta's maternal story ... we would have to begin with the mother" (5). Drawing on Hirsch, Brenda O. Daly and Maureen T. Reddy emphasize in *Narrating Maternity* that even of the limited number of fictional or theoretical texts that do "begin with the mother in her own right, from her own perspective ... [they] seldom hold fast to a maternal perspective; further when texts do maintain this perspective, readers and critics tend to suppress the centrality of mothering" (2-3). Daly and Reddy have coined the term "daughter-centricity" to describe the perspective wherein "we learn less about what it is like to mother than about what it is like to be mothered, even when the author has had both experiences" (2). Within the last three decades, as motherhood studies has emerged as a distinct and established academic discipline, this daughter-centricity has been countered and corrected in both fiction and theory. Indeed, a central aim of motherhood studies is to articulate and theorize "the voice of the mother"—that is, to analyze becoming and being a mother from the perspective and subjectivity of mothers themselves. Adrienne Rich concludes *Of Woman Born* with these words: "The words are being spoken now, are being written down, the taboos are being broken, the masks of motherhood are cracking through" (239). Whether such "unmasking" (Maushart) is conveyed by way of a sociological study of mothers or in a popular motherhood memoir, feminist writers and scholars alike endeavour to unmask motherhood by documenting the lived reality of mothering. In so doing, they counter the daughter-centricity, described by Daly and Reddy above, to create and compose what I term a "matrifocal narrative."

My use of the term matrifocal is drawn from Miriam Johnson's discussion of matrifocality in *Strong Mothers, Weak Wives*. Matrifocal societies, she writes,

> tend to have greater gender equality because of the power of a maternal paradigm. In these societies, regardless of the particular type of kinship system, women play roles of cultural and social significance and define themselves less as wives than as mothers.... Matrifocality however, does not refer to domestic maternal dominance so much as it does to the relative cultural prestige of the image of the mother, a role that is culturally elaborated and valued. Mothers are also structurally central in that the mother as a status "has some degree of control over the kin unit's economic resources and is critically involved in kin-related decision making processes." It is not the absence of males (males may be quite present) but the centrality of women as mothers and sisters that makes a society matrifocal. (226)

A matrifocal narrative, borrowing from Johnson's terminology above, is one in which a mother plays a role of cultural and social significance and in which motherhood is thematically elaborated and valued, and is structurally central to the plot. In other words—and to draw on the work of Hirsch, Daly, and Reddy—matrifocal narratives "begin with the mother in her own right, from her own perspective," and they "hold fast to a maternal perspective"; in addition, a matrifocal reading attends to and accentuates the maternal thematic in any given text.

Maternal writing, as Emily Jeremiah has noted, "entails a publicizing of maternal experience, and it subverts the traditional notion of mother as an instinctual, purely corporeal being. It is thus to be understood as a key tool in the redefinition of maternity in which feminists are engaged" (231). "It is impossible," writes Patrice Di Quinzio, "for feminist theory to avoid the issue of motherhood, and it is impossible for feminist theory to resolve it" (*Impossibility of Motherhood* xx). However, I suggest that a matrifocal perspective in unmasking motherhood and redefining maternity allows for these encounters and explorations. Perhaps, to paraphrase the words of Meryl Coulter, if feminist theory is not the means to a resolution, the matrifocal perspective may well be.

As matricentric feminism is matrifocal in its focus, it is multi- and inter-disciplinary in its perspective. Matricentric feminist theory, as explored in the following chapters, draws from many academic disciplines—including anthropology, history, literary studies, sociology, philosophy, psychology, sexuality studies, and women's studies—as well as from the established schools of academic feminism. Indeed, far from being an island on its own, matricentric feminism is informed by traditional schools of academic feminism and its most prominent theorists: womanist and African American feminism (bell hooks and Patricia Hill Collins); liberal feminism (Ann Crittenden); psychoanalytic feminism (Nancy Chodorow and Jessica Benjamin); queer-lesbian feminism (Baba Copper); cultural-difference feminism (Adrienne Rich and Mielle Chandler); socialist feminism (Mary O'Brien); and third-wave feminism (Ariel Gore).

I am frequently asked what matricentric feminism is. As a new and emergent feminism, it is difficult to define matricentric feminism other than to say that it is explicitly matrifocal in its perspective and emphasis—it begins with the mother and takes seriously the work of mothering—and that it is multidisciplinary and multi-theoretical in its perspective. Below, I gesture towards a possible definition by listing what I see as the central and governing principles and aims of matricentric feminism:

- asserts that the topic of mothers, mothering, and motherhood is deserving of serious and sustained scholarly inquiry;
- regards mothering as work that is important and valuable to society but emphasizes that the essential task of mothering is not, and should not be, the sole responsibility and duty of mothers;
- contests, challenges, and counters the patriarchal oppressive institution of motherhood and seeks to imagine and implement a maternal identity and practice that is empowering to mothers;
- seeks to correct the child centredness that defines much of the scholarship and activism on motherhood and seeks to develop research and activism from the experience and the perspective of mothers;
- commits to social change and social justice, and regards mothering as a socially engaged enterprise and a site of power,

wherein mothers can and do create social change through child-rearing and activism;
- understands mothering and motherhood to be culturally determined and variable, and is committed to exploring the diversity of maternal experience across race, class, culture, ethnicity, sexuality, ability, age, and geographical location; and
- endeavours to establish maternal theory and motherhood studies as an autonomous, independent, and legitimate scholarly discipline.

The above list is only partial and provisional. It is my hope that this book will lead to a more substantive and robust definition of this new feminist field of matricentric feminism.

This book comprises four chapters. The first and most lengthy chapter on maternal theory introduces the reader to the central theoretical concepts of patriarchal motherhood and empowered mothering. By virtue of this aim, the chapter is more descriptive than argumentative. The second chapter on maternal activism provides an overview of the twenty-first-century motherhood movement and, in particular, its theoretical and historical contexts, whereas the third chapter examines the central issues, questions, and concerns of feminist mothering as practice. The relationship of matricentric feminism to the larger discipline of academic feminism is the topic of the final chapter. In this chapter, I document the disavowal and disappearance of matricentric feminism in academic feminism and consider possible reasons for this marginalization and exclusion. Overall, this book, to paraphrase feminist writer and activist Marilyn Waring, seeks to deliver a mode of feminism in which mothers and mothering count.

Chapter One

Matricentric Feminism as Scholarship

Maternal Theory

My first book publication, the edited volume *Redefining Motherhood: Changing Identities and Patterns* published in 1998, opens with Adrienne Rich's oft-cited quote "We know more about the air we breathe, the seas we travel, than about the nature and meaning of motherhood" (11). By 1998, twenty-two years after the publication of Rich's ovarian work *Of Woman Born*, most academic disciplines, from anthropology to women's studies, were engaged in some form of motherhood research. And although scholarship on motherhood in some disciplines still struggled for legitimacy and centrality at the time, there was the recognition that motherhood studies was emerging as a distinct field within the larger disciplines of feminist scholarship and women's studies. Thus, by 1998, when I published my first book on motherhood, I could draw on a canon of motherhood research that was not available to Rich two decades earlier. Much research on motherhood still needed to be done, particularly in the area of marginalized and disadvantaged mothers, yet by 1998, motherhood scholars could claim, to paraphrase Rich, an understanding of the nature and meaning of motherhood.

In the eighteen years from the publication of *Redefining Motherhood* and this book on matricentric feminism, the topic of motherhood has developed from an emergent to an established field of scholarly inquiry. Indeed, today it would be unthinkable to cite Rich's quote on the dearth of maternal scholarship as I did close to twenty years ago. A cursory review of motherhood research reveals that hundreds of scholarly monographs, anthologies, and journal issues have been published on every imaginable motherhood theme. The *Journal of the Motherhood Initiative* and Demeter Press alone have examined motherhood topics in relation to a diverse array of subjects, including the following: sexuality, peace, religion, public policy, literature, work, popular culture, health, carework-caregiving, ethnicity, environment, militarism, young mothers, motherhood and feminism, mothers and sons, mothers and daughters, queer mothers, Muslim mothering, Indigenous mothers, Latina mothers, incarcerated mothers, third-wave mothering, and mothering and domestic violence.

In 2006, I coined the term "motherhood studies" to acknowledge and demarcate this new scholarship on motherhood as a legitimate and autonomous discipline—one grounded in the theoretical tradition of maternal theory developed by such scholars as Patricia Hill Collins, Adrienne Rich, and Sara Ruddick, and one explicitly interdisciplinary in both scholarship and teaching. As an undergraduate student of women's studies in the 1980s, I was expected to know feminist theory and was required to study women's experiences from across a wide variety of disciplines. I remember learning the differences between liberal and socialist feminist theory as well as examining women in courses as diverse as "Women and Film," "Women in Literature," "Women's History," "Women in Society," and "Psychology of Women." Similarly, students and scholars of motherhood studies today must know maternal theory and examine mothers and motherhood across diverse disciplines. This chapter on matricentric feminism as scholarship provides an introduction to maternal theory.

Ultimately I decided to frame this chapter on maternal theory in the context of an undergraduate course on mothering-motherhood that I have taught at York University since 1992. The full year course examines how patriarchal motherhood is oppressive to women and how women may resist such oppression through empowered mothering (appendix A). In the first term, by way of various maternal theories selected, students explore theoretical concepts in order to understand how and why motherhood functions as a patriarchal institution to disempower and oppress mothers. Such key concepts include mothering versus motherhood, reproduction of mothering, maternal thinking-practice, maternal ambivalence, and normative ideologies of good motherhood, such as mother-blame, "bad" mothers, intensive mothering, and the mask of motherhood. The students then read three contemporary novels about motherhood from the standpoint of these theoretical concepts. In the second term, students examine specific practices of maternal empowerment, such as those found among Indigenous, African American, young, queer, and feminist mothers. In this section of the course, students also consider theoretical concepts of empowered mothering, including other-community mothering, queering motherhood, collectivism, matrifocality, hip mothering, homeplace, radical motherhood, and feminist mothering. Organizing the course by way of theoretical concepts—rather than say by chronology or theorist—I found that the students could understand how patriarchal motherhood "works" and how it may be resisted. Such an organization also better prepares students to apply these insights to the fiction read in the course and women's own lived experiences of mothering. The following section organizes maternal theory by key theoretical insights and concepts of the field. It is my hope that my particular approach will serve to illuminate the abundance and acuity of this new scholarly field that we call maternal theory.

Maternal Theory

Disgruntled with using an increasingly costly course kit year after year and with no book on maternal theory available other than the important but very dated Joyce Trebilcot's 1983 collection *Mothering: Essays in Feminist Theory*, I decided to develop an anthology composed of the key texts on maternal theory for my course in 2005. The aim of the book was to bring together for the first time the essential readings in maternal theory. The *Oxford Canadian Dictionary* defines theory as "a supposition or system of ideas explaining something, especially one based on general principles independent of the particular things to be explained" and as "the principles on which a subject of study is based" (1504). For the purpose of the collection, the text in question must develop a supposition or system of ideas independent of the particular issue being discussed in order for it to be considered a theory. This chapter must, in other words, craft a concept, model, or idea that may be applicable to other motherhood texts or contexts. The anthology *Maternal Theory: Essential Readings*, published in 2007, covers a thirty-one-year time period, from 1976 to 2007. The chapters theorize motherhood from three perspectives: motherhood as experience and role, motherhood as institution and ideology, and motherhood as identity and subjectivity. In selecting the chapters, I chose ones that have most influenced the development of maternal theory; writers whose motherhood concepts have shaped the way that we think about motherhood. Such concepts include Adrienne Rich's distinction between motherhood versus mothering, Chodorow's "reproduction of mothering," Sara Ruddick's "maternal thinking," bell hooks's "homeplace," Baba Copper's "radical mothering," Patricia Hill Collins's "other-mothering," Marianne Hirsch's "mother-daughter plot," Sharon Hays's "intensive mothering," Susan Maushart's "mask of motherhood," Ann Crittenden's "price of motherhood," and Daphne de Marneffe's "maternal desire," to name but a few. A highlight of the collection is its attention to diversity. African American, Chicana, Latina, and Indigenous motherhood theories are represented, as are theories concerned with mothers and disabilities, single mothers, working-class mothers, adoptive mothers, and young mothers. This collection is the primary text of my mothering-motherhood course through which students learn the key theoretical frameworks and concepts in maternal theory. In the second term on empowered mothering, students also use my edited collection *Mothers, Mothering and Motherhood across Culture Difference: A Reader*.

Understanding Patriarchal Motherhood

Each year I open my "Mothering-Motherhood" course by asking students to define "good" motherhood in contemporary culture: what does a good mother look like? What does she do or not do? Students usually comment that good mothers, as portrayed in the media or popular culture more generally, are white, heterosexual, able-bodied, married and in a nuclear family with usually one to two children. Words such as "altruistic," "patient," "loving," "selfless," "devoted," "nurturing," and "cheerful" are frequently mentioned. For the students, good mothers put the needs of their children before their own, are available to their children whenever needed, and should the mother work outside the home, her children rather than her career should be at the centre of her life. Good mothers are the primary caregivers of their children: care other than that provided by the mother (i.e., daycare) is viewed as inferior and deficient. Children and culture at large do not see mothers as having a life before or outside of motherhood. As well, although students typically agree that our culture regards mothering as natural to mothers, that same culture paradoxically requires mothers to be well-versed in theories of childrearing. Several students remark that good mothers today are concerned with their children's educational or more general psychological development; good mothers, thus, ensure that their children have many and varied opportunities for enrichment, learning, and self-growth. And, of course, mothers are not sexual! I then ask how many students in the room are good mothers as defined by these normative images of motherhood. (Or if they are not mothers themselves, I ask if they were they raised by this so-called ideal mother.) Seldom has a hand been raised. Of course, we all know that mothers come from all races and ethnicities, that mothers are both young and old, that mothers are both urban and rural, straight and queer, that many women mother with disabilities, that many mothers are poor or working class, that most mothers work outside the home in paid employment, that social and political activism is a part of many mothers' lives, that women mother older children as well as young children, that some mothers live apart from their children, that many women raise children with whom they have no biological relation as with adoption and in blended families, and finally that all these mothers are good mothers who raise their children with love and care equal to that of the normative and idealized "good" mother. However, we also know that normative motherhood, although representative of very few women's lived identities and experiences of mothering, is considered the normal and natural maternal experience: to mother otherwise is to be abnormal or unnatural. Mothers who, by choice or circumstance, do not fulfill the profile of the good mother—they are too young or too old, or they do not follow the script of good mothering—they work outside the home and live apart from their children—are deemed "bad" mothers in need of societal regulation and correction.

In order to illustrate how this discourse of normative mother-hood works, I introduce the students to what I have termed the "ten ideological assumptions of patriarchal motherhood," namely: essentialization, privatization, individualization, naturalization, normalization, idealization, biologicalization, expertization, intensification, and depoliticalization of motherhood. Essentialization positions maternity as basic to and the basis of female identity, whereas privatization locates motherwork solely in the reproductive realm of the home. Similarly, individualization causes such mothering to be the work and responsibility of one person, and naturalization assumes that maternity is natural to women—all women naturally know how to mother—and that the work of mothering is driven by instinct rather than intelligence and developed by habit rather than skill. In turn, normalization limits and restricts maternal identity and practice to one specific mode: the nuclear family. Wherein, the mother is a wife to a husband, and she assumes the role of the nurturer, and the husband assumes that of the provider. The expertization and intensification of motherhood—particularly as they are conveyed in what Sharon Hays has termed "intensive mothering," and what Michaels and Douglas call "the new momism"—cause childrearing to be all consuming and expert driven. Idealization sets unattainable expectations of and for mothers, and depoliticalization characterizes childrearing solely as a private and nonpolitical undertaking, with no social or political import. Finally, biologicalization, in its emphasis on blood ties, positions the birthmother as the "real" and authentic mother.

The ten ideological mandates serve as the framework for the theoretical concepts examined in the course. The theoretical concepts discussed in this chapter are not all the ones covered in *Maternal Theory* or in the course. Rather, I have selected for this chapter the theoretical concepts that I view as most central to the field of maternal theory. With close to twenty concepts covered in this chapter, my discussion of each is, of necessity, brief and cursory. For many of the concepts discussed, an entire book could be written on the subject. Indeed, Demeter Press alone has published books on Sara Ruddick, Patricia Hill Collins and Nancy Chodorow as well as books on intensive mothering, Black motherhoods, queering motherhood, feminist parenting, empowered mothering, Indigenous mothering, neoliberalism, maternal ambivalence, and the wife role. The concepts examined in this section on patriarchal motherhood include the following: mothering versus motherhood; matrophobia; mother-daughter connection; maternal thinking and practice; reproduction of mothering; mothers' relational sense of self; wife role; postfeminist split subjectivity; normative motherhood; intensive mothering; the new momism; maternal ambivalence, and the mask of motherhood.

Patriarchal Motherhood: Key Theoretical Concepts

Mothering versus Motherhood, Matrophobia, and Mother-Daughter Connection: Adrienne Rich

Adrienne Rich's *Of Woman Born: Motherhood as Experience and Institution* is recognized as the first and arguably the most important book on motherhood. The book—a wide ranging, far reaching meditation on the meaning and experience of motherhood that draws from the disciplines of anthropology, feminist theory, psychology, literature as well as narrates Rich's personal reflections on her experiences of mothering—has had a broad and enduring impact on feminist thought on motherhood. Described by Penelope Dixon in her 1991 annotated bibliography on mothers and mothering as "one of the major feminist studies on mothering" (11), *Of Woman Born* has indeed influenced the way that a whole generation of scholars thinks about motherhood.

In *Of Women Born* Rich distinguishes "between two meanings of motherhood, one superimposed on the other: the *potential relationship* of any woman to her powers of reproduction and to children; and the *institution*—which aims at ensuring that that potential—and all women—shall remain under male control" (7). "This book," Rich writes, "is not an attack on the family or on mothering *except as defined and restricted under patriarchy*" (8). The term "motherhood" refers to the patriarchal institution of motherhood, which is male defined and controlled and is deeply oppressive to women, whereas the word "mothering" refers to women's experiences of mothering and is female defined and centred and potentially empowering to women. The reality of patriarchal motherhood, thus, must be distinguished from the possibility or potentiality of empowered mothering. "To destroy the institution is not to abolish motherhood," Rich writes. "It is to release the creation and sustenance of life into the same realm of decision, struggle, surprise, imagination and conscious intelligence, as any difficult, but freely chosen work" (280). In other words, whereas motherhood operates as a patriarchal institution to constrain, regulate, and dominate women and their mothering, mothers' own experiences of mothering can, nonetheless, be a site of empowerment "[F]or most of what we know as the 'mainstream' of recorded history," Rich writes, "motherhood as institution has ghettoized and degraded female potentialities" (33). However, as Rich argues, and her book seeks to demonstrate, this meaning of motherhood is neither natural nor inevitable. "The patriarchal institution of motherhood," Rich explains, "is not the 'human condition' any more than rape, prostitution, and slavery are" (33). Rather motherhood, in Rich's words, "has a history, it has an ideology" (33). Motherhood is, thus, primarily not a natural or biological function; rather, it is specifically and fundamentally a cultural practice that is continuously redesigned in response to changing economic and societal factors. As a cultural construction, its meaning varies with time and place; there is no essential or universal experience of motherhood. Patriarchal motherhood, as described by my students, is neither natural nor inevitable. And since the patriarchal institution is socially constructed, it can be challenged and changed.

The first five chapters of *Of Woman Born* narrate this history of the changing social construction of motherhood, and trace the development of motherhood from neolithic gathering and hunting goddess cultures, when maternity was a site of power for women, through the early agricultural period when women's powers of maternity began to be contained and controlled, to the domestication of motherhood after industrialization. Although recent scholars have clarified and corrected some of the details of this narrative, its overall plot and themes continue to inform contemporary feminist historical readings of motherhood. Feminist historians agree that motherhood is primarily not a natural or biological function; rather, it is specifically and fundamentally an ideological construction that has continuously changed in response to social and economic transformations (O'Reilly, *Mother Outlaws*; Shari Thurer). As an ideological construction, its meaning varies with time and place; there is no essential or universal meaning or experience of motherhood. Works such a Ann Dally's *Inventing Motherhood,* Elizabeth Badinter's *Mother Love* and Shari Thurer's *The Myths of Motherhood* detail how the modern image of the good mother—the "full-time stay at home" mother isolated in the private sphere and financially dependent on her husband—came about as a result of industrialization, which took work out of the home and repositioned the domestic space, at least among the middle class, as an exclusively nonproductive and private realm, separate from the public sphere of work.

In the Victorian period that followed industrialization, the ideology of moral motherhood, which saw mothers as naturally pious and chaste, emerged as the dominant discourse of motherhood. This ideology, however, was race and class specific: only white and middle-class women could wear the halo of the Madonna and transform the world through their moral influence and social housekeeping. After World War II, the time when Rich become a mother, the discourse of the "happy homemaker" made the "stay-at-home-mom-and-apple-pie" mode of mothering the normal and natural motherhood experience. But, again, only white and middle-class women could, in fact, experience what discursively was inscribed as natural and universal. In each of its manifestations, motherhood remains, at its core, a patriarchal institution oppressive to women.

Of Woman Born highlights two features of modern patriarchal motherhood that are particularly harmful to mothers. First, mothering is assumed to be natural to women, and childrearing is seen as the sole responsibility of the biological mother. Second, mothers are assigned sole responsibility for motherwork but are given no power to determine the conditions under which they mother. Mothering, in its current ideological manifestation, regards maternity as natural to women and essential to their beings, conveyed in the belief that women are naturally mothers. As Pamela Courtenay Hall notes, women are believed to be born "with a built-in set of capacities, dispositions, and desires to nurture children ... [and that this] engagement of love and instinct is utterly distant from the world of paid work" (60). This assumption over the last fifty years has given rise to and resulted in the modern ideological construction of "intensive mothering," discussed later in this chapter. For Rich, and more recent theorists, this discourse becomes oppressive to mothers not because children have these needs but because we, as a culture, dictate that only the biological mother is capable of fulfilling them. These two features of the modern ideology of motherhood make mothering oppressive to women because they require the denial of the mother's own selfhood, and deny the mother the authority and agency to determine her own experiences of mothering. Women's mothering, as Rich asserts, is fully controlled and arbitrated by the patriarchal institution of motherhood. As Rich writes: "The institution of motherhood is not identical with bearing and caring for children, any more than the institution of heterosexuality is identical with intimacy and sexual love. Both create the prescriptions and the conditions in which choices are made or blocked; they are not 'reality' but they have shaped the circumstances of our lives" (42).

Rich writes of how she was "haunted by the stereotype of the mother whose love is 'unconditional' and by the visual and literary images of motherhood as a single-minded identity" (23). But she also recognized that "this circle, this magnetic field [of selfless mothers and needy children] in which [she] lived, was not a natural phenomenon" (23). Children need love and care, but it is culture, not children, that demands that the mother be the one to provide them. Rich's eldest son, at age twenty-one, read his mother's journals of early motherhood and commented: "You seemed to feel you ought to love us all the time. But there is no human relationship where you love the other person at every moment." And Rich replied: "Yes I tried to explain to him, but women—above all, mothers—have been supposed to love that way" (23). This is the defining belief of the ideology of patriarchal motherhood that enacts and reinforces the ideological mandates of essentialization, naturalization, privatization, and individualization.

Most women mother in the patriarchal institution of motherhood, in which women's mothering is defined and controlled by the larger patriarchal society in which they live. Mothers do not make the rules, as Rich reminds us, they simply enforce them. Motherhood, for Rich, is an experience of "powerless responsibility." Whether it is in the form of a parenting book, a physician's advice, or a father's rules, a mother raises her children in accordance with the values and expectations of the dominant culture.

Mothers are policed by what Sara Ruddick calls the "gaze of others." Under the gaze of others, mothers "relinquish authority to others, [and] lose confidence in their own values" (111). In *Of Woman Born*, Rich, for example, remembers her mother locking her in the closet at the age of four, for childish behaviour—"[her] father's orders, but [her] mother carried them out"—and being kept too long at piano lessons when she was six, which was "again, at [her father's] insistence, but it was [her mother] who gave the lessons" (224).

Patriarchal motherhood has become the official meaning of motherhood, and as such, it marginalizes and renders illegitimate alternative practices of mothering. As a normative discourse, it polices all women's mothering and results in the pathologizing of those women who do not or cannot perform normative motherhood. Finally, the patriarchal institution of motherhood, as a normative discourse, restrains women's power to challenge and change the oppressiveness of their motherhood experience.

The oppressive and the empowering dimensions of maternity as well as the complex relationship between the two, first identified by Rich in *Of Woman Born*, have been the focus of feminist research on motherhood over the last four decades. Indeed, almost all contemporary scholarship on motherhood draws on Rich's distinction between motherhood and mothering. Within motherhood studies, the term "motherhood" is used to signify the patriarchal institution of motherhood, whereas "mothering" refers to women's lived experiences of mothering as they conform to and/or resist the patriarchal institution of motherhood and its oppressive ideology. Whereas scholars who are concerned with the ideology or institution of patriarchal motherhood investigate policies, laws, ideologies, and normative discourses, researchers who are interested in experience examine the work women do as mothers and consider how mothering may be a site of personal agency and social change.

Laura Umansky, in her study of feminism between 1968 and 1982, outlines two competing feminist views on motherhood: the "negative" discourse that "focusse[s] on motherhood as a social mandate, an oppressive institution, a compromise of woman's independence," and the "positive" discourse, which "argue[s] that "motherhood minus 'patriarchy' ... holds the truly spectacular potential to bond women to each other and to nature, to foster a liberating knowledge of self, to release the very creativity and generativity that the institution of motherhood denies to women" (2-3). Scholars of motherhood have long recognized that Rich's distinction between mothering and motherhood was what enabled feminists to realize that motherhood is not naturally, necessarily, or inevitably oppressive, which is a view held by some second-wave feminists. Rather, if freed from the institutional shackles of motherhood, mothering could be experienced as a site of empowerment and social change. However, and as I examine in my edited collection *From Motherhood to Mothering: The Legacy of Adrienne Rich's 'Of Woman Born'*, there is no discussion of empowered mothering or how its potentiality may be realized in Rich's book. The notable exception is the brief reference Rich makes to her summer holiday in Vermont when her husband was away and she and her sons lived "as conspirators, outlaws from the institution of motherhood" (195). Despite this absence, most scholars agree that although mothering may not be described or theorized in *Of Woman Born*, in distinguishing mothering from motherhood and in identifying the potential empowerment of motherhood, the text interrupts the patriarchal narrative of motherhood and clears the space for the articulation of counter-narratives of mothering, which enables mothers to envision and enact an empowered mode of mothering. And for many scholars, this is the true legacy of Rich's work. The potentiality and possibility of maternal power will be considered in the following section on empowered mothering and then fully in chapter three on feminist mothering.

Matrophobia and Mother-Daughter Connection

In *Of Woman Born*, Rich speaks of the rage and resentment daughters feel towards the powerlessness of their mothers. At the same time the daughter feels rage toward her mother, however, she is expected to identify with her because the daughter is also a woman who, it is assumed, will someday become a mother and wife as her mother did. The daughter resists this identification because she does not want a life like her mother, nor does she wish to be aligned with someone who is oppressed and whose work is so devalued. "Thousands of daughters," writes Rich, "see their mothers as having taught a compromise and self-hatred they are struggling to win free of, the one through whom the restrictions and degradations of a female existence were ... transmitted" (235). Rich calls this distancing between mothers and daughters "matrophobia," or "the fear not of one's mother or of motherhood but of *becoming one's mother*" (236). Rich writes:

> Matrophobia can be seen as a womanly splitting of the self in the desire to become purged once and for all of our mothers' bondage, to become individuated and free. The mother stands for the victim in ourselves, the unfree woman, the martyr. Our personalities seem dangerously to blur and overlap with our mothers, and in a desperate attempt to know where mother ends and daughter begins, we perform radical surgery. (Rich 236)

When a daughter performs this radical surgery, she severs her attachment to her mother. Hence, matrophobia frustrates, if not prevents, understanding and intimacy, empathy and connection between mothers and daughters. "The loss of the daughter to the mother, the mother to the daughter," writes Rich, "is the essential female tragedy. We acknowledge Lear (father-daughter split), Hamlet (son and mother), and Oedipus, (son and mother) as great embodiments of the human tragedy, but there is no presently enduring recognition of mother-daughter passion and rapture" (237). Building on Rich's insights on mother-daughter estrangement, feminist theorists, since the mid-1980s, have focused on the importance of mother-daughter connection and closeness for female empowerment, particularly in the daughter's adolescent years. Writers as diverse as Paula Caplan, Elizabeth Debold, Miriam Johnson, Carol Gilligan, Virginia Beanne Rutter, and Mary Pipher have all argued that a strong mother-daughter connection is what makes possible a strong female self. Virginia Beanne Rutter in her book *Celebrating Girls* argues that high self-esteem in girls is made possible through close relationships with mothers. As Rutter writes: "Mothers can raise girls with a vital, intact feminine spirit.... [The] mother-daughter relationship is the ground for teaching, talking, and sharing the feminine experience and the more we empower that experience, the healthier our girls will be. We need to secure our daughters' sense of self-worth, in their mind and their bodies, so that they will not turn away from us and from themselves" (2, 9-10). These writers maintain that the daughter's empowerment through the valuation of the feminine depends on a close and vital mother-daughter relationship.

Western culture, however, mandates that children separate from their parents in adolescence to enable their achieving an autonomous sense of self. Feminist writers have recently called into question this "sacred cow" of developmental theory, and have argued that it constitutes a betrayal of both mothers and daughters. Elizabeth Debold et al. explain:

> Separation and autonomy are not equivalent ... [daughters] need not separate from mothers emotionally to be autonomous.... Early childhood and adolescence are the two stages of life where separation has been decreed as imperative to the independence and autonomy of children. To mother 'right' women disconnect from their daughters... Rather than strengthen girls, this breach of trust leaves girls weakened and adrift. (36)

What is most disturbing about this pattern of separation and betrayal is its timing. "In childhood," Debold et al write, "girls have confidence in what they know, think and feel" (11). With the onset of adolescence, girls come up against what they call "the wall": "The wall is our patriarchal culture that values women less than men.... To get through the wall girls have to give up parts of themselves to be safe and accepted within society" (12). Daughters are, thus, abandoned by their mothers when they need them the most. Mothers can aid daughters in their resistance to the wall through sustained and sustaining mother-daughter connection. Drawing on the ancient Eleusinian rites of Demeter and Persephone first discussed by Rich, feminist writings on the mother-daughter relationship celebrate the mother-daughter connection and explore how it is achieved and sustained through motherlines and feminist mothering, discussed below and in chapter three.

This feminist aim to fashion an alternative mother-daughter narrative modelled on mother-daughter connection has resulted in perceptive and useful literature on how to raise empowered girls. As well, this counter-narrative has gone a long way to destabilize the patriarchal view that positions mother-daughter disconnection as inevitable and necessary. However, I want to suggest here, and it will be argued as well in chapter three, that these achievements remain partial because of the failure of this new literature to fully comprehend the connection-empowerment trajectory as theorized by Rich. Although Rich champions mother-daughter connection, she recognizes that connection gives rise to the daughter's empowerment only if the mother herself is empowered. "What do we mean by the nurture of daughters? What is it we wish we had, or could have, as daughters; could give as mothers?" (246) asks Rich. She states further:

> Deeply and primarily we need trust and tenderness; surely this will always be true of every human being, but women growing into a world so hostile to us need a very profound kind of loving in order to learn to love ourselves. But this loving is not simply the old, institutionalized, sacrificial, "mother-love" which men have demanded; we want courageous mothering. The most notable fact that culture imprints on women is the sense of our limits. The most important thing one woman can do for another is to illuminate and expand her sense of actual possibilities. For a mother, this means more than contending with reductive images of females in children's books, movies, television, the schoolroom. It means that the mother herself is trying to expand the limits of her life. *To refuse to be a victim: and then to go on from there.* (246)

Karen Payne's edited collection, *Between Ourselves: Letters between Mothers and Daughters,* provides lived examples of Rich's mutual empowerment thesis. One daughter writes: "When Mum finally left Dad she was giving up female martyrdom; she was waving farewell to that womanly virtue of self-sacrifice. And if she could escape that bondage then so could I. In setting herself free, [my mother] set me free" (244). In the same collection, sociologist Jesse Bernard writes to her daughter: "For your sake as well as mine, I must not allow you to absorb me completely. I must learn to live my own life independently in order to be a better mother to you" (272). Or as Judith Arcana, an early feminist theorist whose work was greatly influenced by Rich, advises: "We must live as if our dreams have been realized. We cannot simply prepare other, younger daughters for strength, pride, courage, beauty. It is worse than useless to tell young women and girls that we have done and been wrong, that we have chosen ill, that we hope they will be more lucky" (33).

According to Rich, therefore, what daughters need

> [are] mothers who want their own freedom and ours....The quality of the mother's life—however embattled and unprotected—is her primary bequest to her daughter, because a woman who can believe in herself, who is a fighter, and who continues to struggle to create livable space around her, is demonstrating to her daughter that these possibilities exist. (247)

Courageous mothering, as described by Rich, calls for the empowerment of daughters and mothers, and recognizes that the former is only possible with the later. As Judith Arcana concludes: "If we want girls to grow into free women, brave and strong, we must be those women ourselves" (33). Such mothering works against matrophobia, which is at the heart of mother-daughter estrangement, and is what makes possible reciprocal mother-daughter empowerment.

Maternal Thinking and Practice: Sara Ruddick

I first encountered Sara Ruddick's work in Joyce Trebilcot's collection *Mothering: Essays in Feminist Theory,* which includes two essays by Ruddick: "Maternal Thinking" and "Preservative Love and Military Destruction: Some Reflections on Mothering and Peace." It was spring 1985, and I was the mother of a ten-month-old son just finishing my first master's course on the subject of "Women, Violence, Militarism, and War." I knew then that I wanted motherhood to be my area of expertise, although this would be a hard sell given that my Masters and then my PhD were in the discipline of English. It would be another five years and two more children before I would read *Maternal Thinking* in the summer of 1990. I was reading for my major field comprehensive exam on the topic of women's studies in literature, and I had convinced my committee to substitute books on motherhood on the reading list. My plan was to head to my mother's cottage for three weeks with my three kids—aged one, three and a half, six—and my son's best friend, who was also six and, without my partner, who was home in Toronto, so that I could do some last minute studying for the eight-hour exam to be written in a month's time. I arrived at my mom's small cottage with a pile of books, with four children all under six, and no partner or car, little money, and with a mother, who though adoring her grandchildren, was usually too overwhelmed by them to offer much help. I had the intention to study and rest well. Needless to say, I did not get much rest or studying done in those weeks, but I did read, or more accurately consume, *Maternal Thinking*.

> Today, twenty-seven years later, that original copy of *Maternal Thinking* sits on the desk beside the keyboard as I write this section. The cover features an artist's drawing of a woman with her hand to her head, who is engaged in deep thought, with these words written underneath: "The first attempt to describe, from a philosophical perspective, the thinking that grows out of the work mothers do." For me, and I suspect for most mothers and scholars of motherhood, this is what makes *Maternal Thinking* so life changing and groundbreaking. She theorizes the obvious: mothers think. "The work of mothering," as Ruddick writes in *Maternal Thinking*, "demands that mothers think; out of this need for thoughtfulness, a distinctive discipline emerges" (24). I first read those words on an overcast summer day as my young children played on a near deserted windswept beach. The lines are underlined, the page number is circled twice, and the paragraph remains soiled by sand and water. Yes, mothers think!

Maternal Thinking

Ruddick's concept of maternal practice and thinking—which is divested of biology, nature, instinct, and sentiment—foregrounds what all mothers know: motherwork is inherently an intellectual activity. Ruddick elaborates:

> Like a scientist writing up her experiment, a critic poring over a text, or a historian assessing documents, a mother caring for her children engages in a discipline. She asks certain questions—those relevant to her aims—rather than others; she accepts certain criteria for the truth, adequacy, and relevance of proposed answers; and she cares about the findings she makes and can act on. The discipline of maternal thought, like other disciplines, establishes criteria for determining failure and success, sets priorities, and identifies virtues that the discipline requires. Like any other work, mothering is prey to characteristic temptations that it must identify. To describe the capacities, judgments, metaphysical attitudes, and values of maternal thought presumes not maternal achievement, but a conception of achievement. (24)

"Mothers, like gardeners or historians," Ruddick continues, "identify virtues appropriate to their work. But to identify a virtue is not to possess it" (25). Ruddick explains further:

> Mothers meeting together at their jobs, in playgrounds, or over coffee can be heard thinking. This does not necessarily mean that they can be heard being good. Mothers are not any more or less wonderful than other people—they are not especially sensible or foolish, noble or ignoble, courageous or cowardly.... When mothers speak of virtues they speak as often of failure as of success. Almost always they reflect on the struggles that revolve around the temptations to which they are prey in their work. What they share is not virtuous characteristics but rather identification and a discourse about the strengths required by their ongoing commitments to protect, nurture, and train. (25)

When mothers set out to fulfill the demands of motherwork—what Ruddick defines as protection, nurturance, and training—they are engaged in maternal practice. This engagement, in turn, gives rise to a specific discipline of thought—a cluster of attitudes, beliefs, and values—which Ruddick calls maternal thinking.

Maternal thinking, as Ruddick explains, refers to the "intellectual capacities [the mother] develops, the judgments she makes, the metaphysical attitudes she assumes, and the values she affirms in and through maternal practice" (24). Mothers, in short, are the ones who do the maternal thinking: the remembering, worrying, planning, anticipating, orchestrating, arranging, and coordinating of and for the household. It is mothers who remember to buy the milk, plan the birthday party, and worry that the daughter's recent loss of appetite may be indicative of anorexia. Although the father may sign the field trip permission form or buy the diapers, it is the mother, in most households, who reminds him to do so. Delegation does not make equality and, equally important, delegation also continues to require that mothers have the psychological responsibility for remembering, managing, and meeting the demands of household, family life, and children. Maternal thinking is thus never-ending and difficult to "turn off."

In her examination of maternal thought and practice and their accompanying tasks and concepts of scrutinizing, cheerfulness, holding, welcoming of change, concrete thinking, maternal inauthenticity, and attentive love, among others, Ruddick was the first scholar to examine the experience of mothering, as opposed to the institution of motherhood, and develop a theoretical framework and vocabulary for this analysis. In defining mothering as a practice, Ruddick has enabled future scholars to analyze the experience or practice of mothering as distinct from the identity of the mother. In other words, mothering may be performed by anyone who commits themselves to the demands of maternal practice. As well, this perspective has allowed scholars to study the actual experiences of mothering as apart from, albeit affected by, the institution of motherhood. The word "mother," as Mielle Chandler writes, "[needs to be] understood as a verb; as something one does, a practice" (531). For Ruddick, as Sarah LaChance Adams notes, "it is the practice of mothering that makes one a mother, not a biological or social imperative [and] [t]herefore, the title of 'mother' is not strictly limited to biological mothers, or even women" (727). Ruddick insists, Adam continues, "that true maternal commitment is voluntary and conscious; it is not inevitable, nor is it dictated by nature" (727).

Ruddick's insight has marked a radical rethinking and reframing of the meaning of motherhood in maternal scholarship, as her repositioning of the word "mother" from a noun to a verb degenders motherwork. More specifically, divesting care of biology, Ruddick has enabled scholars to destabilize patriarchal motherhood by dislodging the gender essentialism that grounds and structures it. In so doing, Ruddick's concept of maternal thinking and practice, discussed below, opens up the possibility of male mothering. Ruddick explains that when she uses the term "mother" she is referring to "a person who takes on the responsibility for children's lives and for whom providing child care is a significant part of her or his working life, I *mean* his or her (40). Ruddick maintains that men "really can and often do engage in mothering work (xiii)." Indeed, as Andrea Doucet notes in the introduction to her book *Do Men Mother?*, Ruddick is the most frequently cited proponent of the argument that fathers can, indeed, be mothers. In this, Ruddick's theory has made possible the scholarly field of men and mothering, which is explored at length in Doucet's book and in the recent collection *Essential Breakthroughs: Conversations about Men, Mothers and Mothering*.

The Three Demands of Maternal Practice: Preservation, Nurturance and Training

Sara Ruddick argues that maternal practice is characterized by three demands: preservation, growth, and social acceptance. "To be a mother," continues Ruddick, "is to be committed to meeting these demands by works of preservative love, nurturance, and training" (17). The first duty of mothers is to protect and preserve their children: "to keep safe whatever is vulnerable and valuable in a child" (80). "Preserving the lives of children," Ruddick writes, "is the central constitutive, invariant aim of maternal practice: the commitment to achieving that aim is the constitutive maternal act" (19). "To be committed to meeting children's demand for preservation," Ruddick continues, "does not require enthusiasm or even love; it simply means to see vulnerability and to respond to it with care rather than abuse, indifference, or flight" (19). "The demand to preserve a child's life is quickly supplemented," Ruddick continues, "by the second demand, to nurture its emotional and intellectual growth" (19). Ruddick explains:

> To foster growth ... is to sponsor or nurture a child's unfolding, expanding material spirit. Children demand this nurturance

because their development is complex, gradual, and subject to distinctive kinds of distortion or inhibition. Children's emotional, cognitive, sexual, and social development is sufficiently complex to demand nurturance; this demand is an aspect of maternal work ... and it structures maternal thinking (83).

The third demand of maternal practice is training and social acceptability of children:

[The demand] is made not by children's needs but by the social groups of which a mother is a member. Social groups require that mothers shape their children's growth in "acceptable" ways. What counts as acceptable varies enormously within and among groups and cultures. The demand for acceptability, however, does not vary, nor does there seem to be much dissent from the belief that children cannot "naturally" develop in socially correct ways but must be "trained." I use the neutral, though somewhat harsh, term "training" to underline a mother's active aims to make her children "acceptable." Her training strategies may be persuasive, manipulative, educative, abusive, seductive, or respectful and are typically a mix of most of these. (21)

"In any mother's day," as Ruddick notes, "the demands of preservation, growth and acceptability are intertwined. Yet a reflective mother", she continues, "can separately identify each demand, partly because they are often in conflict" (23). In *Maternal Thinking*, she asks the following questions to illustrate the inherent and inevitable conflicts that arise as a mother seeks to meet the competing demands of maternal practice.

If a child wants to walk to the store alone, do you worry about her safety or applaud her developing capacity to take care of herself? If you overhear your son hurling insults at a neighbour's child, do you rush to instill decency and compassion in him, or do you let him act on his impulses in his need to overcome shyness? If your older child, in her competitive zeal, pushes ahead of your younger, smaller child while climbing a high slide, do you inhibit her competitive pleas or allow an aggressiveness you cannot appreciate. Should her younger brother learn to fight back? And if he doesn't, is he bowing too easily to greater strength? Most urgently, whatever you do is somebody going to get hurt? (23)

Moreover, as Ruddick discusses later in the text, the rival claims of maternal practice become further pronounced when they involve the third demand of training. For most mothers, Ruddick writes, "the work of training is confusing and fraught with self-doubt" (104). It is in the context of the above discussion that Ruddick introduces the central and pivotal concept of inauthentic mothering: "Out of maternal power-lessness and in response to a society whose values it does not determine, maternal thinking has often and largely opted for inauthenticity and the 'good' of others" (103). She elaborates:

> By inauthenticity I designate a double willingness—first a willingness to *travailler pour l'armée* [to work for the army] to accept the uses to which others put one's children; and second, a willingness to remain blind to the implications of those uses for the actual lives of women and children. Maternal thought embodies inauthenticity by taking on the values of the dominant culture. (103)

Maternal inauthenticity, Ruddick explains further, becomes expressed as a "repudiation of one's own perceptions and values" and results in mothers "relinquishing authority to others and losing confidence in their own values and in their perception of their children's needs" (111-112). In the third chapter on feminist mothering, I explore Ruddick's concept of acceptability and authenticity specifically in the context of feminist mothering, and consider the challenge of mothers raising a child to be "acceptable to their social group" as dictated by the demand of training and "produc[ing] a person whom they themselves and those closest to them can appreciate" as a feminist mother (103).

I had the good fortune to be a friend and colleague of Sara Ruddick. Sara was a keynote speaker at several *MIRCI* conferences, including our first one in 1997 on the topic of mothers and daughters. In 2009, I published, in celebration of the twentieth anniversary of Ruddick's book, the edited volume *Maternal Thinking: Philosophy, Politics and Peace*. In 2006, I travelled to New York to interview Sara Ruddick for this volume. The interview, originally taped, became a lengthy conversation written between the two of us via email over many, many months. The conversation opens my edited volume *Maternal Thinking* and ends with these words by Ruddick:

> So we are not as good as we should be, not as good as we could be. We will try to extend our grasp of "other" mothers' lives. And perhaps when we do, we will find that some mothers, acting together and deliberately on behalf of all their children, can weaken just a little the forces of violence that are aimed against us and the forces of destruction that are aimed by us. (36)

I argue, as I conclude this section, that Ruddick's concept of maternal thinking has enabled mothers "to work together" and has made possible the articulation of maternal voices now heard in maternal theory and in the larger field of motherhood studies.

The Reproduction of Mothering and the Maternal Relational Self: Nancy Chodorow

In *The Reproduction of Mothering*, Nancy Chodorow argues that the desire and ability to mother are embedded in the feminine personality and are not acquired through imitation or instruction. Maternal subjectivity, according to Chodorow, is a "relational self," and it is acquired rather than learned through the psychological process of gender formation. Women develop a relational sense of self that is intrinsic to feminine personality and is necessary for mothering because as Chodorow contends, they are mothered by women. Mothers produce in their daughters the relational sense of self that causes women to become mothers. Daughters are psychologically prepared for mothering through their own mother's mothering—hence, the reproduction of mothering. The central and organizing premise of Chodorow's theory is that the pre-Oedipal and Oedipal separation differ for sons and daughters. The length and quality of the pre-Oedipal period is different for boys and girls and this difference, Chodorow argues, is "rooted in women's mothering, specifically in the fact that a mother is of the same gender as her daughter and of a different gender from her son" (98). Along with Freud, Chodorow argues that the pre-Oedipal mother-daughter attachment is more prolonged and intense than the mother-son relationship. Because the daughter and the mother are same gender, the mother perceives and treats her daughter as identical to and as continuous with herself. The sameness and continuity of the pre-Oedipal mother-daughter symbiosis engenders a feminine psychic structure that is less individuated and differentiated. The daughter's sense of self is relational; she experiences herself as connected to others. Chodorow explains:

> Feminine personality comes to be based less on repression of inner objects, and fixed and firm splits in the ego, and more on the retention and continuity of external relationships. From the retention of pre-Oedipal attachments to the mother, growing girls come to define and experience themselves as continuous with others; their experience of self contains more flexible or permeable ego boundaries. Boys come to define themselves as more separate and distinct, with a greater sense of rigid ego boundaries and differentiation. The basic feminine sense of self is connected to the world, the basis masculine sense of self is separate. (169)

The Reproduction of Mothering seeks to answer Chodorow's main question: why do women rather than men come to mother, and what accounts for the differing psychic structures of men and women? In the last fifty pages of her text, Chodorow turns to the question of male dominance. Chodorow argues that male superiority is built into "the definition of masculinity itself" (185). In "mother-involved, father-absent" families, the boy does not learn his gender directly, as his sister does with their mother; rather, he identifies with an abstract, idealized stereotypical concept of masculinity. Furthermore, because masculinity is so elusive, a boy must define his gender negatively: what is not feminine becomes masculine. Upon discovery that the mother is "other" and is feminine, the Oedipal boy must reject her to obtain his masculine identity in the world of the father. The boy also learns from his family and society that masculinity is distinct from, and preferable to, femininity. Chodorow elaborates:

> Masculinity is presented to a boy as less available and accessible than femininity, as represented to him by his mother. A boy's mother is his primary caretaker. At the same time, masculinity is idealized or accorded superiority, and thereby becomes even more desirable. Although fathers are not as salient as mothers in daily interaction, mothers and children often idealize them and

give them ideological primacy, precisely because of their absence and the organization and ideology of male dominance in the larger society. (181)

The psychic structure a boy acquires in a father-absent, mother-involved family is a sense of self that is separate from and superior to others.

Thus, both gender difference and male dominance originate from exclusive female mothering. "The social organization of parenting," Chodorow concludes in her afterword, "produces sexual inequality, not simply role differentiation" (214). Female mothering constructs gendered identities that are both differentiated and hierarchal. The relational sense of self that women inherit from their mothers and bring to their own mothering exacerbates female self-effacement and frustrates women's achievement of an authentic autonomous identity. The exclusive female mothering of boys, Chodorow argues, "generates in men conflicts over masculinity, a psychology of male dominance, and the need to be superior to women" (214). In the final paragraphs of her text, Chodorow develops from her theoretical argument a political strategy. She argues that the involvement of men in early childrearing would halt the reproduction of gender difference and male dominance. Thus, the transformation of the family must be at the top of the feminist agenda. Ultimately, the argument Chodorow makes in *The Reproduction of Mothering* is that relationality is problematic for women because it hinders autonomy, psychological and otherwise. And since daughter-mother attachment and identification is the cause of this relationality in women it is, in her words, "bad for mother and [daughter] alike" (217). Thus, both mother-daughter closeness and connectedness are, for Chodorow, harmful, as they give rise to relationality and work against autonomy. Sons, of course, need to differentiate from the mother; they need to identify with a father to secure a fixed and firm masculine identity.

Significantly, in Chodorow's theory of the reproduction of mothering the "real" world is removed from her psychoanalytic abstraction of family patterns and gender formations. Critics have pointed out that Chodorow's mother-involved and father-absent family is specifically a first-world, white, urban, and middle-class structure. The gendered personalities that this specific family creates thus should not be used, as Chodorow does, to account for universal male dominance and gender difference. Moreover, the theory of mother-daughters' mutual psychological over-identification to explain women's dependent sense of self glosses over women's lived powerlessness in a patriarchal world. In an early review of Chodorow's work, Marcia Westkott comments:

> The important element in the development of feminine personality in a patriarchal context is not identification qua identification but identification "*through weakness.*" It is not just that mothers cannot let go of their daughters, and therefore create mutual dependence; and it is not just that their mothers did the same thing to them. The need of mothers to remain close to their daughters arises because mothers are given few other choices, not just because of an infantile personality structure. The weaknesses stems not only from ego boundaries, but also from a lack of power and choice. What a mother "gives" to her daughter is not just another weak ego boundary, but the weakness and powerlessness of being a mother in a patriarchal society. (9)

Westkott emphasizes that the daughter does not simply identify with a mother who is like her and, thus, obtains a relational sense of self; rather, she identifies with a mother who is weak and powerless and thus develops a sense of self deficient in power and authority. In this early review, Westkott insists that psychological processes are shaped by the social context in which they unfold. But her assumptions of social contexts are themselves problematic. Westkott assumes further, with Chodorow, that women are much too relational and dependent, although she attributes this to culture and not psychology. Westkott's critique of connectedness is, I would suggest, the result of a larger cultural belief that views close mother-daughter connection as harmful and unhealthy, as was discussed in the above section on matrophobia. Indeed as Paula Caplan argues in *Don't Blame Mother:* "Women love connection. But in a society that is phobic about intimacy and extols the virtues of independence, we mistakenly regard connection and closeness as dependency, fusion and merging" (113). Thus, autonomy is equated with independence and connection with dependency.

In her 1974 sociological article, "Family Structures and Feminine Personality," Chodorow explores the interfacing of relationality and autonomy through an examination of cultures with "matrifocal tendencies in family structure." The women observed in her research on matrifocal families (the women of working-class London, Java, and Atjeh) all enjoy high status in their communities. Chodorow writes:

> Women's kin role, and in particular the mother role, is central and positively valued in Atjeh, Java, and east London. Women gain status and prestige as they get older; their major role is not fulfilled in early motherhood. At the same time, women may be important contributors to the family's economic support, as in Java and east London. And in all three societies they have control over real economic resources. All these factors give women a sense of self-esteem independent of their relationship to their children. Finally, strong relationships exist between women in these societies, expressed in mutual cooperation and frequent contact. A mother, then, when her children are young, is likely to spend much of her time in the company of other women, not simply isolated with her children. (63)

The mother-daughter relationships observed in these cultures are also different from those constructed later by Chodorow in her psychoanalytical model. In these three societies, Chodorow elaborates that

> mother-daughter ties ... described as extremely close seem to be composed of companionship and mutual cooperation, and to be positively valued by both mother and daughter. The ethnographers do not imply that women are weighed down by the burden of their relationships or by overwhelming guilt and responsibility. On the contrary, they seem to have developed *a strong sense of self and self-worth, which continues to grow as they get older and take on their maternal role.* The implication is *that ego strength is not completely dependent on the firmness of ego boundaries....* [A] daughter's identification with her mother in this kind of setting is with a strong woman with clear control over important spheres of her life, whose sense of self-esteem can reflect this. *Acceptance of her gender identity involves positive valuation of herself, and not an admission of inferiority.* (62, emphasis added)

Chodorow contrasts the self-assurance enjoyed by the daughters in matrifocal communities to the low self-esteem experienced by the daughters of Western middle-class families: "For the daughter [of] a Western middle-class family," Chodorow argues, "feminine gender identification means identification with a devalued, passive mother, and personal maternal identification is with a mother whose own self-esteem is low" (65).

Chodorow's argument here is crucial and needs to be emphasized. In matrifocal communities, relationality does not equal dependency; mother-daughter identification, far from hindering a strong sense of self in daughters, results in daughters having high self-esteem and valuing themselves as women. In other words, the mother-daughter identification empowers the daughter, and the sense of self she obtains through this identification is one of strength and self-assurance. The daughters are empowered by identification with the mother because mothers are valued in these cultures, and motherhood is not the sole or defining role of women. Women's friendships with one another and their role as economic contributors to the family unit are equally important. Chodorow does not include this argument in *The Reproduction of Mothering*. There she presents mothering as the cause of women's relationality and, hence, dependency. Feminist writers on the mother-daughter relationship, however, have returned to Chodorow's earlier findings to argue that daughters are empowered through connection and identification with their mothers.

Wife Role and Postfeminist Split Subjectivity: Miriam Johnson, Lynn O'Brien Hallstein, and Andrea O'Reilly

Wife Role

In Chodorow's psychoanalytical account, the differential treatment of sons and daughters by their mothers is said to be the cause of both gender difference and male dominance. Miriam Johnson in *Strong Mothers, Weak Wives* argues, in contrast, that "It is the wife role and not the mother's role that organizes women's secondary status" (6). Women's secondary status, she maintains, originates not from the maternal core of women's subjectivity (Chodorow's relational self) but from their heterosexual identity as wives of men. In other words, Johnson maintains that male dominance originates not from the mother-child attachment but from the father-daughter relationship. The relationship between father and daughter, Johnson asserts, "trains daughters to be wives who are expected to be secondary to their husbands" (8). Johnson argues that fathers often romanticize the father-daughter relationship and interact with their daughter as a lover would. Fathers feminize their daughters: daddies teach them to be passive, pleasing, and pretty for men. In Johnson's words, "[The father-daughter relationship] reproduce[s] in daughters a disposition to please men in a relationship in which the male dominates" (184). In other words, "daddy's girls are in training to be wives" (184). Because "daddy's girls" are trained and rewarded for pleasing and playing up to men, they grow up to be male-defined and male-orientated women. Thus, in most so-called normal, (i.e., male-dominant) families, what is experienced is psychological incest. Johnson explains: "The incest is psychological, not overtly sexual. The father takes his daughter over. She looks up to him because he is her father. He is the king and she is the princess. It is all ok because the male is dominant in 'normal' adult heterosexual relations" (173). Johnson argues that these princesses are in need of rescue and the rescuer is the mother. She writes: "If daddy's girls are to gain their independence they need to construct an identity as the daughters of strong mothers as well" (184).

In *The Reproduction of Mothering*, Chodorow attributes women's lack of autonomy to the feminine-related sense of self, which the mother-daughter relationship engendered. In contrast, Johnson argues that women's lack of autonomy originates from the daughter's psychological dependency on her father as a male-orientated "daddy's girl." According to Johnson, far from inhibiting authentic female autonomy, a daughter's identification with her mother produces and promotes that authenticity and autonomy. Chodorow suggests in her article "Family Structures and Feminine Personality," discussed earlier, that daughters are empowered by identification with their mothers in matrifocal cultures. Johnson believes that an empowering mother-daughter identification is also possible under patriarchy if the daughter relates to her mother as a mother and friend and not as the father's wife. Johnson contends that a close mother-daughter relationship is needed to overcome women's psychological inauthenticity as "daddy's girls," and, by implication, women's social oppression in patriarchy. For Johnson, the daughter must identify with the maternal part of her mother's identity rather than the heterosexual one. This identification empowers the daughter in two ways: first, it allows her to step outside her oppressive "daddy's girl" role; and second, it allows her to identify with an adult woman's strength rather than her weakness. In Johnson's view, women are strong as mothers but made weak as wives. In identifying with her mother as mother, the daughter may construct a strong female identity outside of the passive heterosexual one, which is patterned for her by her father and society at large.

For Johnson, it is the wife role, and not the mother's role, that causes women's secondary status in a patriarchal culture. Matrifocal cultures, in contrast, downplay the wife role and emphasize women's mothering; hence, such cultures are characterized by greater gender equality. In matrifocal societies, Johnson writes, "women play roles of cultural and social significance and define themselves less as wives than as mothers" (226). As Johnson continues:

> Matrifocality, however, does not refer to domestic maternal dominance so much as it does to the relative cultural prestige of the image of mother, a role that is culturally elaborated and valued. Mothers are also structurally central in that mother as a status has some degree of control over the kin unit's economic resources and is critically involved in kin-related decision making processes. It is not the absence of males (males may be quite present) but the centrality of women as mothers and sisters that makes a society matrifocal, and this matrifocal emphasis is accompanied by a minimum of differentiation between women and men. (226)

The wife identity is, thus, less pronounced and prevalent in matrifocal cultures because in these societies, women assume an economic role and experience gender equality in the family unit. Patricia Hill Collins writing on African American women (discussed fully below) explores the following: "Black mothers have long integrated their activities as economic providers into their mothering relationships. In contrast to the cult of true womanhood, in which work is defined as being in opposition to and incompatible with motherhood, work for Black women has been an important and valued dimension of Afrocentric definitions of Black motherhood" (48). "Whether they wanted to or not," Collins continues, "the majority of African-American women had to work and could not afford the luxury of motherhood as a non-economically productive, female 'occupation'" (49). Thus, Black women, at least among the urban poor, do not assume the wife role, which Johnson identifies as structuring women's oppression. Moreover, in African American culture, motherhood, not marriage, emerges as the rite of passage into womanhood. As Joyce Ladner emphasizes in

Tomorrow's Tomorrow: "If there was one common standard for becoming a woman that was accepted by the majority of the people in the community, it was the time when girls gave birth to their first child. This line of demarcation was extremely clear and separated the girls from the women" (215-216). The matrifocal structure of Black families with its emphasis on motherhood over wifedom and Black women's role as economic provider means that the wife role is less operative in the African American community and that motherhood, as is discussed later in this chapter, functions as a site of power and empowerment for Black women.

Feminist scholarship on motherhood has rightly identified the need to counter and change the normative discourse of patriarchal motherhood in order for women to achieve empowerment as mothers. However, as Johnson cautions, women must likewise defy and deconstruct traditional partnered relationships, particularly as they are manifested in the normative ideology of the ideal wife in both identity and practice. The normative wife role assumes and expects that 1) the family will be organized around the career of the husband; 2) the career of the wife, should she have one, will be necessarily secondary to that of her husband; 3) the wife is to support her husband's career and its advancement; and 4) the woman is responsible for and performs the many and varied tasks of maintaining the household and homemaking. The normative wife role is particularly detrimental to women in demanding professional careers. It is difficult, if not impossible, for a woman to live up to her career obligations if her career is secondary to that of her husband's, and if she is solely responsible for the care and running of the home and household. Indeed, the findings of my research on academic mothers show that the excessive gender scripts of academe (masculinity) along with conventional marriages (femininity) have created a perfect storm for academic mothers, wherein they find it difficult to achieve academic success—so much so that traditional gendered partnerships become more of a deterrent to academic success than single motherhood. In my recent research on academic motherhood, I explore how the highly gendered scripts of the normative wife and husband role serve to hinder women's employment success. In particular, I argue that in order to make successful academic careers possible for mothers, it is just as critical to challenge patriarchal marriage as it is the masculinist culture of academe; likewise, I propose that women must secure gender equity in the home as well as in the workplace ("I Should Have Married Another Man").

Postfeminist Split Subjectivity

In our introduction to *Academic Motherhood in a Post-Second-Wave Context*, Lynn O'Brien Hallstein and I argue that contemporary women's subjectivity is experienced as a split between new-found gains as unencumbered women (women without children) and old gendered expectations when women become mothers. Thus, at the core of women's post-second-wave split subjectivity is a key tension between women's post-second-wave freedom from pre-second-wave gender discrimination as unencumbered women and ongoing gender-based discrimination once women become mothers. When we use the term "post-second-wave," we mean to suggest "after second-wave feminism" or "as a result of second-wave feminism," and, unlike much popular writing, we do not employ the term to mean that we live in a postfeminist context, which implies that all gender problems have been solved through second-wave feminism. In fact, we mean that our contemporary context is one that is simultaneously split between newfound gains for women—especially for middle-class women with class, race, and sexuality privileges—and old family-life gender patterns and assumptions that discipline both men and women.

More specifically, because they are the first generation of women who are second-wave beneficiaries, contemporary women are living within a cultural milieu that Peggy Orenstein, for example, calls "half-changed," where young women grow up with new expectations about what it means to be female while, simultaneously, traditional patterns, particularly around family life and parenting, remain unchanged. Or, as Julia Wood puts it, "American women's lives are in a 'transitional time' between new roles and expectations and persisting deeply held traditional gender values and roles" (17). Thus, women's post-second-wave split subjectivity is simultaneously divided between real and tangible gender similarity with men and problematic and oppressive gender assumptions primarily connected to family-life issues.

Intriguingly, then, recognizing that contemporary women have a post-second-wave split subjectivity reveals the ways that, on the one hand, the lives of women without children have become more and more similar to the lives of men without children; yet, on the other hand, becoming a mother fundamentally changes that similarity and changes women's lives in ways that most often do not affect many men's lives after they become normative fathers. Shari Dworkin and Faye Wachs describe well the post-second-wave similarity between men's and women's lives. Drawing on the work of Michael Kimmel and speaking in relation to professional life and individual self-care, they suggest: "at the turn of the millennium, men's and women's lives are becoming 'more similar,' at least for the most advantaged. For the privileged, most professions are gender-neutral, and women and men are routinely employed in the same professions, enjoy the same leisure activities, and engage in similar rituals of selfcare" (120). In other words, as gender roles and expectations have changed for both men and women, single or unencumbered—unencumbered with or from children—men's and women's lives are now "more similar," as long as both men and women adhere to the norms and institutional assumptions of professional organizations, including the male organizing systems that undergird academe.

In this new post-second-wave context, "old" gender assumptions about women emerge once women become mothers. And these old gender assumptions contradict and challenge the similarity that now exists between unencumbered men and women. Indeed, feminist writers and scholars (Crittenden; Hayden and O'Brien Hallstein; Hirshman; O'Brien Hallstein, "Second Wave Silences"; O'Reilly, *Mother Outlaws, Rocking the Cradle*; Orenstein; Warner; Williams; Wood) have all shown that even though second-wave feminism opened up access to educational and professional contexts for at least already privileged women, women still have primary responsibility for childcare and childrearing once they have children. Popular writers (Crittenden; Hirshman; Wolf), for example, all argue that this is the case even when women work, even across class lines. As Linda Hirshman puts it: "the assignment of responsibility for the household to women applies in every social class" (11). Ann Crittenden also reveals that women's responsibility for childrearing and care also emerges even if a couple has shared household labour before the arrival of a child. As she argues: "Before the arrival of the first child, couples tend to share the house work fairly equally. But something about a baby encourages the resurgence of traditional gender roles" (25). Ironically, then, many women today—particularly those who are college educated, middle-class and professional—may not actually encounter overt gender discrimination until they become mothers. Contemporary women's subjectivity, then, is split between newfound gains as unencumbered women (women without children) and old gendered expectations when women become mothers.

We argue that one result of contemporary mothers' post-second-wave split subjectivity is that a "new" normative family configuration is emerging—a family arrangement that Miriam Peskowitz first described as a neotraditional family. Neotraditional families appear to be new and even progressive because many contemporary, privileged heterosexual families have both an educated and professional mother and father. This family configuration continues to be problematic, however, since the basic foundation of pre-second-wave family roles and responsibilities still hold once children arrive: mothers continue to be primary caregivers of children in this "new" family type. In other words, although unencumbered women have benefited in real and important ways from second-wave feminism, once women become mothers, many of those women adopt neotraditional family configurations that continue to place the primary responsibility of household labour and caregiving on them, even as they maintain their full-time employment. In new and complex ways, then, even though contemporary women's lives have been freed from a domestic destiny as mothers, women's lives have not been freed from domestic responsibility in their homes. Equally important, neotraditional families are the new norm for many women, and this "new" norm also creates complexity and tension for women because it demands that women simultaneously meet the intensive demands of the new momism, discussed below, while also meeting the intensive and exacting norms and expectations of professional careers.

Normative Motherhood: Intensive Mothering and the New Momism

Building on Rich's insight that motherhood is a cultural construction, I argue in my writing and teaching that normative motherhood discourses are rewritten in response to, and as a result of, significant cultural and economic change. Numerous works detail how the modern image of the "full-time stay-at-home mother"—isolated in the private sphere and financially dependent on her husband—came about as result of industrialization. Industrialization took work out of the home and repositioned the domestic space, at least among the middle class, as an exclusively nonproductive and private realm, which is separate from the public sphere of work. At the end of World War II, the discourse of the "happy homemaker" made "the stay-at-home-mom-and-apple pie" mode of mothering the normal and natural motherhood experience. The view that stay-at-home motherhood is what constitutes good motherhood emerged only in the postwar period to effect a social reorganization and, more particularly, to redesign feminine gender behaviour and roles. During World War Two in North America, there was an unprecedented increase in women's employment to include white, middle-class mothers who had previously not been engaged in full-time employment. Thus, in the war period, mothers were encouraged to work and were celebrated for doing so, particularly in the propaganda films and literature. With the end of the war and the return of the soldiers, women were forced to give up their wartime employment. This was orchestrated and facilitated by an ideological redesign of what constitutes good motherhood. Buttressed by the new psychological teachings, notably Bowlby's attachment theory, two beliefs emerged in the 1950s: 1) children require full time "stay-at-home" mothering; and 2) children, without full time mothering, would suffer from what was termed "maternal deprivation." According to Bowlby, as noted by Shari Thurer in *The Myths of Motherhood: How Culture Reinvents the Good Mother*, "maternal deprivation was as damaging in the first three years of life as German measles in the first three months of pregnancy: mother love in infancy is as important for mental health as proteins and vitamins for physical health" (276).

Sacrificial motherhood, as described by my students earlier in this chapter, thus emerged as the dominant view of good mothering in the postwar period, or approximately seventy years ago. Sacrificial motherhood is characterized by three central themes. The first defines mothering as natural to women and essential to their being, conveyed in the belief, as Pamela Courtenay Hall notes, that "women are naturally mothers, they are born with a built-in set of capacities, dispositions, and desires to nurture children ... [and that this] engagement of love and instinct is utterly distant from the world of paid work" (60). Second, the mother is to be the central caregiver of her biological children. And third, children require full-time mothering, or in the instance where the mother must work outside the home, the children must always come before the job. Sharon Hays argues that intensive mothering emerged in the postwar period. I contend in contrast that even though the origins of intensive mothering may be traced back to this time, intensive mothering, in its fully developed form, developed in the late 1980s and early 1990s. Hays argues that intensive mothering is characterized by three themes: first, "the mother is the central caregiver"; second, "mothering is regarded as more important than paid employment"; and third, "mothering requires lavishing copious amounts of time, energy, and material resources on the child" (8). I would suggest that whereas the first two characterize mothering from postwar to present day, only mothering of the last thirty years can be characterized by the third theme—namely, children require copious amounts of time, energy, and material resources. The postwar discourse of good motherhood demanded that mothers be at home full time with their children; however, such a demand did not require the intensive mothering expected of mothers today. I see the postwar discourse of motherhood—what I term "custodial motherhood" or the "flower-pot" approach—covering the period between 1946 to the late 1980s, and understand it as different from intensive mothering. Intensive mothering, in contrast, emerged in the early 1900s and is practiced by the daughters born after the baby boom era and who become mothers in the early 1990s and onwards. Although intensive mothering emerges from custodial mothering, I emphasize that it is a distinct motherhood discourse specific to its historical period.

To illustrate the difference between custodial motherhood and intensive mothering and to locate this transition in the early 1990s, I share one of my own mothering experiences. In 1988, when my eldest daughter was two, she attended a dance class held on York University campus, where our family lived. The mothers would arrive with large mugs of coffee every Saturday morning, and we would leave our children with the dance instructor. As our toddlers exorcised their rambunctious energy, the mothers enjoyed a much-needed hour of peace and companionship.

Three years later in 1991, I enrolled my youngest daughter in the same program and arrived again with my huge mug of coffee looking forward to that much-needed hour with the other mothers.

However, as I was about to exit the gymnasium after dropping my daughter off, the same instructor explained that I was to stay as this was a "moms and tots" dance class. I do not know who was more surprised and dare I say disappointed that day: my daughter, who was looking forward to an hour with her friends, or I, who would have rather been drinking a cup of coffee hanging out with the other mothers. This is in no way to suggest that I do not enjoy spending time with my daughters or that mothers and their children should not dance together (in fact, I still do, although my children are now adults). I am only suggesting that there is a time and place for everything. Indeed, after experiencing both types of programs, I argue that the one where the children danced with other children without their mothers' interference was more beneficial to both my daughters and me.

Most research on motherhood, however, does not distinguish between custodial motherhood and intensive mothering, or consider how and why the latter emerged in the 1990s; rather, both are characterized as postwar mothering or more generally twentieth-century mothering. To fully understand how patriarchal ideologies of good motherhood function as culturally constructed practices—ones that are continuously redesigned in response to changing economic and societal factors—there must be a distinction made between custodial motherhood and intensive mothering because these two discourses emerged in response to two very different cultural transformations.

Normative motherhood in the postwar era required full-time mothering, but the emphasis was on the physical proximity of mother and child (i.e., the mother was to be at home with the children) and not on the mother needing to be continuously attuned to the psychological, emotional, or cognitive needs of her children. My mother, for example, remembering the early 1960s, recalls "airing" my sister and me on the front porch each morning while she tended to the housework. Domesticity—keeping a clean house and serving well-prepared dinners—was, more so than children, what occupied the postwar mother's time and attention. In the 1950s and 1960s, as well, there was a clearer division between the adult world and the world of children. Children would spend their time out in the neighbourhood playing with other children; children would seldom look to their parents for entertainment or amusement. And children were rarely enrolled in programs, with the exception of the occasional Brownies or club meeting in the school-aged years. Fast forward to the mid-1990s and the type of mothering I received and enjoyed as a child would be regarded as deficient under the new discourse of intensive mothering.

Intensive Mothering

Sharon Hays argues, as noted above, that intensive mothering is characterized by three themes: first, "the mother is the central caregiver"; second, "mothering is regarded as more important than paid employment"; and third, "mothering requires lavishing copious amounts of time, energy, and material resources on the child" (8). Moreover, intensive mothering "tells us that children are innocent and priceless, that their rearing should be carried out primarily by individual mothers and that it should be centered on children's needs, with methods that are informed by experts, labor intensive, and costly" (21). She emphasizes that intensive mothering is "a historically constructed cultural model for appropriate child care" (21). She continues:

> Conceptions of appropriate child rearing are not simply a random conglomeration of disconnected ideas; they form a fully elaborated, logically cohesive framework for thinking about and acting toward children.... [W]e are told that [intensive mothering] is the best model, largely because it is what children need and deserve. This model was not developed overnight, however, nor is intensive mothering the only model available to mothers. (21)

Intensive mothering, in contrast to custodial mothering dictates the following: 1) children can only be properly cared for by the biological mother; 2) this mothering must be provided 24/7; 3) the mother must always put children's needs before her own; 4) mothers must turn to the experts for instruction; 5) the mother must be fully satisfied, fulfilled, completed, and composed in motherhood; and finally, 6) mothers must lavish excessive amounts of time, energy, and money in the rearing of their children. In the introduction to her book *Intensive Mothering*, Linda Ennis perceptively provides concrete examples of how these mandates are enacted in the day-to-day work of childrearing:

> They include but are not limited to mothers doing homework for their children; mothers being friends with their children's friends; mothers' social lives revolving around their children; mothers encouraging children to continually phone or text them; mothers spending all their free time with their children; mothers always putting the children's needs before their own; mothers doing everything for their children such as laundry, driving and

lunches; mothers speaking for their children; all conversations with friends and family revolving around their children; mothers feeling empty after their children leave home for school or move out; mothers who won't allow their children to sleep over at friends' homes or go to overnight camp and/or children who won't leave home for any length of time. (6)

Today, intensive mothering demands more than mere physical proximity of the mother and child: contemporary mothers are expected to spend, to use the discourse of the experts, "quality time" with their children. Mothers are told to play with their children, read to them, and take classes with them. As the children in the 1950s and 1960s would jump rope or play hide-and-seek with the neighbourhood children or their siblings, today's children dance, swim and "cut and paste" with their mothers in one of many "moms and tots" programs. And today, children as young as three months old are enrolled in a multitude of classes—water-play for infants, French immersion for toddlers, karate for preschoolers, and competitive skiing, skating, or sailing for elementary school children, to name just a few. (An article I read recently also recommends reading and singing to your child in utero.) It is not until the rise of intensive mothering that the patriarchal mandates of expertization and intensification become fully enacted and enforced. "We all know the ideal of the good mother," Susan E. Chase and Mary Rogers assert in their book *Mothers and Children: Feminist Analysis and Personal Narratives*, and they proceed to give a list of her characteristics:

> Above all, she is selfless. Her children come before herself and any other need or person or commitment no matter what. She loves her children unconditionally yet she is careful not to smother them with love or her own needs. She follows the advice of doctors and other experts and she educates herself about child development. She is very present in her children's lives when they are young, and when they get older she is home every day to greet them as they return from school. If she works outside the home, she arranges her job around her children so she can be there for them as much as possible, certainly whenever they are sick or unhappy. The good mother's success is reflected in her children's behavior—they are well mannered, and respectful to

others; at the same time they have a strong sense of independence and self-esteem. They grow up to be productive citizens. (30)

Indeed, as Bonnie Fox has remarked:

Expectations about the work needed to raise a child successfully have escalated at a dizzy rate; the bar is now sky high. Aside from the weighty prescriptions about the nutrition essential to babies' and children's physical health, and the sensitivity required for their emotional health, warnings about the need for intellectual stimulation necessary for developmental progress are directed at mothers. (237)

Even though today mothers have fewer children and more labour-saving devices—from microwaves to take out food—mothers spend more time, energy, and money on their children than their mothers did in the 1960s. And the majority of mothers today, unlike fifty years ago, practice intensive mothering while engaged in full-time employment. Mothering today, as in the postwar era, is "expert driven." However, under the ideology of intensive mothering, mothering is more child centred than the "children-should-be-seen-but-not-heard" style of mothering that characterized the postwar period. Contemporary mothering, thus, demands far more from mothers than was asked of them from the 1950s to 1980s.

The ideology of intensive mothering, as Hays notes, "advise[s] mothers to expend a tremendous amount of time, energy and money in raising children" (8). However, as Hays continues, "In a society where over half of all mothers with young children are now working outside the home, one might wonder why our culture pressures women to dedicate so much of themselves to child rearing" (x). Indeed, again to quote Hays, "Today ... when well over half of all mothers are in the paid labor force, when the image of a career women is that of a competitive go-getter, and when the image of the family is one of disintegrating values and relationships, one would expect a de-emphasis on the ideology of child rearing as labor-intensive, emotionally absorbing work" (3). One would expect to locate the ideology of intensive mothering in the postwar period when middle-class mothers, engaged in full-time motherhood, had more time and energy to devote to childrearing. Instead, the emergence of intensive mothering parallels the increase in mothers' paid labour force participation.

Theorists of motherhood and mothers alike, offer various explanations to account for the emergence of intensive mothering over the last twenty-five years. Sharon Hays, for example, argues the following:

> The ideology of intensive child rearing practices persists, in part, because it serves the interests of men but also capitalism, the state, the middle class and Whites. Further, and on a deeper level ... the ideology of intensive mothering is protected and promoted because it holds a fragile but nonetheless, powerful cultural position as the last best defense against what many people see as the impoverishment of social ties, communal obligations, and unremunerated commitments. (xiii)

I argue that intensive mothering emerges in the late 1980s in response to changing demographics of motherhood. Today, for the majority of middle-class women, motherhood is embarked upon only after a career is established and when the woman is in her thirties. For these mothers, the hurriedness of intensive mothering is a continuation of their busy lives as professional women. Whereas once mothers' daybooks were filled with business lunches, office meetings, and the like, now as intensive mothers who are home with their children, their daybooks are full of Gymboree classes, "moms and tots" programs, and library visits. Often these professional, highly educated women, who are unfamiliar and perhaps uncomfortable with the everyday, devalued, invisible work of mothering and domesticity, fill up their days with public activities that can be documented as productive and visible work. With fewer children, and more labour-saving devices and household help, childrearing—or more accurately the enrichment and amusement of one beloved child—becomes the focus of the mother's time and attention, as opposed to cooking and cleaning as it was in my mother's generation. And when these professional women return to their careers, intensive mothering, as practiced in the evenings and weekends, is the way a working mother, consciously or otherwise, compensates for her time away from her children; it bespeaks the ambivalence and guilt contemporary working mothers may feel about working and enjoying the work that they do. As well, intensive mothering's emphasis on enrichment—toys, books, games, activities, programs, camps, holidays, theatre, and so forth for children—has emerged in response to mothers earning an income of their own and having a say on how household money is spent. Mothers, more so than fathers, are the consumers of items children need and want; so as a mother's earnings and economic independence increase, more money is spent on children. As well, mothers today are having fewer children, which makes intensive mothering possible—they can devote all their time and attention to one or two beloved children. Now children must also turn to their mothers, rather than siblings or neighbours, for companionship. Finally, some argue that just as custodial mothering emerged in the postwar period in response to new psychological theories that stressed the need for mother-child attachment, intensive mothering in our time has arisen in response to new scientific research that emphasizes the importance of the first five years of life in the intellectual, behavioural, emotional, and social development of the child. Whatever the economic or social explanation may be, the ideology of intensive mothering measures good mothering in accordance with the amount of time, money, and energy a mother spends on childrearing. Raising one child today, as my mother frequently remarks, demands more time, energy, and money than the raising of four in the postwar period. Indeed, the demands made on mothers today are unparalleled in history.

In her article "Motherhood as a Class Act: The Many Ways in Which 'Intensive Mothering' is Entangled with Social Class," Bonnie Fox argues that intensive mothering requires, signifies, and reproduces middle-class status. From her interviews with forty couples (nine working class and thirty-one middle class), Fox finds that "middle class women are more likely to have the material and personal resources necessary to give themselves over completely to mothering; [thus middle class women] are more likely to develop intensive mothering practices" (251). These resources include not only the obvious one of money—being free from economic pressures and financial worries—but also those of efficacy and time. Middle-class women, Fox argues, come to motherhood with a sense of accomplishment and competence, and thus have "a strong sense of self-efficacy ... to take on and persist in the considerable challenges of intensive mothering" (250). The middle-class women interviewed by Fox also "displayed a sense of ownership of time" and, in particular, successful women in the labour force "felt entitled to spend their time on the baby and able to overcome feelings that they needed to accomplish more than baby care" (255).

Given the nature of intensive mothering, middle-class circumstances and resources—in particular financial security, time and efficacy—seem to be, Fox concludes "the pre-requisites for its accomplishment" (243).

One mother interviewed by Fox remarks: "Having a woman at home full-time is the new marker of being middle class" (256). However, although intensive mothering may signify class privilege, it is, as Fox emphasizes, acutely gendered: "as being home with a baby and doing intensive mothering may detract from women's class status given how much more recognition paid work is regularly shown, it may bolster men's class status" (257). I argue further that different from the postwar era when having a stay-at-home wife marked the achievement of middle-class status, today middle-class status is signified not only by a stay-at-home mother but one who engages in intensive mothering. In this way, intensive mothering is specifically a marker of middle-class status. Fox also considers how mothering practices reproduce social class. She writes that "it is possible that intensive mothering reproduces social class, in that babies cared for in this manner are somehow better prepared for success later in life" (256). However, Fox concludes that "the theoretical and empirical grounds on which to build such a case are not at all obvious" (256). Although I agree with Fox that it is impossible to prove that intensive mothering reproduces social class, I argue that what is at issue here is that middle-class parents believe that intensive mothering does reproduce class status and privilege. Parents are committed to intensive mothering precisely because they believe, to quote again from Hays, that "by lavishing copious amounts of time, energy, and material resources on the child" their children will "succeed" in life and achieve, or perhaps more accurately inherit, middle class status (8).

In her book *Parenting Out of Control: Anxious Parents in Uncertain Times*, Margaret K. Nelson argues that the parenting styles of what she refers to as the "professional middle class" parents compared with those from the "middle" to "working" classes are quite distinct. Parenting among the professional middle classes includes the following:

> A lengthy perspective on a child's dependency, a commitment to creating 'passionate' people, personalized and negotiated guidance in the activities of daily life, respectful responsiveness to children's individualized needs and desires, a belief in the

boundless potential, ambitious goals for achievement and an intensive engagement with children. (7)

By way of contrast, Nelson notes that "the working class and middle class parents are more concerned with skills that will ensure self-sufficiency, and there are clear rules of authority within the family" (8). Why do professional middle-class parents engage in this style of parenting? This mode of childrearing—alternatively called intensive mothering or "helicopter parenting" or in Nelson's words, "parenting out of control"—is due to, according to the author, "anxieties about the children's future, from the nostalgia for the way they imagine families used to live, and from assessment of dangers to children in the world today" (174). Speaking specifically on parents' anxiety about their children's future, Nelson comments:

> anxious to secure their children's competitive advantage in a world marked by increasing anxiety about college acceptance and increasing inequality (and perhaps shrinking options for elite status), professional middle class parents seize opportunities for educational success and enroll even their very young children in a dazzling array of "extracurricular" activities. They assume that their children are, if not perfectible, blessed with boundless potential. In response they nurture children to become the best they can possibly be; they also provide them with the "best" social, cultural and economic capital. (8)

Of interest here, particularly in relation to Fox's argument on the relationship between social reproduction and social class, is Nelson's argument that professional middle-class parents engage in intensive mothering to preserve class privilege so as to ensure, in Nelson's words, "secure status reproduction" (76). Indeed, when mothers engage in intensive mothering, they are, as Hays explains, "grooming their children for their future class position by providing them with the appropriate cultural capital and demonstrating their own class status relative to mothers who cannot afford such luxuries or do not recognize them as an essential element of good childrearing" (159). They are engaging in what Melissa A. Milkie and Catherine H. Warner term "status safeguarding" (66). Thus the issue is not that the intensive mothering reproduces social status and class but that anxious professional middle-class parents in uncertain times practice intensive mothering in the belief that it will.

Nelson attributes parental anxiety about children's future among the professional middle class to several social and economic factors, and all of them centre on giving children a competitive advantage and providing them with social and economic capital. Though not named as such by Nelson, professional middle-class anxiety about their children's future and, in particular, their concern with capital and advantage, I argue, is the result of the specific political and economic context of our times—namely, the ideology of neoliberalism. The ideology of neoliberalism rests on the following assumptions and practices: the rule of the market, as seen in laissez-faire economics and free-trade policies; the cutting of public expenditure for social services, such as education and healthcare; minimal governmental intervention and deregulation; privatization, which results in the public paying even more for its needs; and the elimination of the concept of the "public good" or community with "individual responsibility" (Martinez and Garcia). Susan Braedley and Meg Luxton in their article "Competing Philosophies: Neoliberalism and Challenges of Everyday Life" argue that neoliberalism has negatively affected women in three ways. Melinda Vandenbeld Giles in her introduction to *Mothering in the Age of Neoliberalism* discusses these themes as follows:

> 1) Women's work is so poorly remunerated that women are the majority of poor people in the world and this is only made worse by neoliberal policies. 2) While neoliberalism identifies women only as economic actors, the work of mothering must still be performed and is in fact integral to the reproduction of future neoliberal workers. However, due to the neoliberal commitment of reducing state expenditures such as paid maternity leave and child care, mothers are left with no support systems. 3) Despite the emancipatory potential within the "feminization of society," neoliberalism remains an inherently male paradigm in terms of who controls the capital assets. (6)

Neoliberalism, as Braedley and Luxton write, "allows space for women who are willing or able to be like men, who present themselves as men do and who are able to compete as men do" (15).

Focusing on intensive mothering, rather than mothers and motherhood more generally as do the authors above, I argue that the rise of intensive mothering in the 1990s grows out of the emergence of neoliberalism in the same decade. Once again, the meaning and practice of normative motherhood is rewritten as a result of and in response to significant cultural and economic change. With privatization and deregulation, many of the services once provided by government—schooling, education, culture, arts, recreation, health, fitness and carework—have been downloaded to mothers. As well, with neoliberalism's emphasis on individual responsibility, mothers today are not only responsible for this downloaded work, but they are also responsible for how their children fare under neo-liberalism. If children do not succeed, the blame rests solely with the mother, as it was her responsibility to ensure that they could and should. The forces of neoliberalism and intensive mothering have created the perfect storm for twenty-first century motherhood, as mothers today must do far more work with far less resources. Indeed, neoliberalism has created the "anxious parents in uncertain times" as theorized by Nelson, which is the subtitle of her book, and has produced the practice of intensive mothering, which seeks to alleviate this anxiety and uncertainty through the social reproduction of class privilege and status, as discussed by Fox. And again, these changes in the ideological and material conditions of mothering are due to the larger economic and social transformations brought about by the rise of neoliberalism in the 1990s.

Today's intensive mothering is also, as was custodial mothering in the postwar era, an ideological construction that functions as a backlash discourse, and like all backlash discourses, it functions to regulate women or more specifically in this instance, mothers. Drawing on Naomi Wolf's theory of the "Beauty Myth," I argue that the current discourse of intensive mothering has emerged in response to women's increased social and economic independence, which includes the following: their increased labour participation, their entry into traditionally male areas of work, the rise in female-initiated divorces, the growth in female-headed households, and improved educational opportunities for women that took place in the 1970s and early 1980s. It seems that just as women were making inroads and feeling confident, a new discourse of motherhood emerged that made two things inevitable: that women would forever feel inadequate as mothers and that work and motherhood would be forever seen as in conflict and incompatible. I believe that the guilt and shame women experience in failing to live up to what is in fact an impossible ideal is neither accidental nor inconsequential; rather, it is deliberately manufactured and monitored. Just as the self-hate produced by the beauty myth undercuts and undermines women's sense of achievement in education or a career, the current discourse of intensive mothering gives rise to self-doubt or, more specifically, a guilt that immobilizes women and robs them of their confidence as both workers and mothers. Given that no one can achieve intensive mothering, all mothers see themselves as failures. This is how the discourse works psychologically to regulate (i.e., paralyze) mothers through guilt and shame. And, some mothers, believing that perfect motherhood could be achieved if they "just quit work," leave paid employment. This is how the discourse regulates on the level of the social and the economic.

A few years ago, a colleague shared with me a story that I believe illustrates well the argument I am making here. The woman was at a conference and a presenter was speaking on the merits of intensive mothering. This woman, at the conclusion of the talk, suggested to the speaker that intensive mothering was incompatible with paid work, to which the speaker agreed. The woman than asked, "if a woman cannot practice intensive mothering while employed what is she to do?" The speaker responded, "She should marry a rich man!" Her response forcefully exemplifies how intensive mothering functions as a backlash discourse to undo the achievements of feminism through the redomestication of women. Intensive mothering thus, I argue, emerges as the normative ideology and practice of motherhood in the 1990s, both in response to changing demographics (discussed earlier) and the rise of neoliberalism, and as a backlash to the advancement of women of the earlier decades.

New Momism

Building on Hays's concept of intensive mothering, Susan Douglas and Meredith Michaels define the "new momism" as the following:

> [T]he insistence that no woman is truly complete or fulfilled unless she has kids, that women remain the best primary caretakers of children, and that to be a remotely decent mother, a woman has to devote her entire physical, psychological, emotional, intellectual being, 24/7, to her children. The new

momism is a highly romanticized view of motherhood in which the standards for success are impossible to meet. (4)

The new momism, they continue, has "become unavoidable for one basic reason: Motherhood became one of the biggest media obsessions of the last three decades, exploding especially in the mid-1980s and continuing unabated to the present" (5). However, as Douglas and Michaels go on to explain, "The new momism involves more than just impossible ideals about women's childrearing; it redefines all women, first and foremost, through their relationships to children ... being a citizen, a worker, a governor [is] supposed to take a backseat to motherhood" (22). "The new momism," Douglas and Michaels continue, "insists that if you want to do anything else, you'd better first prove that you're a doting, totally involved mother before proceeding." And they conclude that "the only recourse for women who want careers, or to do anything else besides stay at home with the kids all day, is to prove they can 'do it all'" (22).

In her article, "She Gives Birth, She is Wearing a Bikini," Lynn O'Brien Hallstein argues that "the contemporary new momism is a uniquely post-second-wave, intensive-mothering ideology because it both acknowledges and integrates second-wave rhetoric and ideas" (114). As Douglas and Michaels explain, "embedded in the new momism is the idea that women have their own ambitions and money, raise kids on their own, or freely choose to stay at home with kids rather than being forced to" (5). Thus, Michaels and Douglas emphasize the following as central to new momism:

> the feminist insistence that woman [sic] have choices, that they are active agents in control of their own destiny, that they have autonomy. But here's where the distortion of feminism occurs. The only truly enlightened choice to make as a woman, the one that proves, first, that you are a "real" woman, and second, that you are a decent, worthy one, is to become a "mom" and to bring to child rearing a combination of selflessness and professionalism.... Thus the new momism is deeply contradictory: It both draws from and repudiates feminism. (5)

In this way, post-second-wave women's empowerment, as O'Brien Hallstein explains, "is now entrenched, even acknowledged and utilized, within the new momism" (115).

Locating their analysis in the context of postfeminism—the idea that feminism is no longer needed because second-wave feminism "solved" gender inequity and as a result, women can now "have it all"—Douglas and Michaels suggest that the new momism "has become the central, justifying ideology of what has come to be called 'postfeminism'" (24). Although they are disdainful of postfeminism, Douglas and Michaels also argue that "postfeminism means that you can now work outside the home even in jobs previously restricted to men, go to graduate school, pump iron, and pump your own gas, as long as you remain fashion conscious, slim, nurturing, deferential to men, and become a doting selfless mother" (25). However, in its assertions of female agency and autonomy, the "new momism" denies and distorts the fact that most mothers have little or no choice in the making of their lives. The concept of choice, as feminist theory has shown, is a neoliberal fiction that serves to disguise and justify social inequities, particularly those of gender. For me, the most worrisome part of the new momism is that normative motherhood is constructed as the mother's choice. In their discussion of "choice," Douglas and Michaels write:

> The mythology of the new momism now insinuates that, when all is said and done, the enlightened mother chooses to stay at home with the kids. Back in the 1950s mothers stayed home because they had no choice. Today having been to the office, having tried a career, women supposedly have seen the inside of the male working world and found it be the inferior choice to staying home, especially when her kids' future is at stake. It's not that mothers can't hack it (1950s thinking). It's that progressive mothers refuse to hack it. The June Cleaver model, if taken as a choice, as opposed to a requirement, is the truly modern fulfilling forward-thinking version of motherhood. (23)

The new momism not only enacts and reinforces the essentialization, normalization, and idealization of patriarchal motherhood, but it also distorts and disguises it as an empowered, or in their words "enlightened," mothering.

The discourses of intensive mothering and new momism are oppressive not because children have needs, but because we, as a culture, dictate that only the biological mother is capable of fulfilling them, that children's needs must always come before those of the mother, and that children's needs must be responded to around the clock and with extensive time, money, and energy. Petra Bueskens argues that "Infancy and early childhood are periods of high emotional and physical dependency and, moreover this is not a pure invention of patriarchal science" (81). However, as Petra Bueskens continues, "The problem is not the fact of this requirement but rather that meeting this need has come to rest exclusively, and in isolation, on the shoulders of biological mothers" (81). Indeed, as author Toni Morrison has commented: "If you listen to your children and look at them, they make demands that you can live up to. They don't need all that overwhelming love either. I mean, that's just you being vain about it" (270-271). Although sacrificial motherhood, and in particular intensive mothering, requires the denial of the mother's own selfhood in positioning the children's needs as always before her own, there are other ways to mother—ways that do not deny a mother her agency, autonomy, authenticity, and authority, and allow her both her selfhood and power. This is the subject of a later section on empowered mothering and of the third chapter on feminist mothering.

Maternal Ambivalence and the Mask of Motherhood; Barbara Almond and Susan Maushart

Maternal Ambivalence

In *The Monster Within: The Hidden Side of Motherhood*, Barbara Almond defines "ambivalence" in this way: "[It is] a mental state, in which one has both loving and hating feelings for the same person. It characterizes all human relationships, not just that of mother and child. Being able to tolerate both kinds of feelings, at different times, without having one feeling destroy the other, is a sign of good mental health" (8). Writing specifically on maternal ambivalence, Rozsika Parker defines it as "a complex and contradictory state of mind, shared by all mothers, in which loving and hating feelings exist side by side" (18). Almond argues "that ambivalence itself is not the problem but rather the guilt and anxiety that ambivalence provokes" (24). Mothers fear, in the words of Adrienne Rich, that "hate will overwhelm love" (81). In *Of Woman Born*, Rich relates that her children have caused her great suffering: "It is the suffering of ambivalence: the murderous alternation between bitter resentment and raw edged nerves and blissful gratification" (81). As Rozsika Parker elaborates, maternal ambivalence "is well established in psychoanalytic literature but because cultural expectations and assumptions presume and demand that a mother love her children unconditionally and selflessly the mother who exhibits or admits maternal ambivalence is judged harshly and is the object of shame and disbelief by other mothers and herself" (18). "That mothers have mixed feelings about their children," Almond contends, "should come as no surprise to anybody; but it is amazing how much of a taboo the negative side of maternal ambivalence carries in our culture, especially at this time" (xiii). Moreover, as Almond explains further, "today's expectations for good mothering have become so hard to live with, the standards so draconian, that maternal ambivalence has increased and at the same time become more unacceptable" (xiii). Indeed, although hating someone solely based on her religion, ethnicity, sex or nationality, may be seen as bigoted, if you hate your children, you are, in Almond's words, "considered monstrous—immoral, unnatural, evil" (2).

The patriarchal mandate of naturalization assumes that maternal ability is innate to women: mothers naturally love their children and know how to mother. Drawing on the work of sociobiologist and primatologist Sarah Blaffer Hrdy, Almond argues further that "loving motherhood is not automatically programmed into the female of species" (7). "The guilt produced by the pressure on women to be all-loving and all-giving toward their offspring," Almond continues, "takes a powerful toll on women and on children." She continues: "As women fail in their attempts to fulfill impossible standards of mothering, [t]hey feel angry and disappointed with themselves and, in turn, angry and disappointed with their children" (11). Almond goes on to explain: "Too many women suffer as they attempt to be perfect mothers, an effort driven in part to cover over their ambivalence. Modern 'maternally correct' mothers are literally driving themselves and their offspring crazy in their quest for maternal perfection, which can only be proven by the perfection of their offspring" (7-8). The patriarchal mandate of naturalization assumes that maternal desire and maternal ability are innate to all women, whereas the mandate of idealization requires that all mothers find joy and purpose in motherhood. However, since these mandates prescribe, rather than describe, mothers' lives, mothers experience ambivalence in motherhood.

Mask of Motherhood

Susan Maushart opens her book *The Mask of Motherhood* with a quotation from Betty Friedan's 1963 book *The Feminine Mystique*. "There is a strange discrepancy," writes Friedan, "between the reality of our lives as women and the image to which we are trying to conform" (qtd. in Maushart, xi). This problem, Maushart contends, remains, "in most cases, precisely the same today" (xi). She explains:

> The content of women's daily realities has changed enormously, as has the nature of the images to which we seek to conform. But the identity crisis—the mismatch between expectations and experience, between what we ought to be feeling and how we do feel, between how we ought to be managing and how we do manage—remains as painful and as intractable as ever. (xi)

Looking specifically at women's experiences of motherhood, Maushart examines the contrast and the contradictions between women's expectations of motherhood and their experiences of it.

She argues that mothers today "increasingly bring to the experience expectations that are not simply inaccurate, or ill-informed, but downright disabling ... even delusional" (xiii). The mask of motherhood, Maushart explains, is an "assemblage of fronts—mostly brave, serene, and all knowing—that we use to disguise the chaos and complexity of our lived experience" (2). To be masked, Maushart continues, is "to deny and repress what we experience, to misrepresent it, even to ourselves" (1-2). A woman, as Shelia Kitzinger notes, "who catches sight of herself in the mirror—as it were, unmasked—sees a very different picture. And the message is clear: she is a failure" (qtd. in Maushart, 8). The mask of motherhood confers an idealized and hence unattainable image of motherhood that causes women to feel guilt and anxiety about their own—messy and muddled—experiences of mothering. The mask of motherhood, as Maushart elaborates, "keeps women from speaking clearly what they know and from hearing truths too threatening to face" (7).

The unmasking of motherhood, thus, necessitates what may be termed "an archaeology of maternity": an excavation of the truths of motherhood disguised and distorted beneath the mask (O'Reilly, *Mother Matters*). This requires that mothers unmask themselves and speak truthfully and authentically about their experiences of mothering. Writing on *Of Woman Born*, Maushart comments: "Rich remained acutely aware of the riskiness of the enterprise she had undertaken. Unmasking motherhood, she grasped, was a greater challenge to the feminist imagination than all the other 'women's issues' put together" (239). However, because no mother can live the idealized perfection of the mask of motherhood, to unmask oneself is to "out" oneself as a flawed, if not failed, mother. "Given the punishing rules—and the contemptuous labels for any mom who breaks them," Mary Kay Blakely remarks in her memoir of motherhood, "mothers are reluctant to admit even having bad days, let alone all the miserable details leading up to them" (11). Indeed, as Sara Ruddick emphasizes, the "idealized figure of the Good Mother casts a long shadow on many actual mothers' lives" (31). Indeed, the mask of motherhood exposes the costs and consequences for mothers who seek both to embrace and deny the idealization of patriarchal motherhood.

Empowered Mothering

In *Of Woman Born*, Adrienne Rich, when discussing a vacation without her husband one summer, describes herself and her sons as "conspirators, outlaws from the institution of motherhood" (195). She writes:

> I remember one summer, living in a friend's house in Vermont. My husband was working abroad for several weeks and my three sons—nine, seven, and five years old—and I dwelt for most of that time by ourselves. Without a male adult in the house, without any reason for schedules, naps, regular mealtimes, or early bedtimes so the two parents could talk, we fell into what I felt to be a delicious and sinful rhythm.... [W]e lived like castaways on some island of mothers and children. At night they fell asleep without murmur and I stayed up reading and writing as I had when a student, till the early morning hours. I remember thinking: This is what living with children could be—without school hours, fixed routines, naps, the conflict of being both mother and wife with no room for being simply, myself. Driving home once after midnight from a late drive-in movie ... with three sleeping children in the back of the car, I felt wide awake, elated; we had broken together all the rules of bedtime, the night rules, rules I myself thought I had to observe in the city or

become a "bad mother." We were conspirators, outlaws from the institution of motherhood; I felt enormously in charge of my life. (194-195)

However, upon Rich's return to the city, the institution, in her words, "closed down on us again, and my own mistrust of myself as a 'good mother' returned, along with my resentment of the archetype" (195).

Rich's reflections on being an outlaw from the institution of motherhood and the references she makes to being a "good" and "bad" mother are drawn from the key distinction that she makes between motherhood and mothering discussed earlier in this chapter. In patriarchal culture, women who mother in the institution of motherhood are regarded as "good" mothers, whereas women who mother outside or against the institution of motherhood are viewed as "bad" mothers. In contrast, Rich argues that mothers, in order to resist patriarchal motherhood and achieve empowered mothering, must be "bad" mothers or, more precisely, "mother outlaws." Therefore, and in opposition to the dominant and accepted view on motherhood, Rich defines empowered mothers as good mothers and patriarchal mothers as bad mothers.

This section of the chapter provides an overview of empowered mothering and introduces some of its theoretical concepts, including Black feminist standpoint, motherwork, community-othermother-ing, home place, collectivism, radical motherhood, and queering motherhood. The theoretical concept of feminist mothering is the topic of chapter three. As with the above section on patriarchal motherhood, the theoretical concepts discussed here are only some of the concepts covered in my mothering-motherhood course and in the larger field of maternal theory. The ones selected, I believe, best illustrate how empowered mothering operates as a counter-narrative to resist and reform patriarchal motherhood.

Towards a Theory of Empowered Mothering

In *Of Woman Born*, Rich writes, "We do not think of the power stolen from us and the power withheld from us in the name of the institution of motherhood" (275). The aim of empowered mothering is to reclaim that power for mothers and to imagine and implement a mode of mothering that mitigates the many ways that patriarchal motherhood, both discursively and materially, regulates and restrains mothers and their mothering. However, empowered mothering, or what may be termed "mothering against motherhood," has yet to be fully defined, documented, or dramatized in feminist scholarship on motherhood. Rather, empowered mothering is understood for what it is not—namely patriarchal motherhood. Indeed, as Fiona Green notes, what is still missing from discussions on motherhood is "Rich's monumental contention that, even when restrained by patriarchy, motherhood can be a site of empowerment and political activism" ("Feminist Mothers" 31). A theory of empowered mothering begins by positioning mothers as "outlaws from the institution of motherhood" and seeks to imagine and implement a maternal identity and practice that empowers mothers.

Rich uses the word "courageous" to define a nonpatriarchal practice of mothering, whereas Baba Copper calls such a practice "radical mothering." Susan Douglas and Meredith Michaels use the word rebellious to describe outlaw mothering, and "hip" is Ariel Gore's term for transgressive mothering. In my work, I use the term "empowered mothering" to signify maternal practices that resist and refuse patriarchal motherhood to create a mode of mothering that is empowering to women. Or to use Rich's terminology, an empowered and empowering maternal practice marks a movement from motherhood to mothering, and makes possible a mothering against motherhood.

Interest in and concern for the empowerment of mothers, both in the home and in the larger society, has been a central concern of feminist research and activism worldwide over the last thirty plus years. Feminist scholars contend that motherhood, as it is currently perceived and practiced in patriarchal societies, is disempowering if not oppressive for a multitude of reasons—namely, the societal devaluation of motherwork, the endless tasks of privatized mothering, the current incompatibility of waged work and motherwork, and the impossible standards of idealized motherhood. Empowered mothering is essential for maternal wellbeing, as it enables women to mother comfortably, competently, and confidently. More specifically, empowered mothering enables mothers to more effectively balance motherhood with paid employment; in fact, findings from my study on academic mothers suggest that empowered mothering is more a determinant of employment success than family friendly policies in the workplace (O'Reilly, "I Could Have Married Another Man"). Feminist scholars likewise emphasize that empowered mothers are more effective mothers for children, that such mothers are healthier women and more productive workers, and that empowered mothering is beneficial for families and society at large.

Overall, empowered mothering allows mothers to effect real and lasting change in their lives, in the lives of their children, and in the larger society. However, even as feminist researchers concur that empowered mothering is better for mothers and their children, discussion continues on how empowered mothering, as both practice and politic, may be achieved and sustained (Green, "Developing a Feminist Motherline: Reflections on a Decade of Feminist Parenting"; O'Reilly, *Mother Outlaws, Rocking the Cradle*; Hewett). In other words, how do mothers individually and collectively refuse and resist the ideology and institution of patriarchal motherhood? What makes this possible? Although researchers agree that "the process of resistance entails making different choices about how one wants to practice mothering" (Horwitz, "Mothers' Resistance" 58), the larger question remains: what is needed at both the individual and cultural level to empower women to engage in this process of resistance? Significantly, even though feminist scholars regard maternal empowerment and empowered mothering as essential for women's equality and autonomy in the twenty-first century, there have been few qualitative studies on the subject matter, with a few notable exceptions: one small qualitative study of empowered mothering (Horwitz; discussed below) and two early studies on feminist mothering (Gordon; Green; discussed in chapter three on "Feminist Mothering").

In her book *Modern Motherhood and Women's Dual Identities: Rewriting the Sexual Contract* (2017) Petra Bueskens has theorized how "strategic absence" by mothers beyond the standard work day and/or outside standard work hours reconstructs gendered dynamics in the home. Specifically, she examines how women are in the "default position" in normative families and how leaving—or what she calls "revolving absence"—essentially mandates the contributions of fathers, partners, and others. In her interviews with fifteen "revolving mothers," she finds evidence that fathers gain valuable childcare and domestic skills when they are solely responsible for extended periods of time and that mothers, in turn, negate the effects of the "second shift" when they absent themselves from the family altogether (in her research, for periods of three days to three months).

Interestingly, many of the mothers preferred periods of intensive work combined with periods of intensive mothering, although all of them benefitted from the greater domestic contributions made by partners (and for the single mothers, other carers), which loosened the hold of the default position. Such mothers are engaging in empowered mothering and work practices, which has transformed both sides of the paid-unpaid work nexus. Bueskens further argues that mothers have "dual selves"—maternal selves and individualized selves—and that the strategic absence enables mothers to cultivate and actualize their autonomous selves.

However, these studies on empowered mothering examine the topic largely from the perspective of white, middle-class, heterosexual mothers. Over the last decade, I have sought to develop a theory of empowered mothering that considers how mothers from various cultural positions resist patriarchal motherhood to achieve an identity and experience of maternal empowerment. In the first instance, I argue that empowered mothering functions as an oppositional discourse of motherhood; more specifically, it signifies a theory and practice of mothering that challenges the dominant discourse of motherhood and transforms the various ways that the lived experience of patriarchal motherhood is limiting or oppressive to women. Erica Horwitz, in her qualitative study of fifteen empowered mothers cited above, finds that empowered mothering may be characterized by seven themes: the importance of mothers meeting their own needs; being a mother does not fulfill all of a woman's needs; involving others in their children's upbringing; actively questioning the expectations placed on mothers by society; challenging mainstream parenting practices; not believing that mothers are solely responsible for how children turn out; and challenging the idea that the only emotion mothers ever feel towards their children is love. For my work on empowered mothering I use Wanda Thomas Bernard and Candace Bernard's definition of empowerment, which refers to "naming, analyzing and challenging oppression" (46). Furthermore, for them, empowerment "occurs through the development of critical consciousness," and is concerned with "gaining control, exercising choices, and engaging in collective social action" (46). Most pointedly, the overarching aim of empowered mothering, I argue, is to confer on mothers the agency, authority, authenticity, autonomy, and advocacy-activism that are denied to them in patriarchal motherhood. "Maternal agency," as Lynn O'Brien Hallstein explains in her encyclopedia entry on the topic "draws on the idea of agency—the ability to influence one's life, to have a power to control one's life—and explores how women have agency via mothering" (698). A theory of maternal agency focuses on, as O'Brien Hallstein continues, "mothering practices that facilitate women's authority and power and is revealed in mothers' efforts to challenge and act against aspects of institutionalized motherhood that constrain and limit women's lives and power as mothers" (698). "Authenticity," as explained in Elizabeth Butterfield's encyclopedia entry, "is an ethical term that denotes being true to oneself, as in making decisions that are consistent with one's own beliefs and values [whereas] inauthenticity is generally understood to be an abdication of one's own authority and a loss of integrity." In the context of empowered mothering maternal authenticity draws on Ruddick's concept of the "conscientious mother" (701) and my model of the "authentic feminist mother" (see chapter three), and refers to "independence of mind and the courage to stand up to dominant values" and to "being truthful about motherhood and remaining true to oneself in motherhood" (Butterfield 701; see also O'Reilly, *Rocking the Cradle*). Similarly, maternal authority and maternal autonomy refer to confidence and conviction in oneself, holding power in the house-hold, and the ability to define and determine one's life and practices of mothering, which means the refusal to, in Ruddick's words, "relin-quish or repudiate one's own perceptions and values" (Ruddick 112; see also O'Reilly, *Rocking the Cradle*). Finally, the topic of maternal advocacy-activism foregrounds the political and social dimensions of motherwork, whether such is expressed in antisexist childrearing or maternal activism. As my research identifies agency, authority, autonomy, authenticity, advocacy-activism as the organizing aims of empowered mothering, it also demarcates its defining characteristics or practices by way of four interrelated themes: motherhood, family, childrearing, and activism.

I argue that central to all four attributes of empowered mothering is a redefinition of patriarchal motherhood from various cultural maternal positions and perspectives. Under the theme of motherhood, empowered mothering counters the normative discourse of motherhood as limited to middle-class, married, stay-at-home mothers, to include a multitude of maternal identities, such as noncustodial, poor, single, young, old, and employed mothers, and a variety of motherhood practices, such as the practices of "othermothering" found in African

American culture and the co-mothering of queer households. Likewise, as the normative family is restricted to a patriarchal nuclear structure wherein the parents are married, the children are biologically related to both parents, and the mother is the nurturer and the father is the provider, the family formations of empowered mothers are many and varied: single, blended, step, matrifocal, same sex, and so forth. Furthermore, whereas patriarchal motherhood characterizes childrearing as a private, nonpolitical undertaking, my theory of empowered mothering redefines motherwork as a socially engaged enterprise and a site of power wherein mothers can affect social change, both in the home through feminist childrearing and outside the home through maternal activism. The task of antisexist childrearing foregrounds the political-social dimension of motherwork to emphasize how traditional practices of gender socialization may be challenged and corrected to raise empowered daughters and empathetic sons, while my theme of activism considers how mothers use their position as mothers to lobby for social and political change (see also Hill Collins, Nathanson; Kinser). The attributes of agency, authority, authenticity, autonomy, and advocacy-activism as well as the practices of othermothering, co-mothering, "alternative" maternal identities and family formations, antisexist childrearing, and maternal activism, I argue, enable mothers to challenge and change patriarchal motherhood from various cultural positions, particularly as it is enacted in the ten ideological imperatives discussed above, and to achieve empowered mothering.

Empowered mothering makes motherhood more rewarding, fulfilling, and satisfying for women by affirming maternal agency, authority, autonomy, authenticity, and activism, and by opening up new maternal practices and identities. Such mothering allows a woman selfhood outside of motherhood and affords her power within motherhood. Although it is evident that empowered mothering is better for mothers, it must also be noted that such mothering is also better for children. Mothers who are content with and fulfilled by their lives make better mothers, just as children raised by depressed mothers are at risk. I want to suggest that empowered mothers are more effective mothers. Anyone who has been in a plane knows the routine if oxygen masks are required: put on your mask and then assist children with theirs. This instruction initially seems to defy common sense—namely, that children should be the ones helped first. However, the instruction recognizes that parents must be masked first because only then are they able to provide real and continued assistance to the child: unmasked, they run the risk of becoming disoriented, ill, or unconscious because of lack of oxygen and would be of no use to the child. I see this instruction as an appropriate metaphor for the practice of empowered mothering, since mothers, when empowered, are able to better care for and protect their children.

In her book *A Potent Spell: Mother Love and the Power of Fear*, Janna Malamud Smith references the myth of Demeter and Persephone to illustrate this theme that children are better served by empowered mothers. Demeter, Smith argues, "is able to save her daughter because she is a powerful goddess who can make winter permanent and destroy humankind" (59). "Demeter," she continues, "possesses the very qualities that mothers so often have lacked—adequate resources and strength to protect their children, particularly daughters" (59). Therefore, contrary to patriarchal wisdom, what a child needs most in the world, Smith argues, "is a free and happy mother" (167). Smith explains:

> [W]hat a child needs most is a free mother, one who feels that she is in fact living her life, and has adequate food, sleep, wages, education, safety, opportunity, institutional support, health care, child care, and loving relationships. "Adequate" means enough to allow her to participate in the world—and in mothering…. A child needs a mother who has resources to enable her to make real choices, but also to create a feeling of adequate control—a state of mind that encourages a sense of agency, thus a good basis of maternal well-being, and a good foundation on which to stand while raising a child. Surely, child care prospers in this soil as well as, if not better than in any other. What is more, such a mother can imagine a life of possibility and hope, and can so offer this perspective to a child. [Finally] a child needs a mother who lives and works within a context that respects her labour, and that realistically supports it without rationalizing oppression in the name of safety, or substituting idealization or sentimentality for resources. (240)

Ann Crittenden, who is cited by Smith, elaborates further: "Studies conducted on five continents have found that children are distinctly better off when the mother possesses enough income and authority in the family to make investing in children a priority" (120). "The emergence of women as independent economic actors," Crittenden continues, "is not depriving children of vital support; it is giving them more powerful defenders [and] [d]epriving mothers of an income and influence of their own is harmful to children and a recipe for economic backwardness" (130). To return to the story of Demeter: "It is only because Demeter has autonomy and independent resources," as Smith explains, "that she can protect Persephone" (241). Conversely, "when a culture devalues and enslaves the mother, she can [not] be like Demeter and protect her daughter" (Smith, 244). Therefore, and as Smith concludes: "If we are really interested in improving the lot of children, our best method would be laws and policy that support mothers and mothering" (187). It is, indeed, remarkable, as Smith notes, that "[n]o society has ever voluntarily turned its laws and riches toward liberating mothers" (168).

The free mother valued by Smith and recognized as essential for the wellbeing of children, however, will be not found in the patriarchal institution of motherhood or in the practice of intensive mothering. Patriarchal motherhood robs women of their selfhood and power, and intensive mothering—in its emphasis on excessive time, attention, and energy—makes it difficult, nay impossible, for mothers to be autonomous and independent. Empowered, or to use Smith's term "free," mothering, thus, only becomes possible in and through the destruction of patriarchal motherhood. Such mothers can better protect and defend their children, as Smith observes. As well, and as noted above, empowered mothers can make real and lasting changes in society through social-political activism and in the way that they raise their children. More specifically, empowered mothers challenge and change, in the home and in the world at large, the gender roles that straitjacket children and the harm of sexism, racism, classism, and heterosexism more generally. I believe that patriarchy resists empowered mothering precisely because it understands its real power to bring about a true and enduring cultural revolution.

Amy Middleton, however, in her article "Mothering Under Duress: Examining the Inclusiveness of Feminist Theory," argues that my definition of empowered mothering is problematic because it limits empowered mothering to, in her words, "educated, middle to upper class women with access to financial and human resources" (74). She writes: "These criteria and the way in which they are realized in these women's lives are extremely difficult, and in some cases impossible, for women who do not have access to resources such as substantial finances and good childcare and/or women who are in other situations of duress such as being in an abusive relationship, having a mental illness or being addicted to drugs or alcohol" (74). This criticism suggests that I have been less than clear in my theory of empowered mothering. The terms agency, authority, autonomy, authenticity and advocacy-activism are not to be read as restricted to economic and educational resources. Rather, these terms are to be read in the context of a resistance to patriarchal motherhood. The concept of "authenticity," for example, refers to the refusal to wear, what Susan Maushart terms, the "mask of motherhood." "Authentic" mothering, in contrast, seeks to unmask motherhood and refuses to partake in, what Mary Kay Blakely has termed, "the national game of 'Let's Pretend'—the fantasy in which we are all supposed to pass for perfect mothers, living in perfect families" (12). To be authentic is to be truthful and true to oneself in motherhood.

Similarly, "authority" refers to confidence and conviction in oneself as a mother, and, in this instance, means the refusal to, in Sara Ruddick's words, "relinquish authority and repudiate one's own perceptions and values" (112). As well, "agency" means not power but, in Rich's words "to refuse to be a victim and then go on from there," (246) and "advocacy-activism" refers to any and all forms of formal and informal resistance to patriarchy. My theory of empowered mothering is as available to marginalized women as it is to women of privilege. In fact, I would argue that such agency, authority, autonomy, authority and activism-advocacy of empowered mothering are *more evident* in the maternal practices and theories of mothers who are poor, lesbian, young, or women of colour. Privileged women, I would suggest, with more resources and status in motherhood, are often less able or likely to perceive and oppose their oppression. Furthermore, when I speak of agency and the like I do not mean to say that mothers necessarily have these things but rather that empowered mothers understand that they should have them, and they seek to attain them. Patriarchal mothers, in contrast, do not believe that mothers need or want agency, authority, autonomy, authenticity and activism-advocacy. When I use such terms I mean to signify struggle not necessarily success. Again to quote from Rich: "The quality of the mother's life—however embattled and unprotected—is her primary bequest to her daughter, because a woman who can believe in herself, who is a fighter, and who continues to struggle to create livable space around her, is demonstrating to her daughter that these possibilities exist" (247).This is what a mothering of agency, authority, autonomy, authenticity and activism-advocacy seeks to demonstrate and achieve, and, as such, it is certainly not restricted to women of privilege.

Indeed, what I have discovered in my many years of teaching and researching is that non-normative mothers—whether they are defined and categorized as such by age, race, sexuality, or biology—can never be the "good" mothers of normative motherhood, so they must rely on and develop nonpatriarchal practices of mothering to raise their children. Whether they be shared parenting, co-mothering, communal-othermothering, fictive kin, extended families, or maternal activism, such practices challenge and change the various ways that the lived experiences of patriarchal motherhood cause mothering to be limiting or oppressive to women. The many non-normative mothering practices listed above make mothering more rewarding, if not empowering for women, because these non-normative mothers seldom mother alone or in isolation as they would in patriarchal motherhood, and the work and responsibility of mothering is seldom solely that of the biological mother (as is mandated in patriarchal motherhood).

This is not to say that non-normative mothering is always rewarding or empowering; rather, it is to emphasize that non-normative mothers —who, by choice or circumstance, cannot be the "good" mothers of patriarchal motherhood—must imagine and implement nonpatriarchal mothering practices that, in their very otherness, open up to new possibilities for mothering. Dawn M. Lavell-Harvard concludes the introduction to her book *"Until Our Hearts Are on the Ground": Aboriginal Mothering, Oppression, Resistance and Rebirth* with these words: "We, as Aboriginals, have always been different, we have always existed on the margins of the dominant patriarchal culture, and as mothers we have operated outside of, if not in actual opposition to, their definition of acceptability [and] [w]e are, to use the words of Adrienne Rich, the original mother outlaw" (6). I would suggest that these words are equally applicable to all non-normative mothers; in operating outside, if not in actual opposition to, normative motherhood, these mothers in their very unacceptability show us more empowering ways to mother and be mothered.

Empowered Mothering: Key Theoretical Concepts

Black Feminist Standpoint, Motherwork, Community-Othermothering and Homeplace: Patricia Hill Collins and bell hooks

"During the early stages of contemporary women's liberation movement," bell hooks writes, "feminist analyses of motherhood reflected the race and class biases of participants" ("Revolutionary Parenting" 133). She continues: "Some white, middle class, college educated women argued that motherhood was the locus of women's oppression. Had Black women voiced their views on motherhood, it would not have been named a serious obstacle to our freedom as women. Racism, availability of jobs, lack of skills or education ... would have been at the top of the list—but not motherhood" (133). "Early feminist attacks on motherhood," hooks goes on to explain "alienated masses of women from the movement, especially poor and/or non-white women, who find parenting one of the few interpersonal relationships where they are affirmed and appreciated" (134-135). hooks's argument is important to understand the difference between African American motherwork and motherhood as it is perceived and practiced by the dominant culture.

Significantly, in the preface to the 1986 edition of *Of Woman Born*, Rich revisits the claim that she made in the first edition that "in the mainstream of recorded history, motherhood as institution has ghettoized and degraded female potentialities" and argues that "woman-centred experiences of mothering and acts of mother power can be found throughout history if we look at cultures other than the dominant Western one" (xxv). Rich writes: "Relying on ready-to-hand Greek mythology, I was led to generalize that 'the cathexis between mother and daughter was endangered always and everywhere.' A consideration of American Indian, African and Afro-American myth and philosophy might have suggested other patterns" (xxv). Indeed, as will be discussed below, in African American culture, there are, to use Rich's words, "[maternal] acts of power" and we witness empowered, rather than endangered, relations between mothers and daughters.

Black Feminist Standpoint

"Every culture," Collins explains in *Black Feminist Thought*, "has a worldview that it uses to order and evaluate its own experiences" (10). She continues:

> Black women fashion an independent standpoint about the meaning of Black womanhood and motherhood. These self-definitions enable Black women to use African-derived conceptions of self and community to resist negative evaluations of Black womanhood advanced by dominant groups. In all, Black women's grounding in traditional African-American culture fostered the development of a distinctive African American women's culture. (*Black Feminist Thought* 11)

Black female standpoint has developed in opposition to and in resistance against the dominant view or what Collins calls "the controlling images of Black womanhood." Collins argues that "the dominant ideology of the slave era fostered the creation of four interrelated, socially constructed controlling images of Black womanhood, each reflecting the dominant group's interest in maintaining Black women's subordination" (*Black Feminist Thought* 71). The four controlling images that Collins examines include the mammy, the matriarch, the welfare mother, and the Jezebel. By way of controlling images, as Collins explains, "certain assumed qualities are attached to Black women and [then] used to justify [that] oppression" (*Black Feminist Thought* 7). As Collins further argues:

> From the mammies, Jezebels, and breeder women of slavery to the smiling Aunt Jemimas on pancake mix boxes, ubiquitous Black prostitutes, and ever-present welfare mothers of contemporary popular culture, the nexus of negative stereotypical images applied to African-American women has been fundamental to Black women's oppression. (*Black Feminist Thought* 7)

Black women, according to Collins, may resist these derogatory stereotypes through the creation of a distinct Black female standpoint that is based on Black women's own experiences and meanings of womanhood.

Black female standpoint, Collins argues, develops through the interplay between two discourses of knowledge: "the commonplace taken-for-granted knowledge" and "everyday ideas" of Black women that are clarified and rearticulated by Black women intellectuals or theorists to form a specialized Black feminist thought. In turn, as Collins explains, "the consciousness of Black women may be trans-formed by [this] thought" (*Black Feminist Thought* 20). She elaborates:

> Through the process of rearticulation, Black women intellectuals offer African-American women a different view of themselves and their world from that forwarded by the dominant group.... By taking the core themes of a Black women's standpoint and infusing them with new meaning, Black women intellectuals can stimulate a new consciousness that utilizes Black's women's everyday, taken-for-granted knowledge. Rather than raising consciousness, Black feminist thought affirms and rearticulates a consciousness that already exists. More importantly, this rearticulated consciousness empowers African-American women and stimulates resistance. (*Black Feminist Thought* 31-32)

In other words, the Black female standpoint, which emerges from Black women's everyday experiences and clarified by Black feminist theory, not only provides a distinct "angle of vision on self, community and society" (31-32) but also, in so doing, enables Black women to counter and interrupt the dominant discourse of Black womanhood.

The formation and articulation of a self-defined standpoint, Collins emphasizes, "is [thus] key to Black women's survival" (26). As Audre Lorde argues "it is axiomatic that if we do not define ourselves for ourselves, we will be defined by others—for their use and to our detriment" (qtd. in Collins 21, 45). However, emphasizing the importance of self-definition, Collins recognizes that Black women, as an oppressed group, inevitably must struggle to convey this self-definition, positioned as they are at the periphery of the dominant white, male culture. Collins writes: "An oppressed group's experiences may put its members in a position to see things differently, but their lack of control over ideological apparatuses of society makes expressing a self-defined standpoint more difficult" (*Black Feminist Thought* 26). Black women's standpoint is thus, in Collins's words, "an independent, viable, yet subjugated knowledge" (*Black Feminist Thought* 13).

Collins's standpoint thesis provides a useful conceptual framework for understanding the challenges and possibilities of African American motherhood. To borrow from Collins's paradigm: African American feminist-womanist theorists are intellectuals who take the core themes and develop from them a new consciousness of Black motherhood that empowers African American women to overcome the challenges of Black motherhood and realize its possibilities.

Motherwork

The African American maternal standpoint calls into question the terminology and methodology feminists have traditionally used to talk about mothering. In her 1994 article, "Shifting the Center: Race, Class, and Feminist Theorizing about Motherhood," Collins uses the term "motherwork" to refer to what is usually meant by nurturance, love, or mothering generally. Collins's word choice is a significant one because it foregrounds mothering as labour, and calls attention to the ways in which mothering is socially and politically motivated and experienced in African American culture. In this article, Collins's emphasis is on the ways in which the concerns of what she calls "racial ethnic mothers" differ from those in the dominant culture. Collins identifies the goals of "racial ethnic" mothers as the following: keeping the children born to you; supporting the physical survival of those children; teaching the children resistance and how to survive in a racist world; giving to those children their racial-cultural history and identity; and practicing a social activism and communal mothering on behalf of all the community's children. White feminist writing has traditionally concerned itself with the loss of female identity in motherhood and has argued that only by securing time away from children and creating a life outside of motherhood will women be able to maintain an autonomous identity separate from that of mother. What racial ethnic mothers fight against, in contrast, is not too much time with their children but too little. Forced to work outside the home and frequently employed in jobs, such as domestic service, that separate mothers from their children for days, weeks, or even years, as with overseas domestics, racial ethnic mothers must struggle to claim their identity as mothers and to fulfill the role of mother for their children. Motherwork for many "racial ethnic" women is also concerned with the physical survival of children. Collins explains:

> Physical survival is assumed for children who are white and middle-class. The choice to thus examine their psychic and emotional well-being and that of their mothers appears rational. The children of women of color, many of whom are "physically starving," have no such choices however. Racial ethnic children's lives have long been held in low regard: African-American children face an infant mortality twice that for white infants; and one-half of African-American children who survive infancy live in poverty. In addition racial ethnic children often live in harsh urban environments where drugs, crime, industrial pollutants, and violence threaten their survival. ("Meaning of Motherhood" 49)

Thus, central to the African American standpoint on motherhood is a challenge to the received view that links "good" mothering solely with nurturance. African American mother-work foregrounds the importance of preservation, which is a dimension of motherhood too often minimized and trivialized in dominant discourses of motherhood. However, as Sara Ruddick has argued, the first duty of mothers is to protect and preserve their children—"to keep safe whatever is vulnerable and valuable in a child" (80). "Preserving the lives of children," Ruddick writes, "is the central constitutive, invariant aim of maternal practice" (19). Although maternal practice is composed of two other demands—nurturance and training—this first demand, what Ruddick calls "preservative love," is what describes much of African American women's motherwork. In a world in which, to use Patricia Hill Collins's words, "racial ethnic children's lives have long been held in low regard" ("Shifting the Center" 49), mothering for many Black women, particularly among the poor, is about ensuring the physical survival of their children, and those of the larger Black community. Securing food and shelter and struggling to build and sustain safe neighbourhoods are what defines both the meaning and experience of Black women's motherwork. "Preservation," as Collins explains further is, "a fundamental dimension of racial ethnic women's motherwork" ("Shifting the Center" 48-49). However, normative discourses of motherhood, particularly in their current configuration of intensive mothering, define motherwork solely as nurturance. Though exclusive to middle-class white women's experiences of mothering, the normative discourse of mothering as nurturance has been naturalized as the universal experience of motherhood. Consequently, preservative love, such as that practiced by poor African American mothers, is often not regarded as real, legitimate, or "good enough" mothering. However, for many African American mothers, keeping children alive through preservative love is an essential and integral dimension of motherwork.

Motherwork performed by racial ethnic mothers thus is not to be confused with patriarchal motherhood: an institution that is oppressive to women. As Adrienne Rich writes in *Of Woman Born*: "At certain points in history, and in certain cultures, the idea of woman-as-mother has worked to give women some say in the life of a people or a clan. But for most of what we know as the 'mainstream' of recorded history, motherhood as institution has ghettoized and degraded female potentialities" (13). In contrast, motherwork accords African American mothers authority and centrality; women in this culture are empowered precisely because they are mothers. The valuing of African American mothers and motherwork, however, is specific to the culture itself. From the outside, the many differences of African American mothering are often pathologized as deviant. Normative discourses of mothering position the motherhood experience of white, middle-class women as the real, natural, and universal one. Alternative meanings and experiences of mothering are marginalized and rendered illegitimate. African American mothers do not mother according to the script of what constitutes good mothering—a woman at home, who is financially dependent on her husband and totally responsible for the care of her children, whose mothering is centred on the emotional and intellectual development of children (not just physical), and who sees home and love purely in terms of affection (not politics). Hence, African American mothers are deemed unfit or "bad" mothers.

The African American standpoint on Black motherhood enables and empowers Black women to challenge the devaluation of their motherwork and more specifically the controlling images of Black motherhood discussed above. From this standpoint, Black women are able to resist these negative evaluations of Black motherhood by rearticulating the power that is inherent in Black women's everyday experiences of motherhood. This rearticulation centres on a reaffirmation of the traditional roles and beliefs of Black motherhood and gives rise to an understanding and practice of mothering that serves to empower Black mothers. To this discussion, I now turn.

Othermothering and Community Mothering

Stanlie James defines "othermothering" as "acceptance of responsibility for a child not one's own, in an arrangement that may or may not be formal" (45). Othermothers usually care for children, whereas "community mothers," as Njoki Nathani Wane explains, "take care of the community [by] women [who] are typically past their childbearing years" (112). "The role of community mothers," as Arlene Edwards notes, "often evolved from that of being other-mothers" (88). James argues that othermothering and community mothering developed from, in Arlene Edwards's words, "West African practices of communal lifestyles and interdependence of communities" (88).

This distinct Afrocentric ideology of motherhood, Collins argues, emerged from West African practices of mothering. In West African culture, the private-public distinction of Western culture does not apply and thus, in Collins's words, "[m]othering was not a privatized nurturing 'occupation' reserved for biological mothers, and the economic support of children was not the exclusive responsibility of men" ("Meaning of Motherhood", 45). Rather, mothering involves both the nurturing of children, in the reproductive sphere and the providing for those children in the realm of production." Collins goes on to argue that these complementary dimensions of mothering give women greater influence and status in West African society. She comments:

> First, since they are not dependent on males for economic support and provide much of their own and their children's economic support, women are structurally central to families. Second, the image of the mother is one that is culturally elaborated and valued across diverse West African philosophies, and motherhood is similarly valued. Finally, while the biological mother-child bond is valued, child care was a collective responsibility, a situation fostering cooperative, age-stratified, woman-centered 'mothering' networks. ("Meaning of Motherhood" 45)

Arlene Edwards documents the impact of the experience of slavery on othermothering:

> The experience of slavery saw the translation of othermothering to new settings, since the care of children was an expected task

of enslaved Black women in addition to the field or house duties ... the familial instability of slavery engendered the adaptation of communality in the form of fostering children whose parents, particularly mothers, had been sold. This tradition of communality gave rise to the practice of othermothering. The survival of the concept is inherent to the survival of Black people as a whole ... since it allowed for the provision of care to extended family and non blood relations. (80)

Collins argues that these West African cultural practices were retained and developed by African American mothers and gave rise to a distinct tradition of African American motherhood in which African American mothers do not assume full responsibility for the care of children, nor is such childcare undertaken in the privacy and isolation of a nuclear family. Moreover, African American mothers, according to Collins, combine mothering with paid employment and enjoy greater gender equality in their own households. She explains:

First, the assumption that mothering occurs within the confines of a private, nuclear family household where the mother has almost total responsibility for child-rearing is less applicable to Black families. While the ideal of the cult of true womanhood has been held up to Black women for emulation, racial oppression has denied Black families sufficient resources to support private, nuclear family households. Second, strict sex-role segregation, with separate male and female spheres of influence within the family, has been less commonly found in African-American families than in White middle-class ones. Finally, the assumption that motherhood and economic dependency on men are linked and that to be a "good" mother one must stay at home, making motherhood a "full-time occupation" is similarly uncharacteristic of African-American families. ("Meaning of Motherhood" 43-44)

The practice of othermothering remains central to the African American tradition of motherhood and is regarded as essential for the survival of Black people. bell hooks in her article "Revolutionary Parenting" comments:

> Child care is a responsibility that can be shared with other childrearers, with people who do not live with children. This form of parenting is revolutionary in this society because it takes place in opposition to the idea that parents, especially mothers, should be the only childrearers. Many people raised in Black communities experienced this type of community-based child care. Black women who had to leave the home and work to help provide for families could not afford to send children to day care centers and such centers did not always exist. They relied on people in their communities to help. Even in families where the mother stayed home, she could also rely on people in the community to help…. People who did not have children often took responsibility for sharing in childrearing. (144)

"The centrality of women in African-American extended families," as Nina Jenkins concludes in "Black Women and the Meaning of Motherhood," "is well known" (206).

The practice of othermothering, as it developed from West African traditions, becomes in African American culture a strategy of survival in that it ensured that all children, regardless of whether the biological mother was present or available, would receive the mothering that delivers psychological and physical wellbeing and makes empowerment possible. Collins concludes:

> Biological mothers or bloodmothers are expected to care for their children. But African and African-American communities have also recognized that vesting one person with full responsibility for mothering a child may not be wise or possible. As a result, "othermothers," women who assist bloodmothers by sharing mothering responsibilities, traditionally have been central to the institution of Black motherhood. ("Meaning of Motherhood" 47)

Community mothering and othermothering have also emerged in response to Black mothers' needs and have served to empower Black women and enrich their lives. "Historically and presently community mothering practices," Erica Lawson writes, "was and is a central experience in the lives of many Black women and participation in mothering is a form of emotional and spiritual expression in societies that marginalize Black women" (26). Black women's identity and role as community mothers also, as Lawson explains, "enabled African Black women to use African derived conceptions of self and community to resist negative evaluations of Black women" (26).

The practice of community-othermothering as a cultural sustaining mechanism and as a mode of empowerment for Black mothers has been documented in numerous studies. Carol Stack's early but important book *All Our Kin: Strategies for Survival in A Black Community* emphasizes how crucial and central extended kin and community are for poor urban Blacks. "Black families in The Flats [undisclosed inner-city area in the U.S.] and the non-kin they regard as kin," Stack writes in her conclusion, "have evolved patterns of co-residence, kinship-based exchange networks linking multiple domestic units, elastic household boundaries, lifelong bonds to three-generation households, social controls against the formation of marriages that could endanger the network of kin, the domestic authority of women, and limitations on the role of the husband or male friend within a woman's kin network" (124). Priscilla Gibson's article "Developmental Mothering in an African American Community: From Grandmothers to New Mothers Again" provides a study of grandmothers and great grandmothers who assume the caregiving responsibilities of their (great) grandchildren as a result of the parent being unable or unwilling to provide that care. Gibson argues that "[in]creasingly grandmothers, especially African American grandmothers, are becoming kinship providers for grandchildren with absent parents. This absent middle generation occurs because of social problems such as drug abuse, incarceration, domestic violence, and divorce, just to name a few" (33). In "Reflections on the Mutuality of Mothering: Women, Children and Othermothering," Njoki Nathani Wane explores how "parenting, especially mothering, was an integral component of African traditions and cultures" (111). "Most of pre-colonial Africa" explains Wane, "was founded upon and sustained by collectivism.... Labour was organized along parallel rather than hierarchical lines, thus giving equal value to male and female labour." She continues: "social organization was based on the principle of patrilineal or matrilineal descent, or a combination of both [and] [m]othering practices were organized as a collective activity" (108). Today, the practice of othermothering, as Wane notes, "serves[s] to relieve some of the stresses that can develop between children and parents [and] provides multiple role models for children; [as well] it keeps the traditional African value systems of communal sharing and ownership alive" (113). Othermothering and community mothering, Wane concludes, "can be understood as a form of cultural work or as one way communities organize to nurture both themselves and future generations" (113).

The practices of othermothering and in particular community mothering serve, as Stanlie James argues, "as an important Black feminist link to the development of new models of social transformation" (45). Black women's role of community mothers redefines motherhood as social activism. As Collins explains,

> Black women's experiences as other mothers have provided a foundation for Black women's social activism. Black women's feelings of responsibility for nurturing the children in their extended family networks have stimulated a more generalized ethic of care where Black women feel accountable to all the Black community's children. ("Meaning of Motherhood" 49)

In *Black Feminist Thought* Collins develops this idea further:

> Such power is transformative in that Black women's relationships with children and other vulnerable community members is not intended to dominate or control. Rather, its purpose is to bring people along, to—in the words of late-nineteenth-century Black feminists—"uplift the race" so that vulnerable members of the community will be able to attain the self-reliance and independence essential for resistance. (132)

Various and diverse forms of social activism stem from and are sustained by the African American custom of community mothering. Community mothering, as Arlene Edwards explores in her article "Community Mothering: The Relationship Between Mothering and the Community Work of Women," has been expressed in activities and movements as varied as the Black clubwomen, the civil rights movement, and Black women's work in the church. Drawing on the research of Gilkes, Edwards elaborates: "In reporting on Black community workers, Gilkes found that these women often 'viewed the Black Community as a group of relatives and other friends whose interest should be advanced, and promoted at all times, under all conditions, and by almost any means'" (qtd. in Edwards 88). Wanda Bernard and Candace Bernard theorize Black women's work as educators as a form of social activism. "Education," they argue, "is considered a cornerstone of Black community development, and as such Black women, as community othermothers, have placed a high value on education and have used it as a site for activism" (68). Academic mothers, they continue, "also value education, and use their location to facilitate the education of others. [As well] academic othermothers who operate within an Africentric framework, are change agents who promote student empowerment and transformation" (68). They go on to elaborate:

> Collins's definition of othermothers extends to the work we do in the academy. Othermothering in the community is the foundation of what Collins calls the "mothering the mind" relationships that often developed between African American women teachers and their Black female and male students. We refer to this as mothering in the academy, and see it as work that extends beyond traditional definitions of mentorship. It is a sharing of self, an interactive and collective process, a spiritual connectedness that epitomizes the Africentric values of sharing, caring and accountability. (68)

Collins argues that this construction of mothering as social activism empowers Black women because motherhood operates, in her words, as "a symbol of power." "A substantial portion of Black women's status in African-American communities," writes Collins, "stems not only from their roles as mothers in their own families but from their contributions as community othermothers to Black community development as well" (51). Bernard and Bernard write:

> More than a personal act, Black motherhood is very political. Black mothers and grandmothers are considered the guardians of the generations [and] Black mothers have historically been charged with the responsibility of providing education, social, and political awareness, in addition to unconditional love, nurturance, socialization, and values to their children, and the children in their communities. (47)

Black motherhood, as Jenkins concludes, "is a site where [Black women] can develop a belief in their own empowerment [and] Black women can see motherhood as providing a base for self-actualization, for acquiring status in the Black community and as a catalyst for social activism" (206).

Homeplace

Two interrelated themes or perspectives distinguish the African American tradition of motherhood and enable African American mothers to find empowerment in motherwork. First, mothers and motherhood are valued by and, central to, African American culture. Second, it is recognized that mothers and mothering are what make possible the physical and psychological wellbeing and empowerment of African American people and the larger African American culture. Black women raise children in a society that is at best indifferent to the needs of Black children and the concerns of Black mothers. The focus of Black motherhood in both practice and thought is how to preserve, protect, and, more generally, empower Black children so that they may resist racist practices that seek to harm them and grow into adulthood whole and complete. To fulfill the task of empowering children, mothers must hold power in African American culture, and mothering, likewise, must be valued and supported. In turn, African American culture, understanding the importance of mothering for individual and cultural wellbeing and empowerment, gives power to mothers and prominence to the work of mothering. In other words, Black mothers require power to do the important work of mothering and are accorded power because of the importance of mothering.

African American mothering differs from the dominant model and serves to empower African American mothers because nurturance of family is defined and experienced specifically as an act of resistance in African American culture. In African American culture, as theorist bell hooks has observed, the Black family, or what she terms "homeplace," operates as a site of resistance. She explains:

> Historically, African-American people believed that the construction of a homeplace, however fragile and tenuous (the slave hut, the wooden shack), had a radical political dimension. Despite the brutal reality of racial apartheid, of domination, one's homeplace was one site where one could freely confront the issue of humanization, where one could resist. Black women resisted by making homes where all Black people could strive to be subjects, not objects, where one could be affirmed in our minds and hearts despite poverty, hardship, and deprivation, where we could restore to ourselves the dignity denied to us on the outside in the public world. (42)

hooks emphasizes that when she talks about homeplace, she is not speaking merely of Black women providing services for their families; rather, she refers to the creation of a safe place where, in her words, "Black people could affirm one another and by so doing heal many of the wounds inflicted by racist domination." It was a place where they "had the opportunity to grow and develop, to nurture [their] spirits" (42). In a racist culture that deems Black children inferior, unworthy, and unlovable, providing maternal love to Black children is an act of resistance; in loving her children, the mother instills in them a loved sense of self and high self-esteem, which enables them to defy and subvert racist discourses that naturalize racial inferiority and commodify Blacks as "other" and object. African Americans, hooks emphasizes, "have long recognized the subversive value of homeplace and homeplace has always been central to the liberation struggle" (42). Like hooks, Collins maintains that children learn at home how to identify and challenge racist practices, and it is at home that children learn of their heritage and community. At home, they are empowered to resist racism, particularly as it becomes internalized. Collins elaborates:

> Racial ethnic women's motherwork reflects the tensions inherent in trying to foster a meaningful racial identity in children within a society that denigrates people of color.... [Racial ethnic] children must first be taught to survive in systems that oppress them. Moreover, this survival must not come at the expense of self-esteem. Thus, a dialectal relationship exists between systems of racial oppression designed to strip a subordinated group of a sense of personal identity and a sense of collective peoplehood, and the cultures of resistance extant in various ethnic groups that resist the oppression. For women of color, motherwork for identity occurs at this critical juncture. (57)

The empowerment of minority children through resistance and knowledge occurs at home and in the larger cultural space through the communal mothering discussed earlier. This view of mothering differs radically from the dominant discourse of motherhood that configures home as a politically neutral space and views nurturance as no more than the natural calling of mothers. And in this, African American mothers, despite the oppression that they experience and the many challenges they encounter, find power and worth in their work and identity as mother: indeed, to use the title of Cecelie S. Berry's article, "Home Is Where the Revolution Is."

Collectivism: Kim Anderson

Indigenous theorist Kim Anderson argues that Indigenous women have maintained and revived their own distinct ideology of motherhood. "Through collectivism, spirituality, and the application of sovereignty," Anderson explains, "Native mothers have shaped empowered mothering experiences in spite of the capitalist, Christian, and colonial frameworks that have worked together to support patriarchal western motherhood in Native communities" (762). In contrast to the gendered spheres of patriarchal capitalism discussed earlier—wherein women are assigned to the private, reproductive sphere and men to the public, productive realm—Indigenous economies "are not characterized by a public/private dichotomy, nor were they hierarchical or inherently oppressive to one gender" (762). Rather, "they were understood to be interdependent, equally valuable and flexible" (762). And because, as Anderson goes on to explain, " these economies were upheld through kinship systems, mothers lived and worked in extended families, precluding the possibility of an isolated and subordinate mother as family servant" (763). Indeed, as Amber Kinser comments, "[I]n Indigenous cultures, women's traditional roles have long been recognized and celebrated as powerful" (6). With colonialism, an attempt was made to, in Anderson's words, "fashion Native men, women and families, in the image of Euro-Western people. This entailed moving men towards farming or the wage economy, and training women for their exclusively domestic role" (763). However, Anderson emphasizes that "because the policies of the very same state thwarted Native success in the capitalist system, the gendered transition to public and private spheres never took root" (763). In turn, colonialization and its attendant racist policies and practices meant the Indigenous families and communities had to rely one another for care and support. Indeed, as Memee Lavell-Harvard and Jeanette Corbiere Lavell explain, "For most members of Aboriginal community, everyday survival is still dependent on extensive networks of family and friends who support and reinforce each other" (189). Thus, Indigenous economics and cultures could not and did not subscribe to the Western liberalism of the colonial state and, in particular, to its ethos of individual autonomy. Instead, Indigenous societies revised traditional collectivist interdependencies. Collectivism, as with the concepts of other-community mothering, homeplace and motherwork discussed above, serves to empower Indigenous mothers as their mothering takes place in extended kin networks in which mothers hold economic and cultural prominence. Indigenous women rarely mother in a nuclear family in which they are dependent on their husband's income, nor do they assume sole responsibility for the care of their children. As well, motherwork is recognized as essential for the survival of Indigenous children in hostile colonialized environments, and, thus, it is valued and supported. Moreover, as Anderson explains, family in Indigenous culture, "can be a site of resistance and renewal" as with hooks's theory of homeplace. The concept of collectivism, thus, serves to subvert the mandates of individualization, privatization, and depoliticalization that are enacted in patriarchal motherhood, to make mothering a powerful and empowering identity and practice for Indigenous mothers.

Radical Motherhood and Queering Motherhood: Baba Copper and Margaret Gibson

Radical Motherhood

Much of maternal scholarship identifies exclusive female mothering as the cause of women's oppression in patriarchal motherhood and calls for shared parenting and the degendering of motherwork in order for mothers to be empowered. Nancy Chodorow, for example, as noted above, concludes that "the social organization of parenting produces sexual inequality, not simply role differentiation" (214). Similarly, Sara Ruddick's theory of mothering as practice divests care of biology and seeks to dislodge the gender essentialism that grounds and structures patriarchal motherhood. The critique of exclusive mothering is, likewise, echoed in the feminist sociology on the family and in everyday conversations with women; simply put, mothers are still doing the bulk of domestic labour and childcare in homes around the world. The necessary work of home and community maintenance is performed by mothers whether they work part or full time. Today, however, with the majority of mothers in the paid labour force, households do not have stay-at-home mothers to do the necessary work of social reproduction; hence, the family and work conflict experienced by mothers but by not fathers.

Exclusive female mothering, feminist scholars argue, originates from the gender essentialism of modern motherhood. Contemporary Western patriarchal motherhood, though nuanced in its manifestations, is ideologically quite homogeneous and unambiguous, and is defined by a rigid and uniform philosophy of gender essentialism and the resulting binary opposition of the public and private spheres. A central, if not defining, event in the rise of Western modernity was the emergence of the public-private dichotomy, in which the work of production was assigned to the public sphere and the work of reproduction to the private sphere. This dichotomy was, of course, gender coded: a man belonged in the public realm and was to embody the valued masculine traits of the emergent capitalist and industrial society, whereas a woman was to remain in the home domain and serve as the ornamental wife or, in the lexicon of the day, as "the angel in the house." Significantly, this gender polarity resulted in the emergence, or more accurately the invention, of full-time motherhood. Although this notion of full-time motherhood was largely symbolic—and restricted to middle-class mothers—these mothers acquired moral superiority and cultural prestige (though, of course, not real societal power or respect) in and through their identity as a mother. This gendered schism converged to construct mothering as the natural identity and purpose of women and the family as fundamentally a private unit separate and distinct from the larger public, political, and social world. Douglas and Michaels, as noted above, have termed the twenty-first-century manifestation of this ideology the "new momism."

In sharp contrast to this received explanation for mothers' oppression in patriarchal motherhood, lesbian theorist Baba Copper celebrates and champions exclusive female mothering as a transgressive and transformative mode of mothering. "The practice of motherhood," she writes, "embodies legitimate power—the power of early childhood socialization and a lifelong position of influence on one's children" (186). "Within the context of female-to-female training in motherhood," she goes on to argue, "lies yet another potential—that of strong, women-come-first female bonding. The mother who teaches her daughter how to mother could be an alchemist of culture, vaporizing woman-hating traditions into the gold of feminist change" (186). "First and foremost," Copper writes, "we must acknowledge that the mothering of daughters is of primary importance to us [and] [i]f women come first, then daughters come first" (189). Mothers can and must, in Copper's words, "use their power to commit their daughters to resistance to patriarchal conformity" and "to inoculate them against assimilation into heterofemininity" (186, 192). She argues further that "mothers must model the behavior we expect in [our daughters]" (187). This necessitates, Copper writes, "viewing one's lifestyle not as an extension of who-I-am but of who-I-want-them-to-learn-to-be." She continues: "No mother succeeds in always being how she wants her children to be, but the radical mother structures her lifestyle so that her child has ample opportunity to see her trying" (192). Copper's concept of radical motherhood, though developed from her specific personal experience of a lesbian mother raising a lesbian daughter, nonetheless has relevance and use for all mothers raising daughters. Copper's call for a women-come-first female bonding resonated with the young women in my course, who recalled from their childhood and adolescence many instances of favouritism and privilege accorded to their brothers and how they learned, as daughters, in subtle and not so subtle ways to, in Copper's words, "cater to male supremacy; to serve and submit" (187). Radical motherhood, thus, means, in Copper's words, "involving children in disloyalty to the culture the mother is expected to transmit at the expense of woman-bonding and female empowerment" (191). This "women-come-first" mode of mothering that is enacted through an empowered mother, and which affirms the importance of women, has, I argue, relevance beyond the specific lesbian context of Copper's writing and, indeed, has informed later feminist writings on motherhood, most notably the key theoretical concepts of the "motherline" and "matroreform."

In *Stories from the Motherline: Reclaiming the Mother-Daughter Bond, Finding Our Souls*, Naomi Lowinsky explores "a world-view that is as old as humankind, a wisdom we have forgotten that we know: the ancient lore of women—the Motherline." She goes on to say:

> Whenever women gather in circles or in pairs, in olden times around the village well, or at the quilting bee, in modern times in support groups, over lunch, or at the children's party, they tell one another stories from the Motherline. These are stories of female experience: physical, psychological, and historical. They are stories about the dramatic changes of woman's body: developing breasts and pubic hair, bleeding, being sexual, giving

birth, suckling, menopause, and of growing old. They are stories of the life cycles that link generations of women: Mothers who are also daughters, daughters who have become mothers; grandmothers who also remain granddaughters. (1-2)

Most women today, Lowinsky contends, are cut off from their motherline; they suffer from what she calls "the feminist ambivalence about the feminine" (30). She writes:

Women seemed to want to live their fathers' lives. Mother was rejected, looked down upon. In the headlong race to liberate those aspects of ourselves that had been so long denied, we left behind all that women had been. Many of us who joyfully accepted the challenge of new opportunities discovered in retrospect that we had cut ourselves off from much of what was meaningful to us as women: our mothers, our collective past, our passion for affiliation and for richness in our personal lives. We felt split between our past and our future. (29)

Lowinsky asks that "women integrate their feminine and feminist selves to connect the historical self that was freed by feminism to live in the 'real' world, with the feminine self that binds us to our mothers and grandmothers" (32).

Daughters of the so-called baby boom are the first generation of women, at least among the middle classes, whose lives are radically different from those of their mothers. These daughters, Lowinsky argues, have "paid a terrible price for cutting [them]selves off from [their] feminine roots" (31). By disconnecting themselves from their motherline, these daughters have lost the authenticity and authority of their womanhood. Women may reclaim that authority and authenticity by reconnecting to the motherline:

When a woman today comes to understand her life story as a story from the Motherline, she gains female authority in a number of ways. First, her Motherline grounds her in her feminine nature as she struggles with the many options now open to women. Second, she reclaims carnal knowledge of her own body, its blood mysteries and their power. Third, as she makes the journey back to her female roots, she will encounter ancestors who struggled with similar difficulties in different historical times. This provides her with a life-cycle perspective that softens her immediate situation. Fourth, she uncovers her connection to the archetypal mother and to the wisdom of the ancient worldview, which holds that body and soul are open and all life is interconnected. And, finally, she reclaims her female perspective, from which to consider how men are similar and how they are different. (13)

Virginia Woolf wrote in *A Room of One's Own*: "[W]e think back through our mothers if we are women" (72). Writing about Lowinsky's motherline in her book *Motherless Daughters: The Legacy of Loss*, Hope Edelman emphasizes that "motherline stories ground a daughter in a gender, a family, and a feminine history [and] [t]hey transform the experience of her female ancestors into maps she can refer to for warning or encouragement" (201). Motherless daughters long to know and to be connected to, what Lowinsky calls, "the deep feminine," or in Edelman's words: "that subtle unconscious source of feminine authority and power we mistakenly believe is expressed in scarf knots and thank-you notes but instead originates from a more abstract gendered core" (179). "Without knowledge of her own experiences, and the relationship to her mother's," Edelman continues, "a daughter is snipped from the female cord that connects the generations of women in her family, the feminine line of descent ... the motherline" (200). Rich writes in *Of Woman Born*, "The loss of the daughter to the mother, the mother to the daughter, is the essential female tragedy" (237). In Edelman's work, this loss refers to the daughter losing her mother through death, abandonment, or neglect. In these instances, separation occurs as a result of the mother leaving the daughter. More frequent, in patriarchal culture, is the loss of the daughter to the mother: daughters become disconnected from their motherline through specific cultural practices, most notably matrophopia, as discussed earlier.

"Matroreform," a concept developed by Canadian feminist psychologist Gina Wong, also seeks to work against the estrangement of mother and daughter in and through what she terms a "reformation of patriarchal motherhood." In her article "Images and Echoes in Matroreform: A Cultural Feminist Perspective." Wong argues that the concept of phobia advanced in Rich's theory of matrophobia fails to capture "the real and common experience of feminist mothers" and their refusal "to reproduce or [remain] trapped in the oppressive bonds of conventional motherhood" (142). In the place of matrophobia, Wong articulates a practice or process of matroreform as "an act, desire, and process of claiming motherhood power" (142). She asserts that matroreform is a more appropriate term because it involves a "a progressive movement to mothering that attempts to institute new mothering rules and practices from one's motherline" (135). In essence, Wong suggests that matroreform is a "cognitive, affective, behavioural, and spiritual reformation of mothering from within including removal and elimination of obstacles to self-determination and self-agency" (142).

In her writing on matroreform, Wong illustrates how she engages in the active practice and empowering process in her own mothering to create a meaningful motherline for her and her daughters by engaging in reflective understandings and narratives of her life experiences, despite a previously invisible motherline of her Chinese foremothers because of the cultural dissonance she experienced as a young Chinese Canadian girl living in Montreal. By attending to and sharing her maternal narratives as the mother of daughters and by linking those narratives to reflections and understandings of her relationship as a daughter with her own mother, Wong actively works to forge a strong bond with her daughters. In her practice of embodying matroreform, she strives to create a new feminist motherline. Matroreform is likewise identified as a central process in the feminist mothers' lives studied by Fiona Joy Green in her longitudinal and intergenerational study of feminist motherlines. In her article "Matroreform: Feminist Mothers and Their Daughters Creating Feminist Motherlines," Green explores how a group of Canadian feminist mothers and their daughters dismantle the patriarchal script and revise or reform their own stories of motherhood and daughterhood. She concludes that through the active practice and empowering process of matroreform, mothers can perpetuate an enduring feminist motherline for themselves and their daughters. The concepts of the motherline and matroreform—in their emphasis on mother-daughter connection and empowerment specifically in and through women's shared female identities and histories—illustrate that Copper's theory of radical motherhood provides a useful model of empowerment for all mothers and daughters in patriarchal culture.

Copper's concept of radical motherhood affirms gender difference, positions femaleness as a site of power for women, and regards exclusive female mothering as beneficial to mothers and daughters. Copper does not concern herself with the raising of sons, nor does she consider the place of men in her theory of radical motherhood. Moreover, in reifying gender difference and making mothering the exclusive work and responsibility of women, her theory re-inscribes the essentialism of patriarchal motherhood. However, I suggest that her concept of radical motherhood precisely in its affirmation of exclusive mothering gives to mothers the authority, agency, autonomy, authenticity and activism denied to women in patriarchal motherhood. Radical mothers, as described by Copper, are strong women and empowered mothers. Her concept of radical motherhood thus, I argue, serves as an important model of empowered mothering that is not dependent on men for its realization as is the case with the strategy of shared parenting advanced by Chodorow and others. Moreover, in valuing motherwork and positioning such work as a political practice, radical motherhood demarcates motherhood as a site of power for women and makes possible the feminist motherlines and matroreform necessary for reciprocal mother-daughter empowerment.

Queering Motherhood: Margaret Gibson

Margaret Gibson opens her chapter, "Queer Mothering and the Question of Normalcy" by asking, "who are queer mothers?":

> Are all queer mothers women? Or might "queer mothers' also include intersex, transgender or genderqueer people—or even some cisgender (non-transgender) men? Can queer mothers be partnered and parenting with men? Could queer mothers include all mothers who have sexually stigmatized relationships, including those from polyamorous or kink communities? Or is queer mother a moniker reserved for women with non-heterosexual identities such as lesbian, bisexual or queer? To complicate things further, how do we categorize queer mothers who are not legally (or sometimes socially) recognized as their children's kin? And where do we put queer-identified women who parent but don't identify with the word "mother"? (347)

Such questions trouble the presumed gender, family, and sexual scripts of the dominant relations and make "mother" a contested and unstable social category. Indeed queering, as Gibson explains in the introduction to her book *Queering Motherhood: Narrative and Theoretical*

Approaches, "makes the things we otherwise take for granted suddenly unpredictable, uncooperative, and unexpected" (1). Thus, the concept of queering motherhood extends beyond the experiences of queer or trans parents—although they are central to this endeavor and start in Gibson's words, "where any of the central gendered, sexual, relational, political and/or symbolic components of "expected" motherhood are challenged" (6). To queer motherhood, "is to re-think, re-shape, re-establish notions and practices of [normative] motherhood" (12).

To queer motherhood, thus, is to destabilize patriarchal motherhood, particularly its ideological mandates of essentialization, normalization, naturalization, and biologicalization. Queering motherhood means that not all mothers are women or that there is one right or correct way to create a family. It means as well that the desire and ability to mother is not innate to one sex over the other and that kinship is not defined only by blood. Queering motherhood, thus, makes possible the very identities and practices needed for empowered modes of mothering that were discussed earlier: a multitude of maternal identities, diverse family formations, and a variety of motherhood practices. To queer motherhood is, thus, to empower mothers.

Conclusion

I opened this chapter referencing my book *Redefining Motherhood* and closed it with a discussion of Gibson's concept of queering motherhood. Though not intentional, bookending the chapter this way, I believe, serves as a useful conceptual framework for thinking about what I sought to accomplish in this chapter: to understand, by way of various theoretical concepts, how the institution of patriarchal motherhood, materially and discursively, oppresses mothers and to consider how empowered mothering seeks to redefine patriarchal motherhood by redefining or queering its ideological mandates through specific strategies of resistance, as explained in the theoretical concepts of maternal empowerment. Reading the chapter again as I write this conclusion and rereading now the above convoluted sentence, I realize that I could have been far more precise and concise in my explication of maternal theory. However, as someone trained in literary studies, I believe that it is in the complexities of stories that we arrive at the simple truths. It is my hope that this telling of maternal theory, through its tangled plot and varied characters, provides, if not a simple truth, at least an understanding of how patriarchal motherhood works and how it may be challenged and changed through empowered mothering. Indeed, this is the aim of matricentric feminism, particularly as it is enacted in maternal theory.

Chapter Two

Matricentric Feminism As Activism

The Twenty-First-Century Motherhood Movement

My research on maternal activism began more than a decade ago when I was writing on empowered mothering and maternal empowerment. I recognized then the need and urgency to bring together motherhood organizations to better understand motherhood activism, particularly as it was developing and coalescing to form a twenty-first-century motherhood movement. To this end, the Association for Research on Mothering (now the Motherhood Initiative for Research and Community Involvement) hosted a two-day conference in Toronto, Canada, in October 2008—titled "You Say You Want a Revolution?: The Twenty-First-Century Motherhood Movement"—that brought together twenty-eight motherhood organizations. The objectives of this embedded conference, the first ever on the motherhood movement of the twenty-first century, were threefold. First, we hoped to raise the public profile of the motherhood movement as a potential force for social change. Second, we sought to provide a collective narrative of the history, core concerns, and objectives of the movement in its formative period. And third, we wished to capture the diverse organizational backgrounds, personal perspectives, and visions of those involved in the movement's inception, including independent activists and leaders and founders of groups involved in advocacy, support, education, and consciousness-raising for mothers. Our overall aim was to highlight the scope and diversity of this movement as it moved to create a more equitable world for mothers and their children. At this conference, the International Mothers Network, now the International Mother and Mothering Network, the first ever global consortium of motherhood organizations was formed and officially launched on March 8, 2009—International Women's Day. In 2011, I published *The Twenty-First-Century Motherhood Movement: Mothers Speak Out on Why We Need to Change the World and How to Do It*. Initially, I had planned to include only the motherhood organizations represented at the above conference, but as I researched motherhood activism and as one motherhood group suggested another, the collection grew to include more than eighty organizations and 976 pages. My criteria for the inclusion of chapters in this collection was that they were informed by the values of matricentric feminism (that are now explored in this book) and were committed to improving the lives of mothers and working towards social change for mothers, children, and society more generally. In this, each organization had to view and position itself as an activist and/or advocacy group that sought broad-based change and membership. In defining an organization this way, I looked for groups that not only provided services for mothers but also sought to change the larger meaning and experience of mothering-motherhood and/or addressed a particular social issue that had relevance to mothers' lives in their responsibility and practice of motherwork. Equally important in the selection of organization was that they covered diverse maternal identities and allowed for an international perspective on motherhood activism.

The aim of this chapter on matricentric feminism as activism is to provide an overview of the twenty-first-century motherhood movement and, in particular, its theoretical and historical context. The chapter is organized by way of the following topics: 1) the history and ideological frameworks of the twenty-first-century motherhood movement; 2) the challenges and possibilities of maternalism, a philosophy central to much of twenty-first-century motherhood activism; 3) the specific practices and strategies of twenty-first-century motherhood activism, including strategic essentialism, embodied activism, emotionality, maternal nurturance as resistance, matrifocality, maternal practice, and empowered maternal subjectivity; and 4) motherhood activism in relation to feminism as both theory and practice. Overall, I argue that not only is the twenty-first-century motherhood movement an autonomous social movement distinct from the larger feminist one, but that this movement, in being specifically mother centred and concerned with the empowerment of mothers and social change for mothers, is urgently needed and long overdue. The twenty-first-century motherhood movement, I contend, made possible and gave rise to a specific and much needed theory and politic of feminism for mothers, or what I have termed matricentric feminism.

Defining the Twenty-First-Century Motherhood Movement: What Is In A Name?

If recent scholarship on the twenty-first-century motherhood movement agrees on anything, it is that the term or concept "the twenty-first-century motherhood movement" eludes a precise definition. Discussing the "Call for a Motherhood Movement" paper presented at the 2003 conference held at Bernard College and hosted by the Motherhood Project, Stephanie Wilkinson, co-editor of *Brain, Child Magazine*, writes:

> Over the last six months, I've tried to track the progress of this thing—this shape-shifting, squishy, now-you-see-it, now-you-don't movement—and I've come to think that maybe the Call was more prophetic than prescriptive. All the seeds of schism are outlined there—all the issues that divide mothers working toward a movement. Would a movement be mother-focused or child-focused? Would it be a branch of feminism? What kind of feminism? Would it ask for legal rights for mothers? Would it be aligned with the political left or the right? (5)

"I'd envisioned my quest to find out what was going on in motherhood circles," Wilkinson continues, "as a journey." "At the end, I hoped to find a nice place with a bunch of good people gathered together—kind of like a big family reunion ... [b]ut as I went along, it came to seem more like a road trip between the houses of a bunch of relatives, some of whom don't exactly see eye to eye" (5). Likewise, Judith Stadtman Tucker, editor of the *Mothers Movement Online* website and interviewed in the above article, comments: "There are lots of seeds out there. But I don't believe there is a unifying politics of motherhood. Mothers don't think alike just because they are mothers" (quoted in Wilkinson, 10). Writing in the entry on "The Motherhood Movement" for the *Encyclopedia of Motherhood*, Caroline Gatrell explains the following about the motherhood movement: "[it] is difficult to define in part because of its lack of a political identity, and no officially elected leadership. Furthermore, no single group within the movement claims exclusive knowledge of the needs, beliefs and priorities among mothers within society" (823). "Unlike movements such as women's suffrage or campaigns for more woman-centred birth," she continues, "the motherhood movement today is not focused on any single aspect of women's needs" (823).

Indeed, it would seem that the motherhood movement lacks the criteria—political identity, leadership, common purpose, shared values, and so forth—to qualify as a social movement, particularly when compared to other social movements such as the civil rights movement and feminism. Wilkinson conducted a simple word association experiment for her article that seems to support such an argument. She found that her friends and colleagues associated the civil rights movement with Rosa Parks, integration, Martin Luther King, equality for African Americans; and women's rights with Gloria Steinem, bra burning, and feminism (3). However, when she asked her friends and colleagues with what they associated mothers' rights, their responses were less certain: "maternity leave? ... childcare? I don't know, I'd have to think about it" (3). Wilkinson concludes: "Overall, the results were pretty clear ... if there is a mothers' movement going on, it hasn't reached my neighborhood yet" (3). Judging by the above, it seems that the concept or term "the motherhood movement" appears to be "the problem with no name," to use Betty Friedan's famous quote, or in academic parlance, "a sign without a referent."

However, I argue, that if the motherhood movement is situated in relation to its historical development and in ways specific to its twenty-first-century context, it can be understood to be, in both form and function, a social movement. It should be noted that Wilkinson's article—"Say You Want a Revolution? Why the Mothers' Revolution Hasn't Happened ... Yet"—was written in 2005.

That year, the concept and term "twenty-first-century motherhood movement" was difficult to define or describe with any precision because eleven years ago, this social movement was in its infancy. The majority of motherhood organizations were formed and established only in the first years of the twenty-first century. Similarly, the feminist movement would have been difficult to define and describe in the early-to-mid-1960s. Movements, traditions, and the like are definable only in retrospect when they have become established as such. I argue that in 2016, with a decade plus of maternal activism and the creation of numerous motherhood organizations, the twenty-first-century motherhood movement has become a social movement with its own specific mandate and objectives, which are distinct from the larger feminist movement. However, the shape or character of the twenty-first-century motherhood movement differs from early social movements because of its formation in the twenty-first century. The aforementioned absence of recognizable leaders in the motherhood movement and the apparent lack of a shared agenda are given as reasons why the motherhood movement does not function as a social movement. However, this more diffuse style of organizing is a chosen strategy for many in the motherhood movement; it is reflective of the eclectic and democratic nature of maternal activism. As Linda Jeurgens of the *National Association of Mother Centres* explains, "having a leader for each different area—one working on Social Security, and tax issues, another on universal pre-school bills—might be a more effective idea. You have a number of different champions, each working on their goals" (qtd in Wilkinson 16). And as Enola Aird notes, most in the motherhood movement agree "that the male-power model of leadership needs to be looked at skeptically" (qtd. in Wilkinson 16).

Finally, this movement has developed in the context of rapid technological change, which has resulted in maternal activism being expressed in ways radically different than that of previous social movements. As rallies, marches, meetings, protests, and the like, characterized the activism of second-wave feminism and the civil rights movement, maternal activism, as with other forms of twenty-first-century activism, is often expressed through technology—emails, blogs, websites, Facebook, twitter, online communities, and so forth—and by way of more informal, grassroots, ad hoc, micro, and spontaneous acts of everyday activism. Indeed, many of the organizations described in this collection would not exist without the Internet. In this, twenty-first-century maternal activism is closer to third-wave feminism than to second-wave feminism in its philosophies and practices of social change. Moreover, as will be discussed at length below, maternal activism is often not recognized as activism or dismissed as not "real" activism because of its specific and deliberate maternal stance. In my view, there is no doubt that a twenty-first-century motherhood movement exists. But because it has developed and has expressed itself in ways that do not conform to accepted, traditional, and, more specifically, masculine norms and practices of activism, it remains for many difficult to define and classify.

History

Writing the history of a movement that is only just beginning is a near impossible undertaking. Needless to say, a decade or so from now, the significance of the events that are currently unfolding will be better understood, as they will be placed in the larger thematic and historical trajectory of twenty-first-century maternal activism and, more specifically, the motherhood movement. To decide on a starting date for the motherhood movement appears to be a challenging, if not a problematic task. Several organizations important to contemporary maternal activism—such as Mothers against Drunk Driving, National Association of Mother Centres, and La Leche League—began several years or decades earlier. Likewise, some other organizations—such as Another Mother for Peace, Mothers are Women, The Mothers of the Plaza de Mayo—though not currently active as organizations, are important for a discussion on the twenty-first-century motherhood movement because of the pivotal role they play in contemporary theories and practices of maternal activism. Most agree that 1848, the date of the Seneca Falls convention, marks the beginning of the suffrage movement, or the first wave of feminism. Although there is less agreement on a date or event to mark the inception of second-wave feminism, the year 1968 is usually given as the official date for the beginning of the contemporary feminist movement (while recognizing the activism that preceded and gave rise to it). As well, with each wave, a text is credited for the rise of the movement and becomes a symbol for it: Betty Friedan's *The Feminine Mystique* for the second wave and Rebecca Walker's article "Becoming the Third Wave" for the third wave.

As I read the scholarship on twenty-first-century maternal activism and the eighty-plus motherhood organizations that I included in my edited collection, I looked to find a starting date for this movement or, at the very least, to determine key dates, events, or texts in its development. Although I will now suggest some important moments in the movement's history thus far, I anticipate that in a few years' time, such a trajectory will become clearer. Being called the twenty-first-century motherhood movement, I suspect the year 2000 will be cited as the beginning of this movement. However, in my view, the diverse and disparate maternal activist groups and actions coalesce to create a recognizable entity—something that begins to be called the twenty-first-century motherhood movement—around 2005. Significant dates and events in the history of the twenty-first-century motherhood movement include 1998—when the Association for Research on Mothering and its journal (now the Motherhood Initiative for Research and Community Involvement and the *Journal of the Motherhood Initiative*), the first association and journal on motherhood were formed—and the year 2000, when the Motherhood Project and Mothers Ought to Have Equal Rights and the Million Mom March took place. Two years later in 2002, the Bernard College conference "Maternal Feminism: Lessons for a Twenty-First-Century Motherhood Movement" took place, and the following year, a widely read website, *Mothers Movement Online*, was launched. Other significant dates and events include the 2005 article discussed above on the mothers' movement in *Brain Child Magazine*, and the launching of Demeter Press, the first press on motherhood, and the founding of Moms Rising, both in 2006. In addition, in 2008 the international conference "You Say You Want a Revolution? The Twenty-First-Century Motherhood Movement" was held, in 2009 the International Mothers Network, now the International Mothers and Mothering Network was established, and in 2012 the Museum of Motherhood opened.

As with the feminist movement of the 1960s, both lay and academic publications have played a pivotal role in the development of the twenty-first-century motherhood movement. However, I argue that motherhood scholarship largely predates and has laid the foundation for contemporary maternal activism, particularly as it coalesced to form a unified movement. And it is a departure from the contemporary feminist movement wherein the academic discipline of women's studies was largely born from feminist activism. A cursory review of feminist publications revealed that most were published after 1968—the start of the second-wave feminist movement—whereas with motherhood scholarship, most publications were published before the rise of the motherhood movement at the turn of this century. This is not to say that maternal activism did not exist prior to the twenty-first-century, but it does suggest that the hundreds of books and articles on motherhood published in the 1990s and early 2000s, both lay and scholarly, have provided the knowledge for understanding and responding to the discrimination, devaluation, and dissatisfaction mothers often experience, which has made possible the creation of an organized movement to challenge and change such experiences. Writing in the *Brain Child* article, Wilkinson argues that "If *The Feminine Mystique* was the book that laid the seeds for the women's movement of the 1960's, Ann Crittenden's *Price of Motherhood* (2000) may someday be regarded as the one that did the same for the mothers' movement" (8). In other words, by documenting what Adrienne Rich described years earlier as the patriarchal institution of motherhood, scholarly and literary publications of the mid-1990s to the early 2000s have provided the consciousness and language necessary for maternal activism to coalesce into a social movement. Among the notable publications of these formative years are Sharon Hays's *The Cultural Contradictions of Motherhood* (1996); Dorothy Roberts's *Killing the Black Body: Race, Reproduction and the Meaning of Liberty* (1998); Patrice DiQuinzio's *The Impossibility of Motherhood* (1999); Susan Maushart's *The Mask of Motherhood* (2000); Joan William's *Unbending Gender: Why Family and Work Conflict and What To Do About It* (2000); and Allison Pearson's *I Don't Know How She Does It* (2002), to name but a few.

As the motherhood movement gained momentum from approximately 2005 onwards, it made possible and gave rise to increased writing on motherhood, particularly in lay and literary genres (most notably the motherhood memoir). Significant publications include the following: Susan Douglas and Meredith Michaels's *The Mommy Myth: The Idealization of Motherhood and How it Has Undermined Women* (2004); Miriam Peskowitz's *The Truth behind the Mommy Wars* (2005); Judith Warner's *Perfect Madness: Motherhood in the Age of Anxiety* (2005); Joan Blades and Kristin Rowe-Finkbeiner's *The Motherhood Manifesto: What America's Moms Want and What to Do About it* (2006); Andrea Buchanan's *Mother Shock* (2003); Faulkner Fox's *Dispatches from a Not-So-Perfect Life* (2003); and Naomi Wolf's *Misconceptions: Truth, Lies, and the Unexpected on the Journey to Motherhood* (2003). Throughout this time, the motherhood movement continued to be sustained by numerous scholarly works on motherhood: Pamela Stone's *Opting Out? Why Women Really Quit Careers and Head Home* (2007); Amber Kinser's *Mothering in the Third Wave* (2008); *Women's Studies Quarterly* journal issue "Mother" (2009); and my own *Maternal Theory: Essential Readings* (2007), *Encyclopedia of Motherhood* (2010), and *Twenty-First-Century Motherhood: Experience, Identity, Policy, Agency* (2010), to name but a few. In turn, such motherhood scholarship coalesced to form a specific academic and scholarly discipline, which I termed "motherhood studies" in 2006. As with the development of women's studies as an academic field in the 1970s, motherhood studies, though explicitly interdisciplinary and multidisciplinary, has developed as an autonomous and independent scholarly discipline over the last decade. In so doing, motherhood studies both sustains and is sustained by the twenty-first-century motherhood movement.

Philosophies and Practices of Maternal Activism: Liberal Feminism, Maternalism, Ethic Care Theory

Judith Stadtman Tucker, editor of *Mothers Movement Online*, has written extensively on the twenty-first-century motherhood movement. Tucker advances the concept of "political and ideological grounding" to understand and analyze a motherhood group's identity and its activism. According to Tucker, all motherhood organizations position themselves politically and ideologically in relation to what Patrice DiQuinzio has termed the "trope or discourse of essential motherhood": the view that mothering is essential to women and all women are, or should be, mothers. Susan Douglas and Meredith Michaels, as discussed in the previous chapter, have termed the twenty-first-century manifestation of this ideology the "new momism," which

> involves more than just impossible ideals about women childrearing; it redefines all women, first and foremost, through their relationships to children ... being a citizen, a worker, a governor [and so forth] are supposed to take a backseat to motherhood. (22)

This type of gender essentialism, whether it's conveyed as the "angel in the house" ideology of the nineteenth century or this century's "new momism," naturalizes mothering as "a woman's calling": it is to be performed by the biological mother who must be a wife and nurturer in a heterosexual family, wherein the father is the provider and is not expected to engage in mothering.

Tucker argues that "several strands of political philosophy float through the logic and rhetoric of the emerging Mothers Movement." Moreover, she explains that "the key variables are whether these different frameworks support or contest the dominant ideology of motherhood [described above] and whether they serve as a useful basis for developing advocacy positions that advance rather than obstruct gender equality" (1-2 "Motherhood and Its Discontents"). Tucker elaborates further:

> Frameworks that challenge the dominant ideology of motherhood are attractive because of a growing awareness in popular culture that the idealization of "intensive" selfless mothering detracts from the lived experience of motherhood, isolates fathers from the core of family life, and limits mothers' personal freedom and occupational mobility. Frameworks that align with the dominant ideology of motherhood are politically appealing because they support a plea for better treatment of mothers without posing a serious threat to the status quo. ("Motherhood and Its Discontents" 2)

"Activists and authors currently involved in the articulation of 'mothers' issues,'" Tucker continues, "tend to sample from both conforming and non-conforming frameworks to legitimize their demands for social reforms." She argues further that although there "are any number of philosophies and political theories that feed into the new thinking on motherhood as a social problem, the three predominant influences are liberal feminism, maternalism and feminist care theory" ("Motherhood and Its Discontents" 2).

Tucker then explains in detail how liberal feminism disrupts motherhood's dominant ideology:

> [Liberal feminism] challenges the dominant ideology of motherhood and offers a vocabulary of rights, responsibilities, justice, equity, empowerment and identity.... This framework is essential to their interpretation of mothers as persons with individual and social rights and responsibilities and is fundamental to the articulation of mothers' entitlement to self expression within and beyond the bounds of the maternal role—including self-expression through paid employment or civic engagement ... as

well it qualifies mothers as equal citizens in an ideally egalitarian society ... and provides a context for the strategic separation of the needs and interests of women who mother from the needs and interests of the child they mother. ("Motherhood and Its Discontents" 2)

Motherhood organizations that work from a liberal-feminist or equal-rights paradigm include Moms Rising, Mothers and More, and Mothers Ought to Have Equal Rights. In contrast to liberal feminism, maternalism, Tucker explains, "conforms to the dominant ideology of motherhood and emphasizes the importance of maternal well-being to the health and safety of children" ("Motherhood and Its Discontents" 2). "Maternalism," she continues, "overlaps with what has been called difference feminism—particularly the idea that women are 'naturally' or intuitively more empathic, less exploitative, and more closely attuned to relational ambience than men" ("Motherhood and Its Discontents" 2). "Maternalist politics refers to," as Patrice DiQuinzio elaborates, "political activism and political movements that invoke motherhood as the basis of women's agency" ("Mothering and Feminism" 58). More numerous than equal-rights-based maternal activism (for reasons to be discussed below), groups that work from a maternalist politics include Million Mom March, The Mothers of the Plazo de Mayo, The Mothers of Acari, The Mothers of Laleh Park, Mothers against Drunk Driving, The Motherhood Project, Mainstreet Moms, and Mothers in Charge.

In place of liberal feminism and maternalism, and what she views as their problematic emphasis on individualism and essentialism respectively, Tucker develops and advocates a feminist ethic of care framework: "As with maternalism, a feminist ethic of care designates caring for others as an essential social function. But rather than valorizing maternal sensitivity and altruism as an innate vital resource, a feminist care ethic aims to liberate caregiving from its peripheral status and reposition it as a primary human activity" ("Motherhood Papers" 212). She goes on to explain that "for proponents of the contemporary mothers' movement, grounding the agenda in an ethic of care opens up the possibilities of developing a gender neutral approach to social policy and an opportunity to expand the language of care as a public good beyond the maternalist paradigm ("Motherhood Papers" 201). In positioning caregiving as a social responsibility rather than an exclusive maternal duty, a feminist ethic care framework serves to reinvent normative motherhood and undermine its individualism and essentialism. Although few current motherhood organizations work specifically from a feminist care ethic framework, ones that do include Playground Revolution, Warriors against a Violent Society, The LGBTQ Parenting Network, Welfare Warriors, Feminist.com, and International Feminists for a Gift Economy. Other organizations, although they may be titled mothers' groups, signify a care ethic politics in the way that they position their organizations, in the language they use to describe their mandates, and in the types of activism that they undertake. As Heather Hewitt notes, "The signature tag line of Tucker's *Mothers Movement Online* website reads resources for and reporting for mothers and others who think about social change" (39). As well, Mothers Acting Up, though seemingly a maternalist organization, includes an asterisk after the word "mothers" to include "mothers and others, on stilts and off, who exercise protective care over someone smaller," and Mothers Ought to Have Equal Rights, though working from an equal rights perspective, frequently uses the word caregivers as well as mothers in its literature (Hewitt 39). Other organizations that advance an ethic of care philosophy and practice in their challenge to the essentialism and individualism of normative motherhood include Mother Outlaws, The Latina Mami Collective, Jennifer Schumaker's 500 Mile Walk, and the Australian and Toronto Feminist Mothers Discussion groups. Though working from and advocating a feminist care ethic politic, these organizations continue to use the word "mothers" because as Hewitt notes, "[such] reflects reality—women continue to perform most of the world's motherwork and carework" and affords, in Hewitt's words "a *realpolitik* strategy of identity politics" (39).

Tucker maintains that these competing frameworks have hindered the twenty-first-century motherhood movement's progress and its attempts to develop a cohesive agenda and unified platform to achieve the social change it desires for mothers and motherhood. "The mothers' movement," she argues, "hasn't taken off yet because there's a divide that exists between whether this is a maternalist movement or if this is about the politics of motherhood aimed at resolving the social disadvantages of motherhood" (qtd. in Wilkinson 10). Contrary to Tucker, I suggest that most social movements are characterized by a wide range of differences in politics and ideologies and that the aim of any movement should not be to determine what perspective or agenda is best but how to best position such differences in terms of developing strategies for change. As DiQuinzio writes: "[T]hese tensions are exactly where the movement should begin in refining its ideological commitments, formulating its agenda, and developing strategies for change. Those of us engaged in this movement should not expect to resolve these tensions but rather should be prepared to negotiate and renegotiate them precisely as part of our strategies for change" ("The Politics of the Mothers Movement" 56). The contemporary women's movement has grown and flourished despite (and I would suggest as a result of) the many and diverse feminist ideologies that inform it—liberal, socialist, cultural, queer, womanist, and third wave, to name but a few. Moreover, as Tucker herself argues (as noted above), most organizations draw from all three frameworks, depending on the specific issue at hand, in order to develop the most effective strategy within a particular situation, context, or timeframe.

In her paper "Mother-Activism: Harnessing the Radicalizing Experience of Motherhood to Create Anti-Violent Activists," Susan Logsdon-Conradsen argues that motherhood organizations tend to pick and choose, and mingle and blend the politics and strategies of the different frameworks: "each of these frameworks provides a different pathway a mother may traverse on her path to becoming a mother-activist on any given issue" (4). In the context of mothers opposing violence, the equal-rights framework enables mothers to argue against violence on the grounds that all individuals have the right to live a life free of violence, whereas the maternalist perspective, in emphasizing women's role as caretaker and protector of children, empowers mothers to demand a safe world for their children. "A feminist care theory, with its emphasis on caring for all individuals as a social responsibility," as Logsdon-Conradsen explains, "clearly supports anti-violence activism and the need to protect and advocate for those with less power, including but not limited to children" (4). Moreover, these three frameworks are more complementary than oppositional: they allow for a multitude of perspectives on any given motherhood issue, which makes possible the coalition building necessary for a successful social movement.

"Maternalism is Feminism for Hard Times": The Case Against Maternalist Politics for the Twenty-First-Century Motherhood Movement: Gender Essentialism, and Emotionalism

If any debate has defined current discussions on maternal activism it is the role maternalist politics should or should not play in the twenty-first-century motherhood movement. Most scholars, particularly those writing in the early years of the twenty-first-century motherhood movement—Judith Stadtman Tucker, Heather Hewitt, Patrice Di Quinzio—argue against maternalism as a politic or strategy for maternal activism. "The contemporary mothers' movement," DiQuinzio writes, "should strive to avoid the risks or pitfalls that maternalist politics presents, even if that means sacrificing the advantages of maternalism; advantages that may be dubious anyway" ("The Politics of the Mothers Movement" 58).

Gender Essentialism: Co-Opting Mothers—Normalizing Motherhoods

Critics of maternalism argue that this politic, as it is grounded in the discourse of essential motherhood, serves to reinforce and reify gender difference. Likewise, it renders sacrificial motherhood as both normative and natural. Moreover, as DiQuinzio notes, "maternalism may easily be manipulated or co-opted by others to oppose the interest of mothers; for example, the narrow definition of the "good" mother created from the discourse of essential motherhood may result in only "good" mothers' needs being addressed, whereas the so-called bad mothers and their needs are ignored and demonized ("The Politics of the Mothers Movement" 61). In addition, DiQuinzio explains that mothers and maternal concerns "may be positioned on many sides of the same issue," and thus maternalism may be used to advance causes and organizations that most twenty-first-century maternal activists would regard as antithetical to the objectives of the motherhood movement; mothers in support of war, and organizations such as Security Moms for Bush and Armed InformedMothers, a pro-gun motherhood organization are examples of such" ("The Politics of the Mothers Movement" 61). Moreover, DiQuinzio argues: "maternalist politics risks representing mothers and women as knowledgeable, interested, and entitled to political participation, only as mothers and only when they are acting on behalf of children or other dependent persons" ("The Politics of the Mothers Movement" 61). Finally, critics of maternalist politics worry that because maternalism is not inherently or necessarily feminist in its ideology or practice, it may serve to undermine women's demands for gender equity outside and beyond their role as mothers. As Hewitt argues: "Feminism provides important theoretical underpinnings for current activism. Not to engage with feminist frameworks and history—not to understand its success as well as its failures is to run the risk of forgoing the opportunity to learn valuable knowledge and avoiding the same mistakes" (41).

Emotionalism: A Politics of Grief

Of equal concern to critics of maternalism is its strategy of what may be termed "emotionalism." Michelle Moravec discusses the aforementioned in her article "Another Mother for Peace: Reconsidering Maternalist Peace Rhetoric from a Historical Perspective, 1967-2007." In it, she argues that "while motherhood may provide an emotionally resonant call for motivating peace activists, it undercuts the political efficacy of women working to end war" (9). According to Moravec, the reason for this is maternal peace activists' reliance on gendered constructs of agency and resistance:

> Historically, women's exclusion from politics rested on a belief in women's innate characteristics, such as emotionality, which rendered them too irrational. When women invoke the bonds of womanhood, when they speak from their personal grief, even when they read protest letters in public, they do not become politically efficacious acts. These forms of extra-political activism and emotive arguments run the risk of reinforcing a limited conception of women's participation in the public sphere and reifying the notion that women's true influence lies in persuading men. They reinscribe women's position as firmly on the margins. (24)

She continues:

> The personal voice risks being misheard as an individualized expression of emotion. It threatens to push the debate about

foreign policy deep into the realm of the emotional which is not acceptable in American political discourse. The combination of emotion plus femininity yields even more disastrous political results because women are seen as protesting, not from a position of realpolik but out of fear and anxiety. (23)

Similarly, DiQuinzio argues:

Maternalist politics also tends to become a politics of grief, predicating women's political agency on either the pain or suffering of others or on the pain, suffering, and loss they experience as a result of harm or threats to their children or others for whom they care. But this representation of women's political agency in terms of emotion risks the delegitimation of maternal politics as irrational. ("The Politics of the Mothers Movement" 61)

Critics of maternalism maintain that such a politic—grounded as it is in gender essentialism and in its emotive and child-centred strategies—serves only to reinforce and reify gender difference and render normative and natural sacrificial motherhood, which scholars agree causes mothering to be oppressive to women. As DiQuinzio writes, "maternalist politics based on traditional sentimental representations of motherhood present significant risks and pitfalls for the merging mothers' movement" ("The Politics of the Mothers Movement" 66). She continues: "Sociologist Lisa Brush puts it succinctly when she writes 'maternalism is feminism for hard times.' I take her to mean that maternalism is the feminism we resort to when we can't do any better on behalf of women" (DiQuinzio "The Politics of the Mothers Movement" 66).

A Transgressive Maternalism: Strategic Essentialism, Experiential Maternalism, and a Politics of the Heart

Strategic Essentialism, Experiential Maternalism, and Experiential Essentialism

I argue that maternalism, as both politic and practice, is more nuanced and multifaceted than the above authors suggest. In her article "From Gestation to Delivery: The Embodied Activist Mothering of Cindy Sheehan and Jennifer Shumaker," Natalie Wilson maintains that "motherhood need not be delivered as a static trope that ties women to outdated essential notions of motherhood" (232). Rather than being monolithic, the "trope of motherhood," as Wilson shows, "is varied, heterogeneous and contextual: utilized in various ways by activist movements" (201, 232). Wilson goes on to argue that maternal activism may be characterized by traditional maternalism and what she defines as "activist mothering"—a politically aware and engaged type of mothering (such as feminist mothering, other mothering, maternal thinking, and outlaw mothering). She distinguishes between these two frameworks:

> While maternalism draws on essentialist notions of women as "natural" caretakers of children, and thus is problematic from a contemporary feminist perspective, it nevertheless gave many women an activist voice in society. It allowed mothers to move beyond the "private sphere" and gave them a public voice, albeit a voice that limited the ways in which they could speak.... As an extension of maternalism, activist mothering is aimed at social injustices at all levels and in all places but does not necessarily focus on or emphasize women *as mothers*. While maternalist-based movements chained women to their status as mothers by reifying "motherhood" ... activist mothering moves beyond this limiting frame by using motherhood as a launch rather than a base. (233)

"The maternalist framework employed by earlier activists," she continues, "can be read as a gestation period in which mothers nourished various budding forms of female activism in order to eventually deliver a full-fledged activist agenda" (234). "Hence, maternalism and activist mothering," Wilson emphasizes, "should not be read as two disparate modes but rather as a continuum of activism" (234). I concur that maternalism functions on a historical continuum of motherhood activism and argue that maternalism itself is enacted on a continuum. Maternalism functions more often as a position rather than an identity; in other words, it is performed rather than essentially determined and derived.

Drawing on Judith Butler's theory of the performativity of gender, I argue that motherhood is similarly performed by maternalist activists. Gender, according to Butler, is performed rather than biologically inhabited and, as she explains, such "performativity is not a singular act but always a reiteration of a norm or set of norms, and to the extent that it acquires an act-like status in the present, it conceals or dissimulates the conventions of which it is a repetition" (12). "Essentialist," or good motherhood, is likewise performed by maternalist activists and is used or misused as circumstances dictate and as strategies require. In this, they engage in what Gayatri Spivak calls "strategic essentialism" or "the strategic use of positivist essentialism in a scrupulously visible political interest" (214). "Spivak's strategy," as Michael Kilburn explains, "is deconstructive, like that of a good lawyer: when on defense, prods the prosecution's narrative until the cracks begin to appear and when prosecuting, pieces together the case by understanding the criminal's motivation. [It] is like role-playing, briefly inhabiting the criminal mind in order to understand what makes it tick."

In contemporary maternalist politics, there is a similar deployment of strategic essentialism in Cynthia Edmonds-Cady's concept of "experiential maternalism" and Meghan Gibbons's notion of "experiential essentialism." In her article " Mobilizing Motherhood: Race, Culture and the Uses of Maternalism in the Welfare Rights Movement," Edmonds-Cady distinguishes between the sentimental maternalism of middle-class white women, "Friends" in the welfare rights movement in Detroit, and the experiential maternalism of the "Recipients," the poor Black women directly involved in this movement. According to Edmonds-Cady, the middle-class white women "held traditional [or in the context of this discussion, essentialist] assumptions about women, motherhood and work and "overemphasized a shared gender and motherhood status with the Recipients" (213). In contrast, "the Recipients took a more everyday practical approach to motherhood and their participation in the Welfare Rights Movement" (213). Edmonds-Cady further explains:

> Recipients' use of experiential maternalism represented a pragmatic approach to motherhood as well as a way of emphasizing a desire to help poor women and children. Recipients did not perceive of motherhood as being a separate, romanticized vocation, as did many of the Friends. Instead their experience of poverty and the agency they employed through fighting the racist, classist welfare system allowed them to develop a more politicized activists' view of motherhood. Experiential maternalism was a way of viewing their social movement through the lens of their experiences of discrimination and stigmatization as

poor Black women, while they were simultaneously driven by the critical needs of their children. (214)

In other words, Black women developed experiential maternalism from their specific and lived experiences of poverty and racism and deployed it, in Edmonds-Cady's words, "as a way to reach out to other poor mothers" (219). For these women, maternalism emerged from real and shared experiences of motherwork and not from a romanticized and essential concept of universal motherhood as with the white women. To paraphrase Spivak, these women used maternalism strategically to form, and lobby on behalf of, a community of mothers for a specific political cause: welfare rights. Meghan Gibbons's concept of experiential essentialism draws more from the deconstructive role-playing and decoding dimension of Spivak's strategic essentialism and Butler's concept of subjectivity as performance. In her examination of the Madres de la Plaza de Mayo (Mothers of the Plaza de Mayo) during the military dictatorship in Argentina, and of the organization Another Mother for Peace in the United States during the Vietnam War, Gibbons argues that these maternal activists used and misused the trope of maternal essentialism, and performed "good" motherhood in order to achieve "outlaw" or "activist" mothering. Gibbons explains:

> These women were driven by something that was the product of their experiences (based in the biological and the social) and their treatment as mothers by the state (as citizens whose subject positions in the nation were manipulated to serve nationalist ends). Both groups of mothers showed great sophistication in dealing with the powerful force of essential motherhood. At times they rejected essentialism, but at other times they played on the power that it conferred upon them as mothers. In the end, the mothers rejected this binary and constructed a paradigm that reflected their social and political identities as well as their lived experience. (254-255)

Both groups, Gibbons emphasizes, "used their identities as mothers to authorize themselves to speak publicly about unpopular state policies" (254). But they did so strategically by "manipulating the maternal paradigm that was supposed to control them" (256). As women concerned with the wellbeing of their children, these mothers adhered to the script of normative motherhood, but by doing so in the public sphere and in the context of political protest, they violated the codes and frame (behaving in a nonfeminine manner and in the masculine realm) of this same script. With regard to the madres, "they played on the cultural paradigm of *marianismo*, a Catholic model of ideal womanhood based on the Latin American cult of the Virgin Mary, in order to argue that they were only fulfilling the maternal obligations assigned to them by the state and the Church" (Gibbons 255-256). Moreover in presenting themselves "as pious, self-sacrificing, obedient and devoted to their families" (255) the mothers eventually gained national and international support and respect for their cause. In other words, the madres performed good motherhood in order to enact and achieve outlaw maternal activism. In the context of strategic essentialism discussed above, they decoded and deconstructed what was expected of them as "good" mothers in order to role-play normative maternity to make possible their successful maternal activism. Through this, they re-defined their identities as mothers as well as the larger meaning and practice of political engagement and protest.

A Politics of the Heart: Maternal Nurturance as Resistance and Embodied Activism

Central to maternalist politics is the practice of emotionalism, which has been criticized by earlier scholars on motherhood activism. Many motherhood organizations—madd. umove, Million Mom March, math to name but a few—employ emotionalism and work from what DiQuinzio calls a "politics of grief." Such emotionalism "undercuts the political efficacy of women;" "risks being misheard as an individualized expression of emotion;" "predicates women's political agency on pain and suffering," and "risks the delegitimation of maternal politics as irrational." But is such a characterization of emotionalism just or accurate? As Logsdon-Conradsen argues, "Aren't many types of activism motivated by personal experience?" (21). She further asks:

> Why are mothers questioned for being emotionally motivated, while other activists are not? Does such an elitist perspective, in demanding that activism be based on rationality, not run the risk of devaluing both the feminine and the power of emotion? And is this just another way that society devalues motherhood and holds

up the stereotypically masculine trait of unemotional as more legitimate? (Logsdon-Conradsen 21)

I would argue that emotionalism, similar to strategic essentialism, is an effective practice of resistance and protest if it is employed strategically and situated as a politic rather than a sentiment. Writing on the Madres of Argentina and Another Mother for Peace, Natalie Wilson notes that "emotion transformed the mothers, some of whom were timid housewives before their tragedies, into bold, public actors" (260). In so doing, as Wilson continues, "[they] demonstrated that emotion could be a powerful motive for political struggle and as significantly, by basing their campaigns on emotion, they challenged the privileging of reason in patriarchal culture and politics (260). In this, mothers work from what I have termed a "politics of the heart": a theory and practice that positions motherlove, or more specifically, maternal nurturance, as an act of resistance (*A Politics of the Heart*).

In my previous writings on African American mothering in the fiction of Toni Morrison, I argue that Black mothers view and practice motherlove as a political act of resistance against a racist culture that seeks to harm their children (*Politics of the Heart*). Black mothers recognize that in fiercely loving their children—children who were regarded as unlovable within the institution of slavery and under the discourse of white supremacy—they were able to instill in them a loved sense of self to protect them from the harm of a racist culture. By way of maternal nurturance, Black mothers sought to immunize their children from racist ideologies by loving them so that they could love themselves in a culture that defined them as not deserving or worthy of love. Through loving their children, these mothers instilled them with a loved sense of self and self-esteem, which enabled them to defy and subvert racist discourses that naturalize racial inferiority and commodify Blacks as object and other. This practice of maternal nurturance builds on bell hooks's concept of homeplace as a site of resistance, discussed in the previous chapter. For these mothers, motherlove was not innately derived or determined as in the trope of essential motherhood, but a consciously chosen act of resistance. I argue that the rhetoric and strategy of maternal nurturance in maternalist politics functions in a similar manner: it is a consciously constituted strategy that is motivated by mother love and, as theorized by Sara Ruddick, developed from the central demand of maternal practice—the preservation of children. However, because maternal nurturance is enacted from the heart and not the mind and is developed from the private realm of motherwork and not the public one of social action, it is often not considered as a real or legitimate form of resistance or protest.

As well, as Natalie Wilson has shown, emotionalism informs the highly successful strategy of "embodied activism" that characterizes much of modern motherhood activism. Embodied activism, Wilson explains, emphasizes "the embodied nature of existence" and refers to "a corporeally based political engagement" (235, 236). Activist mothers use their bodies and bodily actions to signify the inherent embodied nature of humanity and to enact their protests. Wilson explains: "Whether using the body as a sort of weapon to blockade factory entrances or as a manifestation of powerlessness and injustice (as when the body is purposefully rendered weak during a hunger strike so as to literally *materialize* various political injustices in ways that are visibly embodied) mothering activists have consistently refused to disembody their activism" (235). Embodied activism, as Wilson continues, "delivers the message that injustices are not abstract wrongs that hurt a particular nation but literal wounds that injure living, breathing bodies" (236). Such activism marks the actions of the Argentine madres, who embodied their grief by wearing posters of their missing children and marching with life-sized silhouettes, which gave a physical presence to the bodies of their disappeared children. Similarly, the organizations Code Pink and Mothers Acting Up enact protest in flamboyant bodily displays (bright pink clothing, walking on stilts etc). Thus, both embodied activism and maternal nurturance are socially motivated and enacted forms of emotionalism through which they serve to transgress the essentially derived gender identity of traditional maternalism to become a consciously chosen political strategy.

A Transformative Maternalism, Matrifocality, Maternal Practice, and Empowered Maternal Subjectivity

Matrifocality

A final concern with maternalism is its alleged child-centred focus and its attendant "It's-for-the-child" justification and rationalization. However, a cursory review of contemporary motherhood organizations demonstrates that the majority of them are mother centred in both perspective and purpose. Many motherhood organizations are concerned with empowering women in pregnancy, childbirth, and breastfeeding, whereas others focus on providing support and community for mothers and on delivering advocacy and activism on their behalf. Others are also firmly mother centred in their commitment to researching, narrating, and performing women's lived experiences as mothers. In this, most contemporary motherhood organizations work from what I have term a "matrifocal perspective," which is one in which a mother plays a role of cultural and social significance, and motherhood is thematically elaborated, valued, and structurally central to the plot. I suggest that the majority of contemporary motherhood organizations may be understood to be political or social modes of matrifocality in that they "begin with the mother in her own right, from her own perspective," and "hold fast to a maternal perspective" (Daly and Reddy). And although children are certainly integral to the agenda or plots of these matrifocal narratives, the mother remains a central character, and her life remains an organizing theme therein.

Maternal Practice

I further suggest that even explicitly child-focused organizations may be considered mother centred in so far as their concern is to better the lives of children. As Sara Ruddick theorized, maternal practice is characterized by three demands: preservation, growth, and social acceptance. If so-called child-focused organizations are located in the context of Ruddick's theory, they function as matrifocal organizations; they are able to aid mothers in their maternal practice, particularly its demand of preservation. An organization that seeks to protect children or support their survival and development in general, likewise, supports mothers by virtue of making motherwork easier. For example, organizations that address issues such as war and militarism, poverty, police-state brutality, drunk driving, environmental degradation, and gun violence empower mothers by enabling them to fully and successfully perform the work they do as mothers. I say this not to romanticize or essentialize motherhood but to remind and emphasize that it is mothers who are responsible for children and childrearing in patriarchal culture. Since it is mothers who do the work of raising children under patriarchy, an organization that seeks to better the lives of children also betters the lives of mothers by improving the working conditions under which mothers perform their reproductive labour.

Demeter and the "Mamazon": Empowered Maternal Subjectivity

In the previous chapter, I discuss how the Demeter-Persephone myth is frequently cited to make the argument that empowered mothers are more effective mothers. As I discuss in chapter three, such a strategy—mothers asking for and being afforded power only if such is used for and on behalf of children—becomes problematic because mothers are accorded agency only to effect social change on behalf of children, with little attention being paid to what this agency does or means for the mother herself in the context of *her own life*. However, I argue that if this strategy is specifically situated in the context of maternal subjectivity, it opens up other possibilities and readings. In her book *Of Woman Born*, Adrienne Rich interprets the Demeter-Persephone myth as it was enacted in the Eleusinian mysteries as representing every daughter's "longing for a mother whose love for her and whose power were so great as to undo rape and bring her back from death" (240). The myth, Rich continues, bespeaks "*every mother's [longing] for the power of Demeter [and] the efficacy of her anger*" (240, emphasis added). In patriarchal culture where there are so few examples, in either life or literature, of empowered mothering, Demeter's triumphant resistance serves as a powerful model of such. More significantly, in the context of this discussion on maternal subjectivity, this anger rendered Demeter powerful, and, in turn, this power made her rage empowering. This enraged power and empowering rage transformed Demeter from being a passive witness to her daughter's abduction to an active opponent against it. As evidenced in many motherhood organizations, the rage or grief that a mother feels as her child is threatened or killed radicalizes and mobilizes the mother, and moves her to social action and political resistance. Mothers develop critical awareness, acquire confidence, build community, and achieve agency in and through their resistance on behalf of their children. In other words, although motherhood activism may originate from a child-centred perspective or purpose, it becomes matrifocal and arguably feminist in the way that it results in and gives rise to an empowered and powerful maternal subjectivity. The Demeter myth, though ostensibly about the rescue of a daughter and her rebirth as she returns from Hades (the place of the dead), also narrates a mother's rebirth in the transformation of her consciousness.

The archetype of the "Mamazon" similarly suggests the possibility of an empowered maternal subjectivity through motherhood activism on behalf of children. The term "mamazon," as Sheri Lucas explains, "was created by merging the meanings of Amazon (the mythical tribe of warrior women who are represented as autonomous and competent, as physically, emotionally and intellectually strong) and 'mama'" (682). When the two are connected, Lucas goes on to explain, "it connotes primal and fierce 'mother bear' instincts; mothering practices that are nontraditional ... and the decision to mother outside of a committed monogamous relationship; and mother-driven political actions, particularly when it is loud, angry and assertive" (683). A "mamazon" identity and practice, Lucas continues, "[is] often considered threatening to conventional definitions of motherhood" (683). The mamazon trope, as with the Demeter archetype, reveals that child-motivated and child-centred forms of motherhood activism do empower mothers and accord them a power not available to women in traditional motherhood. In so doing, this practice of maternalism, though purportedly child centred, transforms both mothers and motherhood and give rises to what I and others have termed a "mother outlaw" and a practice of "outlaw mothering." In the first instance, outlaw or empowered mothering, as discussed in the previous chapter, functions as an oppositional discourse of motherhood; more specifically, it signifies a theory and practice of mothering that seeks to challenge the dominant discourse of motherhood and change the various ways that the lived experience of patriarchal motherhood is limiting or oppressive to women. More pointedly, as explored in the previous chapter, the overarching aim of empowered mothering is to confer to mothers the agency, authority, authenticity, autonomy, advocacy-activism denied to them in patriarchal motherhood. By understanding child-motivated and child-centred activism from the perspective of the Mamazon and the Demeter archetype, it becomes evident that such forms of maternal activism do empower mothers and make possible a powerful matrifocal stance and practice. In so doing, such a perspective reveals that contrary to traditional readings of maternalism, motherhood power is integral and central to maternalist politics and practice.

The Twenty-First-Century Motherhood Movement as Feminist Activism

Motherhood activism—whether such is expressed as maternalism, equal rights for mothers, or as an ethics of care—works to empower mothers; I argue that this makes it feminist. In her article Janice Nathanson contends that maternal activism promotes a feminist agenda in three specific ways:

> First, it exemplifies the very core of feminist ideology –that the personal is political. Second, it helps to negate essential notions of motherhood by transforming views of it from an "isolated or individualized experience... [to] the inspiration for a foundation of visions of large-scale social change" (Orlect 3). And third, whether intentional or not, it upsets traditional gender and power relations. (244)

As discussed at length above, mothers come to political activism as a result of, and in response to, a personal situation or incident in their own lives or that of their children. Activist mothers recognize that their "personal troubles are politically constituted" and that only by political action can such personal troubles be remedied (Nathanson 245). In this, as Nathanson emphasizes, "they [activist mothers] invoke one of feminism's most cherished ideologies—the personal is political" (245). As well, maternal activism, as detailed above, defies and deconstructs essentialist notions of womanhood and motherhood by "reframing motherhood, [by] expanding its boundaries (from private to public), and by endowing it with qualities normally attributed to the public realm" (Nathanson 250). For activist mothers, motherwork is neither private nor mundane, as is assumed and dictated by the normative ideology of patriarchal motherhood. Echoing the above sentiment, Nathanson writes that "mothers, in the process of their activism, take on nontraditional roles in which their action and agency provide a new sense of empowerment that often upsets traditional gender roles" (251). Moreover, "women's activism," as Beth Roy emphasizes, "always challenges domestic as well as public power relations, because by the very act of taking a position in the public domain, women violate their patriarchal assignment to domesticity" (qtd. in Nathanson 251). In each instance, activist mothers redefine motherwork as a socially engaged enterprise and a site of power, wherein mothers can affect social change, both in the home through feminist childrearing and outside the home through maternal activism. Such maternal activism—in rendering the personal political, blurring the boundaries between the private and the public and in inverting traditional gender roles—both disrupts and dislodges the gender essentialism (the naturalized opposition between the masculine-feminine, the private-public) that grounds and structures modern patriarchy. In this, motherhood activism emerges as a specific mode of feminist theory and practice—what I have termed "matricentric feminism."

The Twenty-First-Century Motherhood Movement and the Empowerment of Mothers

The various motherhood organizations of the twenty-first century, though widely diverse in their perspectives and aims, all embrace and advance matricentric feminism. They recognize, albeit with varying degrees of emphasis, that motherhood is disempowering if not oppressive as it is currently perceived and practiced in patriarchal societies for a multitude of reasons—namely, the societal devaluation of motherwork, the endless tasks of privatized mothering, and the impossible standards of idealized motherhood. For example, organizations concerned with maternal health argue that motherwork and female reproduction have a particularly deleterious impact on women's physical and mental health. More specifically, mothers tend to prioritize the needs of other family members to the detriment of their own health—a significant number of mothers experience postpartum depression, and thousands of women die every year globally, and millions more suffer, from debilitating life-long injuries or infections relating to pregnancy and childbirth complications. Similarly, motherhood organizations concerned with mothers and paid work argue that the "second shift," the maternal wage gap, and ongoing employment discrimination all prevent mothers from effectively combining family-care responsibilities and paid employment, which, consequently, inhibits them from achieving agency and autonomy in their lives. Indeed as noted in the introduction, mothers are oppressed under patriarchy as women *and as mothers.* As a result, mothers need a mother-centred feminism organized from and for their particular identity and work as mothers.

Motherhood organizations likewise recognize that mothers are (and have always been) leaders in various social justice movements for children, for families, and for peace and the environment. As well, each organization, even those that are child-centred in perspective, position maternal empowerment as a defining goal of their activism and seek to strengthen the social, personal, and political power of mothers. Each organization, albeit in different ways, seeks to grant women greater authority, resources, and status so that they can adequately care for their children while living full and purposeful lives. Likewise, each is concerned with exploring and addressing both the obstacles to and possibilities for maternal agency to bring about the necessary changes in law, public policy, education, family, health, the workplace, and motherwork in order to afford full and lasting authority, agency, respect, and empowerment for mothers in the twenty-first century. One point they all agree on is that maternal empowerment is needed for healthier mothers, families, and societies.

Conclusion

While writing this section on the twenty-first-century motherhood movement, I am reminded of Adrienne Rich's groundbreaking distinction between two meanings of motherhood discussed in the previous chapter. Like Rich, motherhood organizations begin with the realization that motherhood, as it is currently perceived and practiced in patriarchal societies, is disempowering if not oppressive for a multitude of reasons. However, like Rich, they also recognize that mothering holds much potential for the empowerment of mothers, particularly the power of mothers to effect real and lasting change in their lives, in the lives of their children, and in the larger society. Both Rich and motherhood organizations maintain that empowered mothers are more effective mothers for children, that empowered mothers are healthier women and more productive workers, and that empowered mothering is beneficial for families and society at large. To realize and maximize the power of mothers, the organizations develop a plethora of theories and strategies that gives mothers what is denied to them in patriarchal societies: the agency, authority, authenticity, autonomy, and advocacy-actvism that were explored in the previous chapter. Overall, motherhood organizations seek empowerment of and for mothers that in varied and diverse ways, "names, analyzes and challenges oppression by way of the development of critical consciousness [and through] gaining control, exercising choices, and in engaging in collective social action" (Bernard and Bernard 46). From this stance of maternal power, mothers are empowered to not only challenge and change patriarchal motherhood, as Rich advocates, but transform the society in which they live in order to improve their own lives as mothers. From the perspective of Rich's theoretical model, the twenty-first-century motherhood movement emerges as a viable and necessary social movement; it empowers mothers to better their lives, those of their children, and the larger society. Indeed, the twenty-first-century motherhood movement shows us why we need to change the world and how to do it.

Chapter Three

Matricentric Feminism As Practice
Feminist Mothering

This chapter, developed from my published works on feminist mothering as well as from my recent reflections on the subject matter, is to be read as an overview of the central issues, questions, and concerns of feminist mothering as practice. In so doing, it looks at feminist mothering from the perspective of both children and mothers. The chapter is divided into five sections. The first section looks at the problematic of defining feminist mothering and develops a possible theory of feminist mothering. The following two sections examine the meaning and practice of feminist mothering for daughters and sons. As these sections explore the rewards of feminist mothering for children, the fourth section considers its risks. The final section calls for a mother-centred mode of feminist mothering that regards the empowerment of mothers as its primary focus and aim.

Feminist Mothering: From the Problematic of Definitions to the Possibility of Practice

Mothering and Motherhood

Central to *Of Woman Born*, as discussed in the opening chapter, is the distinction Rich makes between patriarchal motherhood and the possibility or potentiality of feminist mothering. Although much has been published on patriarchal motherhood since Rich's inaugural text—research that documents why and how patriarchal motherhood is harmful, indeed unnatural, to mothers and children alike—little has been written on the possibility or potentiality of feminist mothering. "Still largely missing from the increasing dialogue and publication around motherhood," as Fiona Green writes, "is a discussion of Rich's monumental contention that even when restrained by patriarchy, motherhood can be a site of empowerment and political activism" ("Feminist Mothers" 31).

The introduction to my edited volume *Feminist Mothering* opens with a review of publications on motherhood in the mainstream media. These books would suggest that the selfless and doting mother of yesteryear has, like the eighteen hour bra, fallen out of fashion. These authors, particularly those that write in the self-help genre, call for a new style of mothering, one that advocates balance and admonishes guilt. Bria Simpson, for example, asserts in *The Balanced Mom: Raising Your Kids without Losing Your Self* that "We need to continue, rather than deny, the development of ourselves to be fulfilled" (2). She goes on to write: "As you try so fervently to help your children develop into their best selves, I encourage you to refocus some of that energy into living *your* best life" (3). Likewise, Amy Tiemann, in her book *Mojo Mom: Nurturing Your Self While Raising a Family*, claims that "all women need to continue to grow as individuals, not just as Moms" (xvi). Overcoming the guilt of motherhood is the focus of many books, as with the bestselling book, appropriately titled *Mommy Guilt: Learn to Worry Less, Focus on What Matters Most, and Raise Happier Kids* (Bort et al.). Other writers challenge the excessive child centredness of contemporary parenting practices and call for a more "children should be seen and not heard" philosophy of childrearing. Christie Mellor in *The Three-Martini Playdate: A Practical Guide to Happy Parenting* for example, asserts:

> You were here first. You are sharing your house with them, your food, your time, your books. Somewhere, in fairly recent memory, we have lost sight of that fact. Somehow a pint-sized velvet revolution was waged under our noses, and the grown-ups quietly handed over the reins. We have made concession after concession, until it appears that well-educated, otherwise intelligent adults have abdicated their rightful place in the world, and the littlest inmates have taken over the asylum. (12)

She goes on to say that "it is time to exert a little autonomy and encourage some in your child" (13). Other writers advocate shared parenting. In *How to Avoid the Mommy Trap: A Roadmap for Sharing Parenting and Making it Work* (2002), Julie Shields argues that *"the best alternative to parenting by mother is parenting by father"* (17). She goes on to explain:

> Since fathers can parent, too, we should not start from the assumption that mothers, and mothers alone, must choose whether to work, cut back, or hire a replacement caregiver. Instead, we can change our approach to seeking ways to provide babies the best start in life, at the same time, giving mothers *and* fathers the best opportunity for happiness, individually and together. (19)

Whether the emphasis is maternal autonomy, shared parenting, less guilt, and more balance, these writers challenge traditional or, in academic parlance, patriarchal motherhood practices. Similar to Betty Friedan, who exposed "the problem that has no name" more than fifty years ago, these writers insist that women must achieve and sustain a selfhood outside of and beyond motherhood. And similar to Adrienne Rich, who attributed mothers' exhaustion and guilt to the isolation of patriarchal motherhood and its impossible standards of perfection, these writers, likewise, recognize that mothers require more support and less judgement if they are to obtain satisfaction in motherhood.

However, although these authors certainly challenge patriarchal motherhood, they do not use the word "feminist" in this critique, nor do they call their new mother-positive mode of mothering a feminist practice. Given this, can these new models of mothering be called feminist mothering? Does the mother have to identify as a feminist for her mothering to qualify as a feminist practice? Or more pointedly, is there a practice of feminist mothering without a politic of feminism? And who decides and determines this?

I opened *Feminist Mothering* with such questions to illustrate the difficulty of defining a feminist practice of mothering. Although a challenge to patriarchal motherhood has been a central concern of feminist scholarship since at least Rich's book *Of Woman Born* in 1976, there has been very little academic discourse on the subject of feminist mothering as practice. This dearth of research is, indeed, perplexing and troubling. A review of feminist scholarship on motherhood reveals that only four books have looked specifically at the topic of feminist mothering: *Mother Journeys: Feminists Write About Mothering*, edited by Maureen T. Reddy et al; Tuula Gordon's book, *Feminist Mothers*; Rose L. Glickman's *Daughters of Feminists*; and Fiona Green's *Feminist Mothering in Theory and Practice 1985-1995: A Study in Transformative Politics*.[1] The 2006 volumes of the journals *off our backs* and *Journal of the Association for Research on Mothering* include articles on feminist mothering in their issues on "Mothering and Feminism." Likewise, two of my edited volumes—*Mother Outlaws: Theories and Practices of Empowered Mothering* and *From Motherhood to Mothering: The Legacy of Adrienne Rich's* Of Woman Born—incorporate sections on feminist mothering. In 2006, I edited a book specifically on the subject of feminist mothering; as well my book *Rocking the Cradle: Thoughts on Motherhood, Feminism, and the Possibility of Empowered Mothering* examines the topic of feminist mothering.

In my writing, I use the term feminist mothering to refer to an oppositional discourse of motherhood, one that is constructed as a negation of patriarchal motherhood. A feminist practice of mothering, therefore, functions as a counter-narrative of motherhood: it seeks to interrupt the master narrative of motherhood to imagine and implement a view of mothering that is *empowering* to women. Feminist mothering is, thus, determined more by what it is not (i.e., patriarchal motherhood) rather than by what it is. Feminist mothering may refer to any practice of mothering that seeks to challenge and change various aspects of patriarchal motherhood that cause mothering to be limiting or oppressive to women. As noted in the opening chapter, Rich uses the word "courageous" to define a nonpatriarchal practice of mothering, whereas Copper calls such a practice "radical mothering." Susan Douglas and Meredith Michaels use the word "rebellious" to describe outlaw mothering, and "hip" is Ariel Gore's term for transgressive mothering. For this chapter, the term "feminist" is used—though with a proviso as explained below—to signify maternal practices that resist and refuse patriarchal motherhood to create the practice of feminist mothering. Or, to use Rich's terminology, a feminist maternal practice marks a movement from motherhood to mothering and makes possible a mothering against motherhood.

What is in a Name?: Defining Feminist Mothering

Feminist mothering, as noted above, functions as an oppositional discourse: its meaning is constructed as a *negation* of patriarchal motherhood. In other words, an understanding of feminist mothering is determined more by what it is not (i.e., patriarchal motherhood) rather than by what it is. However, since feminist mothering, in its origins and function, is a counter-narrative, I believe a more direct and specific definition of this mode of mothering is needed. In her book *Feminist Mothers*, the first book length study of the subject matter, Tuula Gordon in her concluding chapter "What is a Feminist Mother?" observes, "[I]t seems impossible to conclude by explaining what a feminist mother is, or to answer the underlying question of how people conduct their lives according to alternative ideologies, in this case feminism" (148). However, Gordon does say that her study of feminist mothers reveals some "particular factors":

> The way in which [mothers] challenge and criticise myths of motherhood; the way in which they consider it their right to work: the anti-sexist (and anti-racist) way in which they try to bring up their children; the way in which they expect the fathers of the children to participate in joint everyday lives; and the way in which many of them are politically active. (149)

Gordon goes on to conclude:

> Feminism emphasizes that women are strong, that women have rights as women, and they can support each other as women. Thus "feminist mothers" have been able to develop critical orientations towards societal structures and cultures, stereotypical expectations and myths of motherhood. They do that in the context of exploring how the personal is political, and with the support of the networks of women which place them beyond "collective isolation." (150)

Rose L. Glickman in her 1993 book *Daughters of Feminists*, likewise, emphasizes that feminist mothering must be understood as lived resistance to the normative and stereotypical expectations of both motherhood and womanhood. She writes: "[For these feminist mothers] there is no 'apart from their feminism' and no matter how ordinary their lives seem from the outside to the casual observer, *their feminism was a profound defiance of convention....* Flying in the face of tradition, feminist mothers expected their daughters to do the same" (emphasis added, 22). "The mothers' struggle," Glickman continues, "to shake off the dust of tradition was the basic dynamic of the daughters' formative years" (21).

In her book *Feminist Mothering in Theory and Practice 1985-1995*, Green examines the lives of sixteen self-identified feminists living in the mid-1990s who, in Green's words, "purposely [chose] to mother in ways that [were] informed by and embody their feminism" (4). Green's book centres on three interrelated issues: how feminism informs mothers' understanding and practice of motherhood; how feminist mothering may be understood as a form or an act of feminist pedagogy; and how parenting informs the feminism of mothers. In examining these three issues, Green identifies four common themes in the interviews: participants understand motherhood to be an institution and experience; they consciously mother as feminists; they practice elements of feminist pedagogy; and they engage in feminist praxis while mothering (76). For me, the most illuminating and instructive concepts that emerge from Green's study are what may be termed the "dialectical and transformative nature of feminist mothering" and Green's notion of "mothering as pedagogy."

Feminist theorists, as Green writes, "have established an inherent contradiction in motherhood; while motherhood is strongly associated with access to an internalization of patriarchal power, it simultaneously is a place where women can create their own mothering strategies to challenge various dominant power strategies" (57). Significantly, the mothers, in language and tone evocatively similar to those of Adrienne Rich, speak passionately and often about this contradiction. The mothers make visible what is often invisible about institutionalized motherhood: they acknowledge the confining aspects of motherhood; recognize how regulatory elements of the institution are harmful to woman and children; and speak to the low self-esteem, self-blame and self-hatred of internalized oppression. However, as the women identify and catalogue the many ways that motherhood is an oppressive and a repressive institution, they, in and through this critique, "create some distance from it and make space within mothering to mother in ways that are suitable to them," and in so doing "engage in a self-reflexive creating of subjectivity to redefine motherhood for themselves" (84). Such transformative practices include the following: mothering outside of heterosexual relationships; living apart from the father and mothering alone; rejecting the wife role expected of mothers; renouncing the belief that mothers are totally responsible for the character of the child; challenging the assumption that mothers will raise their children according to patriarchal expectations; developing feminist styles of childrearing; creating other models for family; and practicing nonauthoritative ways of parenting. When defined on its own terms, mothering becomes, to borrow from Green, "a dynamic place for creativity" (113). What Green's study shows is that patriarchal motherhood is neither completely oppressive nor non-negotiable. In it, mothers do find room to practice agency, resistance, and renewal. In this, the women's stories and Green's study realize the hope that Rich spoke to more than forty years ago—mothers have "managed to salvage for [them]selves [and] for [their] children, even within the destructiveness of the institution ... the tenderness, the passion, the trust in our instincts, the evocation of a courage we did know we owned" (280).

A second illuminating and instructive concept developed in Green's work is that feminist mothers practice feminist pedagogy. Green contends that such feminist pedagogy is observable in five aims or acts of feminist mothering: teaching children to think analytically about the world; analyzing and providing alternatives to gender inequality; prompting egalitarian relationships that advance collaborative learning; fostering empowerment and self-governance; and encouraging collective action. Feminist teaching is integrated in the motherwork of feminist mothering. However, feminist mothers not only instruct their children on the various elements of feminist pedagogy, they model or embody them. Green artfully weds Sara Ruddick's earlier and central concept of mothering as practice with the more recent writings in motherhood studies on maternal agency and activism. A central theme of motherhood studies today is the repositioning of mothering as a private and nonpolitical undertaking to one with profound political and social dimensions. Scholars today explore how mothers, by way of maternal agency and activism, use their position as mothers to lobby for social and political change. Whether such work is in the home or in the world at large or is expressed as antisexist childrearing and maternal activism, activist and empowered mothers redefine motherwork as a socially and politically engaged practice through which cultural change is made possible. Green in her insistence to reframe the popular feminist slogan—the pedagogical is political—and in her emphasis on the centrality and importance of modelling and mentoring feminism shows that indeed motherwork for feminist mothers is a transformative practice in that it both embodies and instructs upon the possibilities of and for social and political change.

Green's book reveals that indeed feminist mothers "are challenging motherhood, creating alternatives in mothering that transform the lives of mothers and of children and changing the meaning of both mothering and feminism" (4). Reading Green's book, I am reminded of Maureen Reddy's *Everyday Acts against Racism*, in which she explains that she chose the phrase "everyday acts" as her title to "emphasize the daily, the ordinary, as opposed to extraordinary" dimensions of anti-racist parenting (ix). She concludes her introduction citing political scientist Howard Zinn: "When changes take place in history, they are not the result of a few heroic deeds, but of small actions—all that persistence creates a great social movement" (qtd. in Reddy xiii). What Green's work shows, or perhaps more appropriately teaches, to paraphrase Zinn, is that the politic, praxis, and pedagogy of feminist mothering, while expressed as everyday acts, are indeed the heroic deeds of a great social movement.

Whether it manifests itself in combining motherhood with paid employment, insisting that fathers be involved in childcare, engaging in activism, creating a life outside of motherhood—feminist mothering, as these studies document, has developed in response to the mother's dissatisfaction with and dislike of traditional motherhood. Commenting on Gordon's study, Ericka Horwitz in her thesis "Mother's Resistance to the Western Dominant Discourse on Mothering" observes: "Her [Gordon's] findings suggest that mothers can hold beliefs that are not in agreement with those promoted by the dominant discourses on motherhood. Gordon alerts us to the possibility that *the process of resistance entails making different choices about how one wants to practice mothering*" (emphasis added, 58). Tuula Gordon, Rose Glickman, and Fiona Green look specifically at mothers who identify as feminists, whereas Horwitz in the above thesis and her later chapter "Resistance as a Site of Empowerment: The Journey Away from Maternal Sacrifice" is interested in "the experiences of women who believe they were resisting the dominant discourse of mothering ... [but] who may or may not see themselves as feminist" (44, 45). Empowered mothering, thus, signifies a general resistance to patriarchal motherhood; feminist mothering, however, refers to a particular style of empowered mothering in which this resistance is developed from and expressed through a feminist identification or consciousness. Although the two seem similar, there are significant differences that warrant further elaboration. It is to this discussion that I now turn.

Feminist Mothering Versus Empowered Mothering

In her chapter, "Resistance as a Site of Empowerment" (noted above), Erika Horwitz argues that although resistant, empowered mothering is characterized by many themes, they all challenge patriarchal motherhood. These themes include the following: the importance of mothers meeting their own needs; being a mother does not fulfill all of women's needs; involving others in their children's upbringing; actively questioning the expectations that are placed on mothers by society; challenging mainstream parenting practices; not believing that mothers are solely responsible for how children turn out; and challenging the idea that the only emotion that mothers ever feel towards their children is love. In the opening chapter, I argue empowered mothering begins with the recognition that both mothers and children benefit when the mother lives her life and practices mothering from a position of agency, authority, authenticity, and autonomy. In emphasizing maternal authority and ascribing agency to mothers and value to motherwork, this perspective defines motherhood as a political site, wherein mothers can bring about social change through the socialization of children and the world at large through political-social activism. Empowered mothering, thus, calls into question the dictates of patriarchal motherhood. Empowered mothers do not regard childcare as the sole responsibility of the biological mother, nor do they regard 24/7-mothering as necessary for children. They look to friends, family, and their partners to assist with childcare and often raise their children with an involved community of what may be termed "co-mothers" or "othermothers." As well, in most instances, these mothers combine mothering with paid employment and/or activism; thus, the full-time intensive mothering demanded in patriarchal motherhood is not practiced by these mothers. As well, many of these mothers call into question the belief that mothering requires excessive time, money, and energy: they practice a mode of mothering that is more compatible with paid employment. As well, they see the development of a mother's selfhood as beneficial to mothering and not antithetical to it as is assumed in patriarchal motherhood. Consequently, empowered mothers do not always put their children's needs before their own, nor do they look only to motherhood to define and realize their identity. Rather, their selfhood is fulfilled and expressed in various ways: work, activism, friendships, relationships, hobbies, and motherhood. These mothers insist on their own authority as mothers and refuse the relinquishment of their power as mandated in the patriarchal institution of motherhood. Motherhood, in the dominant patriarchal ideology, is seen simply as a private and, more specifically, an apolitical enterprise. In contrast, mothering for these mothers is understood to have cultural significance and political purpose. Building on the work of Sara Ruddick, these mothers redefine motherwork as a socially engaged enterprise that seeks to effect cultural change through new feminist modes of gender socialization and interactions with daughters and sons.

Feminist mothering differs from empowered mothering in so far as the mother identifies as a feminist and practices mothering from a feminist perspective or consciousness. A feminist mother, in other words, is a woman whose mothering, in theory and practice, is shaped and influenced by feminism. Thus, although there is much overlap between empowered and feminist mothering, the later is informed by a particular philosophy and politic—namely feminism. In the Horowitz study, the women's demands that their husbands be more involved or that they need time off from motherhood do not derive from a larger challenge to gender inequity. For example, one woman in the study remarks that "If I was going to love that baby, have any quality of time with that baby, I had to get away from that baby. I had to meet my own needs" ("Resistance as a Site of Empowerment" 48); and another mother chose "to paint her nails while her baby cried in her crib because 'she has needs and wants'" (47). These women resist patriarchal motherhood in order to have, in one woman's words, "a higher quality of life," or in the words of another "to [become] a better mother for my children" (52). The reasons for their resistance are more personal than political and, as a consequence, are not developed from an awareness of how motherhood functions as a cultural or an ideological institution to oppress women in patriarchal society. These mothers resist patriarchal motherhood simply to make the experience of mothering more rewarding for themselves and their children. In so far as this aim challenges the patriarchal mandate of maternal selflessness, sacrifice, and martyrdom, these mothers resist in demanding more time for themselves and support from others. However, these demands do not originate from a feminist desire to dismantle a patriarchal institution. In contrast, feminist mothers resist because they recognize that gender inequity, in particular male privilege and power, is produced, maintained, and perpetuated in patriarchal motherhood. As feminists, feminist mothers reject an institution founded on gender inequity, and as mothers, they refuse to raise children in such a sexist environment. Thus, although in practice the two seem similar (i.e., demanding more involvement from fathers and insisting on a life outside of motherhood), only with feminist mothering does this involve a larger awareness of, and challenge to, the gender (among other) inequities of patriarchal culture.

Although the above discussion helps to distinguish between empowered and feminist mothering, it begs the larger question of how to define feminism itself. Feminism, as scholars of women's studies are well aware, is composed of many perspectives and positions: socialist, liberal, radical, womanist, third wave, to name but a few. For my purpose here, I use a very open-ended definition of feminism: the recognition that most cultures are patriarchal and that such cultures give prominence, power, and privilege to men and the masculine, and they depend on the oppression and the disparagement of women and the feminine. Feminists are committed to challenging and transforming this gender inequity in all of its manifestations—whether they are cultural, economic, political, philosophical, social, ideological, sexual, and so forth. As well, most feminisms (including my own) seek to dismantle other hierarchical binary systems, such as race, (racism), sexuality (heterosexism), economics (classism) and ability (ableism). A feminist mother, therefore, in the context of this definition of feminism, challenges male privilege and power in her own life and in the life of her children. In her own life, the mother would insist on gender equality in the home and on a life and identity outside of motherhood. As well, it would mean that the important work of mothering would be culturally valued and supported and that mothers, likewise, would perform this motherwork from a place of agency and authority. In the context of children, feminist mothering means dismantling traditional gender socialization practices that privilege boys as preferable and superior to girls and that socialize boys to be masculine and girls feminine. Feminist mothering, thus, seeks to transform both the patriarchal role of motherhood and that of child-rearing.

However, the word "feminism" remains troubled. In her book on feminist daughters, Glickman writes:

> I ruled out daughters whose mothers' lives can surely be described as feminist, but who reject the label. Once, in my search for Latina daughters, I spoke with the head of a Latino women's health collective. She said she couldn't help me because "although we have the consciousness, in our culture we don't use the word." The consciousness without the word is not what I'm looking for. (xv-xvi)

However, the word "feminist" often excludes the mothering experiences of women of colour, as the above incident demonstrates. The term "feminism"—as African American scholars Patricia Hill Collins, bell hooks, and others have argued—is understood to be a white term for many Black women. As one daughter, a woman of colour, in Glickman's study comments: "[Feminism] has overwhelmingly, statistically, benefited white women disproportionately to women of colour" (168). And another daughter states: "Here you are reading all these feminist writers who are telling you to bust out of the kitchen and get into the work force. What does that have to do with the majority of women of colour who have always been in the kitchen *and* the work force at the same time?" (169). Indeed, the mothers of colour in Gordon's study emphasize that "Black women are critical of feminism dominated by white women for ideological, political and strategic reasons" (140). The question thus remains: how does one develop a specific study of feminist mothering without excluding the many women—women of colour and working-class women—who eschew or disavow the word "feminism"? Although I do not believe that there are easy answers to such questions, I see a broader understanding of feminism to include womanist, antiracist, and global feminist perspectives as a way to begin talking about women of colour and their specific theory and practice of feminist mothering.

A Practice of Feminist Mothering

Feminist mothering seeks to challenge and change the many ways that patriarchal motherhood is oppressive to women. Numerous feminist scholars have detailed the various ways that patriarchal motherhood constrains, regulates, and dominates women and their mothering. I organize these themes under eight interrelated rules of "good" motherhood as dictated by contemporary patriarchal ideology. They are the following: 1) children can only be properly cared for by the biological mother; 2) this mothering must be provided 24/7; 3) the mother must always put children's needs before her own; 4) mothers must turn to the experts for instruction; 5) the mother must be fully satisfied, fulfilled, completed, and composed in motherhood; 6) mothers must lavish excessive amounts of time, energy, and money in the rearing of their children; 7) the mother has full responsibility but no power from which to mother; and 8) motherwork and childrearing more specifically are regarded as personal and private undertakings with no political import. The patriarchal ideology of motherhood makes mothering deeply oppressive to women because it requires the repression or denial of the mother's own selfhood; moreover, it assigns mothers all the responsibility for mothering but gives them no real power from which to mother. Such "powerless responsibility," to use Rich's term, denies a mother the authority and agency to determine her own experiences of mothering. Moreover, in defining mothering as private and nonpolitical work, patriarchal motherhood restricts the way mothers can and do create social change through feminist childrearing and maternal activism.

Feminist mothering refuses this patriarchal profile and script of "good" mothers and "good" mothering. And in so doing, it challenges and changes the various ways patriarchal motherhood becomes oppressive to women, as noted in the eight themes above. Although feminist mothering functions as an oppositional discourse, thus defying definition, it is characterized by several themes that coalesce to form a specific theory of feminist mothering. In *Of Woman Born*, Rich writes: "We do not think of the power stolen from us and the power withheld from us in the name of the institution of motherhood" (275). "The idea of maternal power has been domesticated," Rich continues, "in transfiguring and enslaving woman, the womb—the ultimate source of the power—has historically been turned against us and itself made into a source of powerlessness" (68). The central aim of feminist mothering is to reclaim that power for mothers.

Feminist mothering refers to a particular style of empowered mothering in which resistance is developed from and expressed through a feminist identification or consciousness. A feminist mother, as discussed above, seeks the eradication of motherhood as she recognizes that it is a patriarchal institution, in which gender inequality, or more specifically the oppression of women, is enforced, maintained, and perpetuated. Feminist mothering is, thus, primarily concerned with the empowerment of mothers. A theory of feminist mothering, therefore, begins with recognition that a mother must live her life and practice mothering from a position of agency, authority, authenticity, and autonomy. A feminist standpoint on mothering affords a woman a life, a purpose, and an identity outside and beyond motherhood, and it does not limit childrearing to the biological mother. Likewise, from this standpoint, a woman's race, age, sexuality, or marital status does not determine her capicity to mother. A feminist theory on motherhood also foregrounds maternal power and confers value to mothering. Mothering from a feminist perspective and practice redefines motherwork as a social and political act. In contrast to patriarchal motherhood that limits mothering to privatized care undertaken in the domestic sphere, feminist mothering, more so than empowered mothering, regards mothering as explicitly and profoundly political and social.

Feminist mothering is also concerned with feminist practices of gender socialization and models of mother-child relations so as to raise a new generation of empowered daughters and empathetic sons. However, as will be discussed in more detail in the final section of this chapter, these two aims of feminist mothering—empowerment of mothers and antisexist childrearing—are specifically interdependent. A review of feminist thought on motherhood, however, reveals that a critique of the institution of motherhood and a concern with new modes of childrearing have developed independently of each other and that feminists committed to the abolition of motherhood and the achievement of mothering have seldom considered what this means for the mother *herself*, apart from the issue of childrearing.

Fiona Green in her research on feminist mothering interviews feminist mothers who, in Green's words, "live Rich's emancipatory vision of motherhood" ("Feminist Mothering" 130). Driven by their feminist consciousness, their intense love for their children and the need to be true to themselves, their families, and their parenting, "[these] feminist mothers," Green writes, "choose to parent in a way that challenges the status quo" (130). They do so, according to Green, by way of two different approaches: "overt strategies of resistance" and "subversive strategies of resistance" (130). To illustrate the first strategy, Green gives the example of a lesbian lone parent who births and raises a child without any connection to a man. "No man ever called the shots in my home," the woman explains, "nor did a man ever support me in any way ... that is really breaking the rules in the patriarchy" (131). According to Green, this is "a deliberate act of resistance to dominant conceptions and practices of mothering" (131).

The second strategy is less overt. With this approach, mothers "under the cover of the institution of motherhood effectively challenge patriarchy, and their subversive activity often goes unnoticed" (132). Green provides examples of two heterosexual married mothers to illustrate this strategy. One raises a son to make him consciously aware of social injustices, whereas the second mother "actively encourages the nurturing and non-competitive tendencies of her son, while supporting her daughter in her pursuits of maths and science" (133). The second, subversive strategy, thus, seems to focus on childrearing undertaken by women in the institution of motherhood, whereas the overt strategy involves a challenge to the institution itself and is concerned with the empowerment of the mother. In the example of overt resistance, when discussing the mother's choice to rear her daughter with an othermother during a difficult time in her daughter's adolescence, Green comments that this mother "enjoyed a level of freedom and strength that she would not have experienced had she conformed to patriarchal [motherhood]" (132).

I refer to Green's research because it illustrates well the way the two demands of feminist mothering both interface and underpin one another. Feminist mothering seeks to dismantle motherhood *for mothers themselves* so that they may achieve empowerment in mothering. That is reason enough to abolish motherhood. However, in so doing, mothers are also invested with the needed agency, authenticity, autonomy, and authority to undertake the feminist childrearing that they desire. Feminist mothers recognize that the changes pursued in childrearing are made possible only through changes in mothering. By way of a conversation with my two daughters—Erin and Casey—when they were teenagers, I now explore the interface between the empowerment of mothers and antisexist childrearing, and Rich's argument that the latter depends on the former. More specifically, I argue that in order for mothers to mentor feminism for their daughters, they must model it themselves.

"As Daughters We Need Mothers Who Want Their Own Freedom and Ours." Feminist Mothering of Daughters: Modelling and Mentoring Feminism

From the mid-1980s to the mid-1990s, the literature on mothers and daughters, as discussed in the opening chapter, recognizes this connection between mentoring and modelling—that mother-daughter connection empowers daughters if the mother with whom the daughter is identifying is herself empowered. "What do we mean by the nurture of daughters? What is it we wish we had, or could have had, as daughters; could give as mothers," asks Rich:

> Deeply and primally we need trust and tenderness; surely this will always be true of every human being, but women growing into a world so hostile to us need a very profound kind of loving in order to learn to love ourselves. But this loving is not simply the old, institutionalized, sacrificial, "mother-love" which men have demanded; we want courageous mothering. The most notable fact that culture imprints on women is the sense of our limits. The most important thing one woman can do for another is to illuminate and expand her sense of actual possibilities. For a mother, this means more than contending with reductive images of females in children's books, movies, television, the schoolroom. It means that the mother herself is trying to expand the limits of her life. To refuse to be a victim: and then to go on from there. (246)

Similarly, sociologist Jesse Bernard once wrote to her daughter: "For your sake as well as mine, I must not allow you to absorb me completely. I must learn to live my own life independently in order to be a better mother to you" (272). Judith Arcana in her book *Mothers and Daughters* writes: "We must live as if our dreams have been realized. We cannot simply prepare other, younger daughters for strength, pride, courage, beauty. It is worse than useless to tell young women and girls that we have done and been wrong, that we have chosen ill, that we hope they will be more lucky"(33). According to Rich, daughters need mothers who "want their own freedom and ours. The quality of the mother's life—however embattled and unprotected—is her primary bequest to her daughter, because a woman who can believe in herself, who is a fighter, and who continues to struggle to create livable space around her, is demonstrating to her daughter that these possibilities exist" (247). Whether it is termed "courageous mothering," as Rich describes it, or "feminist mothering," this practice of mothering calls for the empowerment of daughters and mothers, and recognizes that the former is only possible with the latter. As Judith Arcana concludes: "If we want girls to grow into free women, brave and strong, we must be those women ourselves" (33).

As a mother of two feminist daughters, I read all the feminist literature on mothers and daughters and increasingly became intrigued by the connection made in the scholarship between modelling and mentoring feminism. I am the mother of three children: a son, Jesse, aged thirty-two; and two daughters: Erin, aged twenty-nine, and Casey, aged twenty-seven. I had my children quite young—between the ages of twenty-three and twenty-eight when I was an undergraduate and later a graduate student. I write this chapter as a fifty-five-year-old heterosexual woman of Irish, Scottish, and English descent, who has been in a common-law relationship with the children's father for thirty-four years.

I am a mother, a feminist, and a feminist mother. My daughters proudly self-identify as feminists. Yet how did my daughters become feminists? Or, more specifically, what was the relationship between my feminist mothering and their becoming feminists? What I am interested in exploring here is not my feminist mothering per se but my daughters' perceptions and experiences of being raised by a feminist mother. In particular, I want to examine, in the context of our lived lives as a feminist mother and feminist daughters, the argument made by Rich that feminist mothering must first be concerned with the abolition of patriarchal motherhood so as empower mothers. Only then is feminist childrearing made possible. In other words, how did my identity as a feminist and my work of feminist mothering give rise to the feminism of my daughters? How did they become feminist? Was it through antisexist childrearing (i.e., raising empowered daughters), as is the focus of more contemporary writers, or was it through my being a feminist and being a mother who sought to mother against the institution of patriarchal motherhood and practice feminist mothering? Was it my challenge to patriarchal motherhood that afforded me the agency and authority to impart my feminism to my daughters and to practice antisexist childrearing? I will return to these questions after a summary of my daughters' observations.

Feminism: "A Saturated Reality"

The comments of Erin and Casey discussed below are drawn from an eighty-minute taped discussion when they were eighteen and sixteen years of age, respectively. The discussion took place as we sat on the floor of Casey's bedroom and was informally structured. I asked a general question and then asked them to take turns in answering the question. I instructed them to answer the questions honestly. And although I agree that an interview between a parent and child can never be fully candid, I do believe that our interview was as honest as one could be, as my daughters and I enjoy an intimate and very open relationship.

I opened the interview with general questions. How would you define a feminist mother? What does she do or not do? What is feminist mothering? Erin commented:

> A feminist mother quietly incorporates feminism into the child's life. And it is not like feminism is a separate thing; it is the makeup of the world that you live in because everything that you do is textured by feminism and the entire way that you grow to see the world is being shaped for you through a feminist perspective.... so things like absence of teen magazines lying around the house or books written by women piling up in front of you that you could read at your leisure. I would say a feminist mother makes feminism something that is a normal part of your life.

Casey similarly commented:

> I remember when I was in grade eight this girl came up to me and said your mom is a feminist eh? She was so confused and concerned as to why my mom was a feminist or what feminism even was. But in some way or another, every mother incorporates feminism as basic survival because girls need feminism, whether it is called feminism or not, to survive. It is absolutely essential to the survival of girls.

When I asked them for specific examples of feminist mothering from their own childhood, Erin and Casey mentioned examples of antisexist childrearing. Casey remembered in grade three not listening to the Spice girls or playing with Barbies as her friends did and wearing track pants and being made fun of because of this by her fashion-conscious friends. Erin also remembered when she was in grade five and received a Barbie doll and understood "in some vague way that it was a symbol of patriarchy." Both commented on how all their friends received plastic makeup sets in elementary school, whereas they did not. Although Erin did play with girl toys as she grew up, there was, she explained, "more variety; the toys were more geared to my personality and not my gender, for example I collected coins ... that is a dorky thing for a girl to do." Casey remembered not knowing how to put on makeup or nail polish like the other girls, who knew how to: "I remember not knowing how to do this.... I never got those lectures on beauty. I didn't start wearing makeup until grade eight. I am now glad that I [never learned like the other girls] because now I can do whatever the fuck I want with it." When I mentioned to them that I did wear makeup and wore fashionable clothing Erin remarked: "You were a femme feminist, but you didn't force it on us. Being a girl didn't mean that ... it could mean what we wanted it to mean." "Other mothers," Erin went on to say, "want [their] daughter to exist successfully in patriarchy, so the daughter has to be feminine. You had different hopes for us, different than that." Erin noted further that "while you might have worn fashionable clothing ... but then you walked off to work and talked about issues to me ... what I noticed about you was not that you were or were not fashionable ... but that you were constantly expressing your mind."

Significantly, even these examples of antisexist childrearing also convey learning feminism by way of it being modelled to them. When I asked about their earliest memory of being raised by a feminist mother, Erin said: "You worked. Work was a normal part of your life, the same as Dad's if not more so. It didn't seem weird that you went out to work. When kids of stay-at-home moms came to our house they saw not a fresh batch of muffins but a brand new batch of graded essays." Casey, too, remarked that she was proud that her mom worked, although she was teased by others because of this. Wanting to understand more on modelling feminism, I asked them about how they perceived the relationship of me and their father growing up. They both agreed that in some ways our relationship was traditional. When they were young, their father disciplined, for example, but they both emphasized that they were still not like other families. Erin remarked: "You both cooked dinner ... and he was always the one doing the dishes ... [also] dad had really long hair. That was weird among my friends. I have seen dad cry; most people don't." Speaking on how opposite-sex relationships are structured by traditional gender roles, Erin commented that although those were present in my and their father's relationship, "you never took it ... you were always a bitch ... and would fight back ... [the idea] that he was the 'man' would only go so far ... you would scream and yell and say 'excuse me I don't think so'.... We saw it [traditional roles] happen, but we also saw that if it does happen the woman can say no.... I will do it my way."

When asked how the general feminist belief that patriarchy is wrong and women should be equal to men was conveyed to them, Erin commented: "It was in everything we did and around us. I was a girl and I knew that boys would think they were better than me and I knew they weren't." Erin continued:

> The message was that it was great to be a girl. A lot of girl pride was given to me. Books. Goddess worship was a big thing. You always said thank the Goddess. Just the idea that a woman could be worshiped like that. Around the house there were goddesses everywhere. You also talked about being a mother.... This sense of pride of being a woman was in the things you said, things that were up on the wall, subtle ways, in books, comments. It saturated our existence.

Casey agreed: "It was constantly everywhere. Saturated feminism, as you say. When I was little, I ignored it as I wanted to be a 'normal' girl." Yet Casey went on to say that when she was in kindergarten, a boy would not stop bothering her, and she warned him to stop or she would cut open his finger. He said that she would not fight back because she was a girl, to which Casey replied, "wanna bet." Speaking of her own experiences of coming to feminism, Erin said:

> I was always a freak. I couldn't avoid it because it was so saturated. I didn't realize that I was doing feminist things; it was just the way I acted. I was a loud girl. If I had something to say I said it. Feminism did make it harder for me growing up because it

made me different but it was so worth it in the end. I came out the other side of all that. I am my own person. The girls I grew up with are still playing all those games. Still trapped in that world ... still don't say what they think.

Casey commented:

I feel the same way. [It was] worth it in the end, though going through it was hard particularly in elementary school. I was always a freak. I couldn't be pretty. I just failed. I didn't know how to dress 'normally.' As you grow older you come to appreciate it more. I live in this world without being swallowed up.

Central to their understanding of feminist mothering was "being allowed to express myself" and being supported in this. Talking about how she stopped shaving her armpits, Erin said: "[you were] okay with it. Other girls are told it is disgusting and unclean and their mother wouldn't let them." Both Erin and Casey emphasized the development of critical thinking. Casey remarked: "I always had arguments with dad on music and movies. I never sat and accepted things that are supposed to be accepted. They gave us access to information to make our own opinions. Just because you have strong opinions doesn't mean that I would have your own opinions ... because we grew up in this household that was possible." Erin explained that the difference was that she and her sister were "treated like people instead of being treated like children." She continued:

Other parents just say NO and while we got that to a degree, I would argue, argue. Say what I wanted to say; not told to shut up just because you are a kid.... People think if you are raised in a feminist setting, ideas are put in your head. In our family, we were encouraged to think for ourselves ... that was the big thing ... encouraged to think about things. Even if you disagreed, we would argue it to the end. We were encouraged to think for ourselves ... to come up with our own opinions, despite the fact that the world is trying to shove other ideas down your throat.

At the conclusion of the interview, I explained the research questions of this section and asked them to speak directly to the question. How is feminism learned? Is it modelled or taught? I explained to them Rich's argument that more important than feminist childrearing is the mother seeking to achieve in her own life what she wishes for her daughters. In response to this, Erin commented:

> That is what I mean when I said our reality was totally saturated with it. It was shown, not just told (though we were told as well). I agree with you, definitely 100 percent. If it had just been talked about, it would not have been the reality that it was. Feminism was the world I lived in because of the fact that you were a feminist in what you did and acted. I mean I remember you going out with your friends ... and me saying "I want you to stay home and be a good mother and baby me," and you saying mothers need to go out too. This is what feminism is, the acting and living ... not just the told. Feminism was expressed to us in the way you lived your life. And the way you set things up ... we saw it everywhere. That is how it became our reality. Instead of something we talked about, it was what everything was.

Casey remarked: "When I was young, I was resentful that my mom wasn't home making me cookies. I am now glad you worked and was not home baking cookies." In response to Casey's comment, I asked them to consider how patriarchy views feminist mothers as "bad" mothers in putting their lives before those of her children. Erin said: "Anybody who said you put your career first would be a liar ... no way in hell you put your career first. You were an involved mother ... and you had a career. What is so amazing is that you were so involved with kids and did a career." She went on to explain:

> When I was little there were times that I said come play with me and you said I have to do this.... It was not a big deal. [The] times that you weren't there, I never felt neglected. I never ever felt that way. I think it is a demonizing idea that they put out against women who work and decide to be a mother. It is completely possible to do it ... you did both very well.

I also asked them to think about another common assumption on the mother-daughter relationship found in some feminist writings—namely, mothers represent to the daughter patriarchal oppression, and, hence, the daughter must turn against the mother to become a "free" woman. Adrienne Rich termed this sentiment "matrophobia": "The fear not of one's mother or motherhood but of becoming one's mother"

(235). In response, Erin said: "Never felt your life was inhibited ... you got what you wanted ... had three kids still managed to suck fun out of life." Erin continued: "In this, you were a role model to me ... you have your cake and eat it too. [The belief] is that a woman is not allowed to be a mother and get a PhD ... and you always did it all ... that is inspiring to me ... I knew that I could have it all ... which I do." Speaking specifically on what impact, if any, being raised by a feminist mother had on whether she plans to be a mother, Erin concluded: "You definitely made motherhood something I want to do ... I know it is a lot of work, but you have shown that it is possible to be a mother and have your own life."

From the above commentary, it is evident that my daughters perceived and experienced their upbringing as antisexist childrearing and that my daughters understood their childhood in this way. They both mentioned several times that my partner and I did not "girl" them in their upbringing. (Casey spoke about how fishing, playing with frogs, and getting dirty in the mud were a normal part of her childhood.) As well, they commented on how they did not experience the "normal" sexist feminization of daughters. (They didn't play with Barbies, wear makeup or listen to the Spice Girls.) As well, both of them emphasized the importance of being offered alternative—empowered—examples and images of womanhood (feminist books and music, Goddess figures, and so forth). But equally, my daughters spoke about how they learned feminism directly from the way that I lived my life. This came up far more than I had anticipated. What they remember about me is "working, standing up to traditional gender roles and always talking about issues." They saw me living a life outside of motherhood. As Erin remarked: "You had a long relationship with dad, work, friends, partying. You did everything. You never had a shitty nonlife." My daughters, in watching me live my life, learned that feminism was possible, doable, and normal. And, as importantly, they learned that motherhood does not, and should not, shut down other dimensions of a woman's life: work, sexuality, friendship, activism, leisure, and so forth. Listening over and over again to my daughters' voices as I transcribed the interview, I finally "got" Rich's insight at a deeply personal level. To paraphrase Rich: the quality of my life—however embattled and unprotected it might have been—was my primary bequest to my daughters because in believing in myself, in fighting, and in struggling to create liveable space around me, I demonstrated to

Erin and Casey that these possibilities exist. Feminist mothering of girls is not about choosing blue over pink or trucks over dolls but about living, to use the title of Marilyn Waring's work, as if women counted. And more specifically, in the context of motherhood, feminist mothering demonstrates to our daughters that women have a selfhood outside of motherhood and have power within motherhood.

This story is that of me and my two daughters. What I learned in interviewing my daughters is not generalizable to all women. Moreover, the routes by which daughters come to feminism are many and varied: feminist mothering is just one of many. However, what I take from this narrative, and what I believe may be of use to others who likewise seek to imagine and achieve feminist mothering, is that the future we wish for our daughters must be struggled for today in our own daily lives. We must be the changes that we seek. Would my daughters have become feminists in patriarchal motherhood? The interview findings suggest that such would not have been possible or not to the degree that I, as a feminist mother, would wish. In patriarchal motherhood, feminism would not have become "the saturated reality" of my daughters' upbringing. I certainly could not have lived and modelled a feminist life in patriarchal motherhood, nor would I have had the agency and authority to impart feminist childrearing to my daughters. I believe that what our daughters need most from us is not self-sacrifice or selflessness, as preached in patriarchal motherhood, but selfhood and, yes, a healthy dose of selfishness. A mother who insists on "a life of her own" tutors her daughter that she, too, is deserving of the same. Or to conclude with Erin's words: "What you have shown us is that it is possible to be a mother and have your own life." That is the lesson we, as mothers, must impart to our daughters by living it ourselves.

Feminist Mothering of Sons: "The Strongest Lesson I Can Teach My Son is the Same Lesson I Can Teach My Daughter: How to Be Who He Wishes to Be For Himself"

"Few subjects provoke anxiety among feminists," Robin Morgan writes, "as the four-letter word *sons*" (38). Morgan continues: "We've thought and talked about, written and read about, mothers and daughters but with a few notable exceptions we've averted our eyes from the Other Touchy Subject. Yet that subject goes to the heart of practicing what we claim to believe, that 'the personal is political'. It goes to the crux of power and of patriarchy —even though it also grazes the living nerves of love" (38). Has feminism," as Babette Smith asks in her book *Mothers and Sons,* "failed the mothers of sons" (ix). Nancy Backes argues in her article "Beyond the 'World of Guilt and Sorrow,'" that whether or not feminism has failed sons or not, it has, indeed, forgotten them. "Although [the mother-son] relationship is one of life's most permanent and powerful relations," writes Backes, "mothers and sons have not been much studied" (28). The mother-son relationship is, it would seem, as Linda Forcey notes in her book *Mothers and Sons,* "a taboo topic" (2).

As both a feminist mother of a son and an academic who teaches and researches the mother-son relation, I have often wondered and worried about this absence of the mother-son relationship in feminist writings. Have mothers in our academic and personal interest in the mother-daughter relationship wronged our sons, let them down, or simply forgotten about them? Have we in our negligence or disinterest, academic and otherwise, given our sons up to patriarchy, done to them what we have spent our lives fighting against for ourselves and for our daughters? I know that I have spent far more time over the past three decades thinking about mothers and daughters than mothers and sons while I raised my own two daughters. However, as I wrote my articles, edited my books on mothers and daughters, and designed and taught a course on the topic, and as I sought to raise my girls in a feminist fashion, my son and my concerns for him as a male child in a patriarchal culture were always there, hovering, phantom-like, just beyond full consciousness or articulation. As with other mothers of sons and women who care deeply about boys today, I worried about my son Jesse and wondered whether he would be okay in a world that seemed destined to harm and maim him emotionally, spiritually, and, increasingly, physically as he grew into manhood. As time passed, I became more and more disturbed by the feminist silence surrounding mothers and sons and by my own inability, or perhaps unwillingness, to theorize the mother-son relation and my relationship with Jesse as I had done for mothers and daughters in general, and my two daughters in particular. In 1998, I initiated an international conference on mothers and sons, and in 2011, I edited the book *Mothers and Sons: Feminism, Masculinity and the Struggle to Raise our Sons,* both in an attempt to make sense out of, at least from an academic point of view, the disturbing and puzzling silence surrounding mothers and sons. I wanted to begin a feminist dialogue on what I felt to be an urgent and timely matter. However, as I worked on the book, identifying and investigating the salient issues of this new and emerging field of inquiry, my own story as a feminist mother of a son kept intruding on and interrupting the trajectory of my theoretical ponderings like some postmodern ellipse. I realized then that my understanding of the mother-son relation would remain fragmentary and partial until I remembered, recollected, and relived my own narrative. I needed to sort out how feminism had shaped the mothering of my son and how being a mother of a son has redefined my feminism. I realized that in order to understand the bigger picture—feminist theory on mothers and sons—I needed to sketch my own mother and son portrait. To that portrait, I now turn.

This narrative is my own; my son Jesse, now thirty-two, has his own story that I hope will be told at another time and place. I found myself pregnant with my first child, my son Jesse, in the fourth year of my bachelor of arts degree at the age of twenty-two. Motherhood was something I had planned to do at thirty-something, only after both the career and the guy were firmly established. I was not supposed to become pregnant this way: young, poor, and in a dating relationship. Well, we decided to have the baby, and three weeks later, I found myself setting up house (if such is possible in student residence) with this man, obscenely happy, and eagerly awaiting the birth of this child. I believed my life would go ahead as planned. I reassured my mother that with my child in daycare at six weeks, my studies would resume as scheduled. I did not know then, could not have known then, how completely pregnancy and, later, motherhood would change, completely and forever, life as I knew it.

In the early months of pregnancy, I was horribly ill with unrelenting nausea; in the later months, I developed the serious condition of pre-eclampsia, which necessitated the daily monitoring of my blood pressure. I wrote a brilliant paper on the plight of "fallen women" in Victorian literature as my feet swelled and my back ached; the ironies, in retrospect, are splendid. Labour destroyed any remnants of complacency left over from my prepregnant self. I hemorrhaged during labour, and I never before had experienced such pain, terror, or aloneness, nor have I since. When my son was finally born, pulled from my body with forceps, my spouse held him as I watched the doctors attempt to repair my ripped and torn self.

Nothing, as any new mother will tell you, can prepare you for the numbing exhaustion and physical dislocation of new motherhood. Nor can anyone warn you about how deeply you will fall in love with your child. Motherhood, as Marni Jackson so aptly puts is, "is like Albania—you can't trust the descriptions in the books, you have to go there" (3). Motherhood radicalized and politicized me; it brought me to feminism. Although I had identified as a feminist for a number of years, motherhood made feminism real for me and radically redefined it. At twenty-three, I knew in my gut, although I could not yet fully articulate it, that my feminism was to be centred on motherhood. I believed as well that if feminism required of women, in either thought or deed, a repudiation of motherhood, I did not want to be a part of it. If I had to deny or downplay my maternal self (as if such were possible) to "make it," I was not interested in playing the game. Quoting Audre Lorde, I believed, as I do now, that "the master's tools will never dismantle the master's house" (110). Although I now realize, many years later, that had I been willing to cleave off my maternal self and "pass" as a nonmother, my stay in academe—as a graduate student, contract faculty, and later as tenured faculty—would have been a great deal easier, though far less rewarding.

I became a mother through the birth of a son. All the while pregnant, as I increasingly identified with the radical feminist celebration of sisterhood, I deeply longed for a daughter. As I marched with my girlfriends on International Women's Day, I believed I marched for and with my unborn daughter Sarah. However, as the days of my pregnancy passed, and as I caressed my swelling belly and talked to my unborn child, I knew with an uncanny certainty that she was a boy. Lesbian author and poet Jess Wells in her appropriately titled narrative "Born on Foreign Soil," movingly recounts the displeasure and dismay, fear and panic, she felt upon learning through ultrasound and amniocentesis that her assumed-to-be girl was in fact a boy: "I was profoundly disappointed," writes Wells, "I wept. I sobbed to my friends" (20). Wells wondered, "What did mothers and sons have in common? What could they do together?" She worried, as a "separatist, punk dyke, a radical feminist" that she would be, in her words, "spawn[ing] a member of the oppressing class" (21). As my son was pulled from my body and I was told "it's a boy," there was a disappointment, but as I came to know and love my son, he was no longer a boy, but simply, for better or worse, Jesse.

With my first pregnancy, I lost what I refer to today as my feminist innocence. I discovered that feminism has, at best, an ambivalent relationship to motherhood. When feminist friends and women's studies classmates learned of my unplanned pregnancy, I was greeted with sentiments of pity and concern, and when I spoke with joy and pride about my pregnancy and, later, my children, my colleagues seemed suddenly suspicious of my feminism and made me feel as if I had in some irrevocable and fundamental way failed feminism. I had "sold out," been duped, gone over to the other side, or—in the language of current feminist discourse—fallen prey to the false consciousness of patriarchal ideology. Being a mother of a son made my motherhood identity all that much more problematic. Once at a union meeting shortly after the birth of our son, a woman with whom I had recently developed a friendship, stopped by to chat, and upon learning that the baby she cooed at in the carriage was a boy, she looked straight at me and said "what a shame and waste it was that a good feminist like me was now going to spend her life raising a man" and with that, she turned and walked away. Sixteen years later in 2001 when I was discussing the topic of our mothers and sons conference at the International Women's Day Fair in Toronto, two women dismissed both me and the topic of sons with a laugh that implied that a feminist would have to be an utter fool to spend her time worrying about boys. Although views such as these are no doubt rare, I do believe they bespeak a larger feminist discomfort or disinterest in the topic of mothers and sons. Be that as it may, I can say with complete certainty, after years of teaching and researching the topic of motherhood, that feminists have been far more interested in daughters than in sons, although as of late there has been an emergent feminist interest in sons. My purpose in writing this section on mothers on sons is not to explore the reasons for such silence or to chart the emergence of this new field of feminist inquiry. Rather, I am interested in exploring, from a personal viewpoint, how my identity as a feminist influenced the mothering of my son and how, in turn, my identity as a mother of a son shaped my feminism. I turn now to the first question.

My son Jesse, now thirty-two, would be regarded as a "feminist success story." He and I enjoy a close and intimate relationship. He is sensitive and kind, wise and gentle, witty and affable, empathetic and thoughtful, reliable and generous, hard-working and yet fun-loving. He models in both his behaviour and demeanor so-called masculine and feminine attributes. He is adamantly antiracist, antielitist, anticlassist, feminist, and, in particular, antiheterosexist in his politics. Occasionally, I am congratulated on raising such a fine feminist son; more often I am asked "how I did it?" This question, each time I am asked it, leaves me feeling baffled, anxious, and strangely off centre. I do not believe it is possible or desirable to format a blueprint of feminist mothering; mothers do not need yet another normative discourse of the "good mother." Moreover, we know that a whole array of influences—the media, popular culture, genetics, peer groups, schools, extended family, and the like—have as much say, if not more, in how our children "turn out." At the same time, however, I realize that my son's feminine sensibilities and feminist leanings are surely no accident in a patriarchal culture that does its utmost to ensure that boys are anything but feminine and feminist.

Jesse, with his many professional successes (a master's degree and teaching-volunteering overseas for several years), his adventurous spirit (he has travelled to more than seventy countries, most on his own), and his love of his immediate and extended family (to praise only a few of his many attributes and achievements) would do any mother proud. But what I marvel at is his determination to be himself, his refusal to give into peer pressure, and his unwillingness to compromise his principles. Given that he has lived in a very conservative, very white, rural community since the age of eight, and attended schools that were often racist, sexist, and consistently homophobic, his conviction and courage are admirable. I remember how he was teased about his long hair, and ridiculed about his odd parents—those "leftie, shacked up, hippies on the hill." I also recall the many times Jesse came home from school or baseball practice deeply upset and troubled by the "fag" jokes and queer bashing that he encountered on the playground. But I also remember a son who, in grade seven, wrote and presented a speech about Rosa Parks and won the school speech award. In grade eight, he did a major research report on homophobia; in grade ten, he wrote for his social studies assignment an essay on genital mutilation. No doubt, such views are anomalies and aberrations in our very straight (in all senses of the word), conservative "Pleasantville-like" community, and, no doubt, we, his leftie parents, must bear some responsibility or credit (depending on who you are) for our son "turning out this way."

However, to return to the questions asked above—the impact of my feminism on the mothering of my son, or the related question "how did

I raise him to be a feminist"—I still find myself circling, uncertain how to proceed. First, I cannot honestly say that I consciously raised him to be a feminist. With my daughters, my feminist mothering was overt, explicit, and to the point. For example, with my middle girl, an avid reader, I would buy for her, as she began to read independently, only books by women; it was a justified censorship, I reasoned, given that she would be reading plenty of male-authored books in later life. Over dinner, in the car, I informed them of the injustices of patriarchy and catalogued women's achievements. No topic was taboo: a normal dinner conversation in our household, from the time they could sit up in a highchair, would shift from the witch burnings to suffrage in the time it takes to say "pass the broccoli please." Every film, music video, song, commercial they have seen has been analyzed "to death"—each's misogyny, homophobia, or racism was tracked and exposed. I used to change the endings of fairy tales when I read to the children at night in order to allow the princess to "live with the prince only after she got her PhD." When my eldest daughter was thirteen, I temporarily pulled her from her school in an act of protest when the principal prohibited her from wearing a particular top, saying it was "distracting to the boys." The mothering of my girls has been actively and adamantly feminist, and my daughters unequivocally identify themselves as feminists.

With my son, the relationship between my mothering and my feminism has been less direct and perhaps more complicated. Although Jesse has certainly been a part of thousands of conversations about women, feminism, and patriarchy, he has not been schooled and cautioned about patriarchy with the same rigour and thoroughness as my daughters have, nor has his autonomy—emotional, economic, or otherwise—been as emphasized in his upbringing as it was for his sisters. Nonetheless, my son, as noted above, has feminine characteristics and feminist political leanings. How did this come to be in a patriarchal culture? The answer, despite the seeming complexity of the question, is, I think, quite simple and straightforward. My son has a clearly defined feminine dimension to his personality because such was allowed and affirmed in his upbringing. My son, since his birth, has been an exceptionally sensitive child who has needed a great deal of attention and care—emotional, physical, or otherwise. In his first year of life, he spent more times in my arms and at my breast than he did in his crib. He could not fall asleep at night without me lying in bed beside him until his early school years. Two and half years after my son was born, I would watch my newborn daughter sitting in her infant chair alone for hours on end contentedly playing with her fingers and toes: I was convinced there was something profoundly wrong with her. At the tender age of one, she put herself to bed and has done so ever since. She announced to me at the age of two that "she was the boss of herself" each and every time I asked her to do something. At the same age, my son would not leave my side. I remember one day, I suggested to my son (age three), as we walked past the playground, that he should go in and have a play while I nursed his sister. He looked at me quite terrified, and backing away from the playground gate, he proclaimed with feigned stubbornness that he would not go in there. When I, quite baffled by his behaviour, asked him why, he explained: "because children were in there." (We ended up waiting until the daycare kids left before going in for a swing and some sand play.) This image always stands in sharp contrast to the memory of my youngest daughter, also three, running through the same playground in a blur of winter hats and scarves as I waited to pick her up from daycare.

I do not recall these events to prescribe "what a good mother should do" but rather to illustrate that my son from birth was already a child with so-called feminine sensibilities. But it would be dishonest of me to say that raising such a child, boy or girl, was easy. I believe that with every child there is a difficult, or as the parenting books would delicately put it, "challenging" age or stage. With my son, it was, without a doubt, his first five years. He needed so much time, care, and attention that his seemingly endless demands left me exasperated and exhausted, trapped in those bad-mother days that Mary Kay Blakey describes so poignantly. However, despite my fatigue, irritability, and anger, I more often than not held and comforted him when he cried, cuddled him at nights, stayed close to him physically and emotionally, and honoured and protected his shy and sensitive personality—not because I was a "good mother," not even because I was a feminist mother wanting to raise a "good" man, but simply and quite honestly because it seemed to be the decent, normal, and only thing to do. When a child (boy or girl) cries, you give comfort; when a child feels lonely, you provide companionship; when a child is afraid you offer reassurance; such was my basic—but looking back now—eminently reasonable childrearing philosophy at the age of twenty-three when I first became a mother.

On my son's first day of kindergarten when he asked if I could stay with him, I simply said "yes," found a comfortable rocking chair (I had my six-week-old daughter with me), nursed my baby, and spent a morning in kindergarten as I had done a quarter century before. A few years later, when we moved and my son changed schools in December of grade three, I went with him, at his request, to his classroom on his first day and stayed with him. This time my visit was shorter; after ten or fifteen minutes, my son, with tears still falling from his eyes, told me that he would be okay now and that I could go. No doubt we were an odd sight that morning: me, a thirty-something mother, sitting in one of those straight-back school chairs kindly provided by the teacher, beside my son, in his place in a row of desks, tears streaming down his face with me trying to act as if my heart was not breaking. I am sure that many people thought that, in mothering my child this way, I was spoiling him; or worse, because he was a boy, I was coddling and emasculating him, was tying him to my apron strings, and was turning him into a "Mama's boy." No doubt I worried about that, too. But what I remember most about raising my son is loving him. That meant making sure he felt loved, protected, and good about himself. My son grew up with the knowledge that it was quite all right to be a sensitive boy and, indeed, quite normal to need your mother.

Today, when people describe my son, what is mentioned more often than any other aspect of his personally, is a "sense of groundedness," not necessarily self-confidence, but a self-acceptance and assurance in being who he is. I realize now that in my resistance to traditional practices of masculinization, I was modelling for my son the authentic mothering that Judith Arcana, Adrienne Rich, and Sara Ruddick, among others, argue is necessary for a daughter's empowerment, and, I would add, it also makes possible a son's self-assurance and acceptance in being different. Audre Lorde writes about the power of such feminist mothering in her now-classic "Man Child: A Black Lesbian Feminist's Response":

> The strongest lesson I can teach my son is the same lesson I can teach my daughter: how to be who he wishes to be for himself. And the best way I can do this is to be who I am and hope that he will learn from this not to be me, which is not possible, but how to be himself. And this means how to move to that voice within himself, rather than to those raucous, persuasive, or threatening voices from outside, pressuring him to be what the world wants him to be. (77)

In allowing my son to be who he was, in affirming this difference and doing so despite social demands to the contrary, I raised my son "feminist," or, at the very least, I raised a son comfortable with the so-called feminine dimension of his personality. My son is also, in his political views and personal ways, very feminist. His feminist beliefs are for him simply the normal way to see the world. Jesse and his sisters have been raised with socialist, antiracist, antiheterosexist, and feminist values, which seem to them to be merely sensible. All individuals—and my vegan daughter would add, species—are deserving of respect and equality; each is entitled to a fair share of the world's resources, is valued for her or his differences across race, class, ability, sexuality, and gender, and is deserving of a full life of meaningful work, good friendships and loving family. I, along with my spouse, have sought to model in my day-to-day living and to teach to my children what Carol Gilligan and others have defined as an "ethic of care"—a world view based on the values of love, respect, fairness, peace, and decency. These values have been fed to them, if you will, since they were babes in arms, served alongside their Pablum and later bagels and cream cheese. Feminism for my son is not a politic or an identity but rather a lens through which he views and understands the world. When my children started to encounter sentiments of racism, homophobia, and sexism they were surprised, incredulous, and, indeed, quite confused. They could not understand why seemingly smart people, in the lingo of the schoolyard, could be "so stupid"; "all people are equal, good, etc." they reasoned, thus, the person saying otherwise must be the fool. Of course, as they grew, they came to realize that what they understood to be the sane, sensible, normal, and natural way to be in the world—good, fair, and decent to people regardless of race, class, and so forth—was not seen as such by most of the children in our very conservative community. My children now understand that in their community and in the world generally, what seems to them perfectly sensible is, in fact, a particular political stance, and one that is not shared by most. My son supports feminism not because he is a feminist per se but because for him that is what any sane and sensible person would do. I could not agree more.

In the conclusion to "Who Are We This Time?," Mary Kay Blakey writes: "If I've taught [my sons] something about women and justice, my jock sons have taught me something about being a sport. In our ongoing discussions of gender politics, I've looked at the issues as urgently as ever, but through the lens of love and hope rather than anger and despair" (40). My feminism, too, has been rethought, reworked, and redefined through the mothering of my son, most significantly in terms of the way I understand gender difference. Prior to my son's birth, I identified with a radical feminist theory of gender difference that positioned "the feminine" and "the masculine" as more or less fixed and oppositional categories with the former superior to the latter. Crudely put, I saw the feminine as good, the masculine as bad. I understood women were, more or less, feminine and men masculine as a consequent of patriarchal gender socialization. I defined myself as "feminine" and was happy to do so. However, as my son grew and he seemed far more "feminine" in his disposition than his two sisters, my complacent and simplistic understanding of gender difference was called into question. My son was both feminine and masculine, so too were his sisters. I learned through being a mother of a son that gender is not pure, essential, or stable; as postmodernism teaches us, gender is fluid, shifting, and contested. As I came to appreciate the inevitable instability of gender, I continued to define myself as feminine and regarded it as superior, although I now concede that these preferred traits were available to men as well as to women.

As my son grew and I started to spend more time with him "hanging out," I realized that the two of us were alike in many ways and that our similarities were to be found in our so called shared masculine characteristics. This came as quite a surprise, as I had never considered myself "masculine" in any sense of the word. However, with Jesse, I saw myself in a different light and came to realize that many of my personality traits are, indeed, masculine. I am adventurous, assertive, ambitious, more rational than emotional, carefree, usually confident, and often competitive. I pride myself on my independence, resolve, intelligence, and resourcefulness, and I attribute the successes I have had in life to my drive, tenacity, stamina, resiliency, self-sufficiency, and willingness to take risks. My friends joke that I am type-A personality personified. I realize now that although I always knew I had this type of personality, I would not self-identify as such because to do so would mean admitting to being masculine. However, over the last few years, as Jesse has grown into a man and has begun to demonstrate many of these traits, I have named them in myself and come to see them as good and desirable as long as they are balanced with feminine characteristics. Being the mother of a kind son, I have come to realize that the masculine is not inherently evil, and through this realization, I have been able to discover and honour dimensions of my personality that were before unknown or shameful to me.

When Jesse was a teenager, he and I joined the local gym. We went four to five days a week for several years in the hour between picking him up from school and the time when my daughters' school day ended. Like many women my age, I grew up hating my body. As a teenager I was a compulsive dieter; in my twenties, as I came to both feminism and motherhood, I saw my body as an enemy—an instrument of patriarchal power and control. By my late thirties, I had, more or less, forgotten about, given up on my body, and lived, as do many academics, completely in my head. By working out in the gym, I have come to trust, love, respect, challenge, and honour my body as I have my mind. I feel, in an odd way, reborn, as if I have been introduced to a new self, a self more complete and whole, strong and brave. From our time at the gym together, Jesse and I developed a close bond based on something that is uniquely our own. No doubt many of the young men at the gym, most of whom went to Jesse's high school, found it odd that a mom and her teenage son would hang out at the gym together. But my son and I delighted in each other's company, took pride in each other's accomplishments, and had great deal of fun doing so.

One year while Jesse and I were regular attendees at the gym, I started horseback riding lessons with my youngest daughter—an activity that I would not have undertaken without this new confidence and trust in my body, particularly because I was thrown from a horse when I was thirteen, never to ride again. After our first lesson, my aching hamstring muscles let me know that I would have to change my workout routine in order to strengthen these muscles. So one day at the gym, I tried some machines that I had not used before. At one point, I dragged Jesse over to a machine and asked him to explain how it worked. The machine required that you lie on your back and, with your legs extended push up and down a press that has weights attached to it. There is a partial and a complete lift. On my back, with Jesse beside me, I did the partial lift, and then at my signal, he released the lever to the full lift. When the weight came down, my weak hamstring muscles could not push the press up; so there I lay, my thighs almost pressed to my face, unable to move. Jesse and I finally managed to lift the weight and release me. I remember both of us laughing out loud, to the surprise and chagrin of the guy jocks who take working out very seriously. At that moment, as I looked at my son, I thought about this narrative and had one of those rare but profoundly wondrous moments of joy and revelation. It felt right and good to be me, the mother of this man. Reflecting on this today, I realize that what was revealed to me in that moment was precisely the thesis of this narrative: my son has made me a better person and, hence, a better feminist, and my feminism has allowed him to become the good man he was meant to be.

I would like to conclude this section on feminist mothering of sons by recalling two memorable moments from my son's teenage years. The first occurred in the summer of 1995 when I attended a session on mothers and sons at a women's studies conference in Scotland. Presented at the session was a preliminary report of interviews the presenters had conducted with feminist mothers of sons. Although the details of their research are evidently important, of significance to me were their conclusion and the discussion that followed. The feminist mothers of sons interviewed for this study, the presenters concluded, although they had initially been committed to feminist childrearing, had all, more or less, given up in their attempt to challenge and circumvent their sons' becoming sexist and traditionally masculine. They provided numerous quotations to illustrate the frustration, disillusionment, and resignation felt by these mothers. But all I can remember is the rage and despair I felt when I heard those words. In the question period, I raised my hand and struggled to vocalize the rush of emotions in my heart: "I know that it is hard to go up against patriarchy but we can't give up so quickly and easily. Our sons deserve more ... our world deserves more.... The struggle to save our daughters from patriarchy has been equally as tough, but we have not given up on them ... we can't just give up on our sons." My remonstrance fell largely on deaf ears. Most in the audience agreed with the presenters, some reasoned that our time would be better spent on our daughters; others suggested that perhaps mothers, even feminist ones, secretly take pride in their sons' traditional masculinity and, thus, do not really want to change things. Still others cautioned that perhaps feminist mothering would turn our sons into misfits, causing them to be miserable.

I left the room shaking and immediately went to a payphone to call home and talk to Jesse. My spouse answered the phone, and before I could get a word in edgewise, he relayed the various newsworthy events of our children's final day of school before summer holidays. The most significant news was that our son—our child who proudly and publicly affirmed his differences every chance he got—had been chosen by his classmates in a year-end ceremony as "the person most liked by others." Politically, I find these contests offensive, but at that moment, I felt vindicated and wanted to rush back in the room—I think I would have, had the session been still on—and say "told you so!" Or more reasonably, I would have tried to explain to them that my feminist mothering had not made my son a freak; in fact, it had enabled him to take pride in his differences and become through his uniqueness and his self-acceptance, the type of person that people genuinely like. The second event is more an image than a story. In the summer of 1998, my son, my mother, and I spent two weeks in Norway and then a week in London as part of my conference and research travels. My son, like myself, is an avid traveller; since the age of eight, he had accompanied me on numerous research "road trips" throughout the United States. But this was his first time overseas. My mother, likewise, loves to travel, and she and I have travelled a great deal together. However, this was the first time we—a fourteen-year-old son, thirty-eight-year-old mother, and a sixty-eight-year-old mother and grandmother—would be travelling together. Our trip would include a weekend jaunt to Svalbard—as close as you can get to the North Pole (a two hour flight from northern Norway)—a five-day journey down the coast of Norway in a coastal steamer, four days in Tromsö (the location of the conference), a day in Bergen and Oslo, and finally a week in busy London. Although I eagerly awaited the trip, I wondered whether we were up to one another's company for a full three weeks: bunking together in the same room (on the boat, our "room" would be the size of a closet) and all the time moving by boat, train, and airplane. As well, I was concerned that my son, in his youthful exuberance, would wear my mother out the first day and that he would not survive one of her shopping excursions. I need not have worried. Although there were the usual upsets as there always are when people travel together, this journey will remain one of my fondest memories of motherhood. There are hundreds of photos from this trip and even more photos in my mind, each more beautiful than the last, but I would like to conclude this narrative with just one. It is that of my son, my mother, and me on the top deck of the steamer standing by the railing of the ship, close to breathless in awe of the scenery before us. As we stood there, my son placed one of his arms around me and the other around my mother and, gesturing to the fjords across the water, said, "Isn't it beautiful?"

For me the beauty of the moment was less in the fjords than in the three of us together standing arm in arm. Although countless circumstances brought us to that moment, I now know, as I conclude this section, that what made that moment truly possible was the feminist mothering of my son.

The Paradox of Feminist Mothering and the Promise of A Feminist Maternal Practice: "Worth It In The End"

As the above two sections on the feminist mothering of sons and daughters look at the rewards of feminist mothering for children, this section considers its risks. It considers whether feminist mothering fosters or undermines the aims of maternal practice. My writing on feminist mothering frequently draws on my experience of raising three children in a feminist household. Of interest to me in my reflections is how my children came to be feminists in a patriarchal culture. All three of my children, as noted above, identify as feminists. In the above section, I explored my challenge to traditional practices of male socialization that mandates both mother-son disconnection and "macho" masculinity in boys as well as my antisexist parenting practices and the need for mothers to model a feminist life in order to mentor the same for their girl children. The emphasis of my writing, thus, has been on how my children came to be feminists with little attention paid to the effects of that in their own lives. Even though I discussed at some length how my children were frequently ridiculed, bullied, and ostracized for their feminist practices and beliefs, I did not theorize on how this related to the larger requirements of motherwork—namely the preservation, nurturance, and socialization of children.

When my children became teenagers and young adults and the assaults on them became more frequent and hateful, I began to think about how my feminist mothering seemed to be in conflict with my maternal practice. More specifically, I struggled with how I could reconcile the demands my motherwork—keeping my children safe and ensuring that they have a sense of belonging in their culture—with the desires of my feminism, which would mean raising my children to challenge that very same culture and put themselves at risk in doing so. Preoccupied with and perplexed by this inherent and perhaps irresolvable paradox of feminist mothering, I returned to the writing of Sara Ruddick to consider whether feminist mothering could be understood as a form of maternal practice.

In *Maternal Thinking*, Sara Ruddick argues, as explored in the opening chapter, that motherwork is characterized by three demands: preservation, nurturance, and social acceptance. "To be a mother," argues Ruddick, "is to be committed to meeting these demands by works of preservative love, nurturance, and training" (17). "In any mother's day," Ruddick continues, "the demands of preservation, growth and acceptability are intertwined [and yet] a reflective mother can separately identify each demand, partly because they are often in conflict" (23). Moreover, as discussed in the opening chapter, the rival claims of maternal practice become further pronounced when they involve the third demand of training. For most mothers, Ruddick writes, "the work of training is confusing and fraught with self doubt" (104). It is in the context of the above discussion that Ruddick introduces the central and pivotal concept of inauthentic mothering. "Out of maternal powerlessness and in response to a society whose values it does not determine, maternal thinking," Ruddick writes "has often and largely opted for inauthenticity and the 'good' of others" (103).

Maternal inauthenticity, Ruddick explains further in *Maternal Thinking*, becomes expressed as a "repudiation of one's own perceptions and values" and results in mothers "relinquishing authority to others and losing confidence in their own values and in their perception of their children's needs" (111-112). Locating Ruddick's concept of acceptability and authenticity specifically in the context of feminist mothering reveals the contested terrain of this demand of maternal practice. How can mothers raise a child to be "acceptable to their social group," while at the same time "produce a person whom they themselves and those closest to them can appreciate" (103). In other words, a macho aggressive son would be deemed acceptable to the social group of patriarchy, but he would not be deemed as such by the feminist mother or those closest to her.

Irreconcilable Differences?: Feminist Mothering and Maternal Practice

Reading and rereading Ruddick over the last two decades as my children grew from toddlers to young adults I become increasingly troubled and perplexed by the apparent conflict between the expected social acceptability of my children and my own authenticity as a feminist mother. If I raised my children to belong to their larger patriarchal culture, I would be untrue to myself as a feminist mother. But if I raised them to be feminist, my children could not achieve the social acceptance mandated by maternal practice and achieve a sense of belonging in the world as adults. As a mother, I am committed to the safety, wellbeing and social acceptability of my children, yet as a feminist, I knowingly and deliberately raise my children to be critical of the dominant culture and to cause, as a result, possible harm—physical and psychological—to my children.

Over the last several years, as my feminist children, and in particular my daughters, became teenagers and the assaults upon them became more frequent and hateful, I came to realize that feminist mothering does undermine and run counter to the demands of preservation, nurturance and, in particular, training, as dictated by and demanded in maternal practice. I struggled with how I could reconcile the demands of my motherwork—keeping my children safe and ensuring that they have a sense of belonging in their culture—with the desires of my feminism, which means raising my children to challenge that very same culture and put themselves at risk in doing so. In other words, how can I be an authentic mother while still assuring the social acceptability of my children?

As a feminist and as mother I experience daily this contest of allegiance. When my daughters challenge a sexist remark, I applaud them as feminists, yet as a mother, I worry that this will only heighten their social isolation. And that they will spend another Saturday night sad and alone, shunned by their peer group for "being such a freak." When my daughters share yet another story of how yet another man accosted them in the subway or on a street corner and how they told him off or stared him down, I applaud their confidence and courage as feminists but worry about their safety as a mother. That my daughters stand up to sexist teachers, police officers, and bus drivers who objectify and belittle them, and speak up against racists and homophobes. makes me proud as a feminist but worries me as a mother. As a woman who was raised to believe that if you "don't have anything nice to say, don't say anything all" my daughters' confident outspokenness both awes and alarms me. As a mother I do find myself continually tempering their feminism by saying: "yes you can tell men off when they make obscene comments about your breasts but when you do so be sure that you are with at least one other person, that it is daylight and in a public space, and that you can run away if you have to." Not that they listen, of course.

When my eldest daughter was eighteen, she and her girlfriend (as in lover) set out to attend the International Women's Day march only to find themselves mistakenly at a rally by the right-wing group "Focus on the Family," which was arranged to protest the legalization of same-sex marriages in Canada. Safety would have dictated that my daughter and her girlfriend leave this rally of a thousand right-wing homophobes, but, instead, they stood on the opposite corner, just the two of them, and yelled "we're queer and we're here," with much kissing thrown in for good measure. When my youngest daughter was eighteen, she told a guy off for grabbing at and making offensive comments about her breasts while on a downtown street. In response, he said to my daughter "your mother is a whore," and my daughter, in turn, spit on the ground near his shoe in retaliation. The man then punched my daughter in the face knocking her to the ground. When my daughter told me the story, my initial, though unspoken, thought, trained as I was to be a nice girl, was "why didn't you walk away? Why did you have to spit?" As a mother, I can understand such a response—no mother wants to have her daughter hit—but as a feminist mother, such thought was hypocritical given that I had raised my daughters since the cradle to stand up for themselves and speak up and act against sexism and misogyny.

The constant violence and harassment experienced by my daughters reveals the consequences, and I would add dangers, of raising daughters to be feminists in a world hostile to empowered women. Rich has argued that as feminist mothers, we worry that we may turn our sons "into misfits and outsiders" (205). I would argue that as feminist mothers, we do make our children—both sons and daughters—misfits and outsiders and that this is in direct conflict with our responsibility as mothers to ensure the safety and social acceptability of our children. My constant worry about the inherent and seemingly irreconcilable conflict between feminism and motherwork, therefore, is more than academic. My children's difference, deliberately produced by my feminism, does put my children at risk and renders them outsiders to their culture, which forfeits my supposed commitment to maternal practice and its demands of preservation, nurturance, and social acceptability.

Writing on this paradox of feminist mothering, I am reminded of the work of Black mothers of sons who speak of a similar paradox. Marita Golden in her book *Saving our Sons: Raising Black Children in a Turbulent World* says this of her son. "The unscathed openness of Michael's demeanour was proof that he had been a protected, loved child. But this same quality was also suddenly a liability, one that he had to mask" (95). Nurturing Black sons to be confident and proud, mothers recognize that these same traits—because they may be misconstrued as insolence, obstinacy, and arrogance by other Black youth, police, or whites—put their sons at risk. Golden realizes that this paradox of mothering Black sons necessitates a new mode of mothering. A feminist mother, I believe, must likewise develop a new mode of mothering and teach her children to be true to themselves by modelling such in her own life. For Rich, this means the mother herself trying to expand the limits of her life. To *refuse to be a victim*: and then to go on from there (246).

Having spent over thirty years committed to both maternal practice and feminist mothering, I have yet to resolve the paradox of feminist mothering. However, what I have come to understand is that feminist mothering may be seen an expression of maternal practice. Although feminist mothering does, in the first instance, run counter to the safety and social acceptability requirements of maternal practice, it does, in allowing our children to grow outside and beyond the gender straitjackets of patriarchal culture, foster the nurturance of children, the second demand of maternal practice, which enables our children to become happy and healthy adults. Moreover, what I have learned as a feminist mother is that we must teach our children not only how to resist patriarchy but as importantly how to keep safe and sane in so doing. We need to model to our children our own lived resistance and to share with them our stories of success and sorrow. And most importantly we must create a feminist community and work towards a feminist world so that our children will have that sense of belonging that is essential for wellbeing and makes possible resistance.

As a mother of grown children, I can speak about feminist mothering with some measure of composure and confidence. My kids have turned out just fine and are, more or less, content with their lives. They have not sprouted two heads or morphed into antisocial loners as a result of being raised by a feminist mother. This is not to say that feminist mothering has been easy; on the contrary there were many days, and even more nights, that I wondered and worried whether I was doing right by my children by raising them to be such strong feminists. And, of course, my children likewise suffered as a result of being raised in a feminist household, particularly as they grew up in a rural and very conservative community. But, ultimately, I believe that feminist mothering has made me a better mother and my children, better people. As Casey commented: "I feel it was worth it in the end." Like my daughters, I, too, believe that feminist mothering is more about rewards than risks and that it is indeed "worth it in the end." And in this, feminist mothering may be seen as a full and complete expression of maternal practice.

Feminist Mothering and Mothers: Towards a Mother-Centred Practice of Feminist Mothering

Realizing the Promise of the Demeter Archetype

In *Of Woman Born*, Rich argues that the institution of motherhood must be abolished so that the "potential relationship of woman to her powers of reproduction, and to children" could be realized. (13). Although maternal scholars have heeded Rich's call, I believe that the radical impetus and implications of Rich's vision have yet to be fully realized. Feminist mothering, in Rich's view, must be primarily concerned with the empowerment of mothers. For Rich, the central reason for feminist mothering is to free mothers from patriarchal motherhood. In contrast, much of the current literature on feminist mothering is concerned with antisexist childrearing or, more specifically, raising empowered daughters and relational sons with little attention paid to the mother herself or the conditions under which she mothers. Although Rich certainly was interested in antisexist childrearing, as shown in her two chapters on mothers and daughters and mothers and sons, the over-arching purpose of *Of Woman Born* is to abolish patriarchal motherhood so that women can achieve an empowering and a feminist experience of mothering. This mother-centred, and I believe far more radical, vision has become lost in our current preoccupation with antisexist childrearing. Moreover, having made the oppression of mothers in patriarchal motherhood tangential to their goal of antisexist child-rearing, feminist theorists now find themselves in the impossible situation of trying to achieve feminist mothering without first having abolished patriarchal motherhood.

Rich's concern was mothers and dismantling patriarchal motherhood so as to make mothering less oppressive for mothers. However, she also realized that the achievement of antisexist childrearing also depended on the abolition of patriarchal motherhood. Mothers cannot facilitate changes in childrearing in an institution in which they have no power, as in the case with patriarchal motherhood. Antisexist childrearing necessitates motherhood itself being changed; it must become, to use Rich's terminology, "mothering." In other words, only when mothering becomes a site, a role, and an identity of power for women is feminist childrearing made possible.

In dismantling patriarchal motherhood, mothers are invested with the needed agency and authority to create the desired feminist childrearing. Only then does antisexist childrearing become possible. A challenge to traditional gender socialization is, of course, integral to any practice of feminist mothering. However, I argue, as Rich did forty years ago, that the empowerment of the mother must be the primary aim of feminist mothering if it is be a truly transformative theory and practice. To fully and completely liberate children from traditional childrearing, mothers must first seek to liberate themselves from traditional motherhood; they must, to use Rich's terminology, mother against motherhood.

Feminist literature on motherhood has allowed for new progressive styles of childrearing and has generated maternal activism. Despite this, I believe that it has not gone far enough in its attempts to transform motherhood *for the mother herself* and to realize fully the maternal power and fury promised in the Demeter archetype. In its emphasis on childrearing and in its strategy of rationalization, current thinking on feminist mothering fails to develop a revolutionary model of mothering that takes as its aim and focus the empowerment of *mothers*. I believe that we need to develop a more radical and militant politic that is—in the style of the Demeter archetype—more discordant, direct, and defiant in our critique of patriarchal motherhood.

Adrienne Rich in *Of Woman* Born interprets the Demeter-Peresphone myth, particularly as it was enacted in the Eleusinian mysteries, as representing every daughter's "longing for a mother whose love for her and whose power were so great as to undo rape and bring her back from death" (240). As well, the myth, Rich continues, bespeaks "*every mother's [longing] for the power of Demeter [and] the efficacy of her anger*" (emphasis added, 240). In patriarchal culture, where there are so few examples in either life or literature of empowered mothering, Demeter's triumphant resistance serves as a model for the possibility of mothering first imagined by Rich in *Of Woman Born*. However, as I reflect on the triumphs and tribulations of feminist mothering, I question whether my research and that of feminist scholarship on motherhood more generally have truly and fully actualized Demeter's maternal power and fury.

In her book *Mother without Child: Contemporary Fiction and the Crisis of Motherhood*, Elaine Tuttle Hansen argues that "the story of feminists thinking about motherhood since the early 1960s is told as a drama in three acts: repudiation, recuperation, and, in the latest and most difficult stage, to conceptualize an emerging critique of recuperation that coexists with ongoing efforts to deploy recuperative strategies" (5). Using Hansen's metaphor, I want to argue that as feminist theory moves from a repudiation of patriarchal motherhood to a recuperation of motherhood (i.e., the formation of feminist mothering), we must not lose sight of what should be the primary and central aim of our challenge to patriarchal motherhood: the empowerment of mothers. In other words, as repudiation and recuperation define the first two acts of the feminist resistance to motherhood, the final act must be expressed as a revolution of motherhood for mothers themselves. I believe we have lost this focus, and our tone has become tame and timid and our manner cautious and circuitous. Instead of demanding changes for mothers, we are now requesting them on behalf of children.

Antisexist childrearing and maternal activism on behalf of children are significant and essential tasks of feminist mothering. However, maternal activism on behalf of children and feminist childrearing for children do not in any real manner address the needs of mothers. More specifically, I argue that in defining feminist mothering in this manner we have, consciously or otherwise, discounted and disregarded what must be the first and primary aim of feminist mothering: the empowerment of mothers. Feminist scholarship has documented well how and why patriarchal motherhood is oppressive to mothers; however, when this same scholarship seeks to imagine a feminist mode of mothering, the focus inexplicably shifts from the mother to children (antisexist childrearing) and/or to a world apart from the mother (maternal activism). In the first stage of repudiation as theorized by Hansen (discussed above) the mother and her discontent were the focus; however, in the second stage, recuperation, the mother frequently becomes instrumental to larger, and seemingly more important, objectives of social change. In other words, mothers are accorded agency to effect social change through childrearing or activism, but little attention is paid to what this agency does or means for the mother herself in the context of her own life.

Equally troubling is the way much of this literature justifies and rationalizes the reasons for feminist mothering. Too often, the demand to empower mothers is recast as a strategy for more effective parenting. Erika Horwitz, as discussed above, argues that empowered mothering is characterized by women insisting on "the importance of mothers meeting their own needs" and the realization that "being a mother does not fulfill all of women's needs." However, in most instances, the mothers' demands for agency and autonomy are repositioned as requirements of the children. As one mother in Horwitz's study explains, she resisted patriarchal motherhood "to make me a better mother for my children" (52). Janna Malamud Smith, as well, draws on the myth of Demeter and Persephone but does so to argue that children are best served by empowered mothers. Rereading my own work, I recognize that I too have been complicit in this questionable tactic of rationalization and justification. My feminist mothering, as explored above, is defined and defended as necessary and essential *for children.* Like much of feminist scholarship on motherhood, my campaign for feminist mothering centred on how this would benefit children, most notably by arguing that empowered mothers are more effective mothers.

Although I do believe that feminist mothers are more effective mothers and that antisexist childrearing and maternal activism are worthwhile aims and are made possible by dismantling patriarchal motherhood, I still wonder and worry why the rhetoric of rationalization has become the strategy of choice among feminist activists and scholars today and why our campaigns for social change centre on children and not on ourselves as mothers. Why can we not simply demand that motherhood be made better for mothers themselves? Why are our demands for maternity leave, for flex-time, or for greater involvement of partners in the home always couched and explained as being for and about the children? Why are mothers' demands for more time, money, support, and validation only responded to when they are seen as benefiting children? I realize that this rhetoric is often employed strategically by feminists to make gains for mothers that otherwise would not be possible in a patriarchal culture. Patriarchal culture only accords mothers resources if they use them on behalf children; the mother can take time for herself if this makes her a better mother for her children. Although I appreciate the utility of this tactic, it still deeply troubles me. Such a strategy will certainly backfire. Moreover, and most importantly, real change for mothers can not be achieved if it is always defined as for and about children. I am not suggesting that we do away with a strategy that has proven effective, but I do believe that we must, likewise, lobby for and on behalf of mothers in order to secure and guard a place for mothers between the proverbial baby and the bathwater. Only as an empowered and enraged Demeter, can we, I believe, achieve a truly transformative and transgressive feminist practice of mothering.

Conclusion

In her article, "Developing a Feminist Motherline: Reflections on a Decade of Feminist Parenting," Fiona Joy Green, reflecting on the experiences shared by the feminist mothers she interviewed, observes, "I am struck by the need to continue sharing and recording feminist motherline stories to ensure that the difficult, yet rewarding work of feminist mothering remains a communal and political endeavour" (18). She goes on to say:

> A feminist motherline provides the space and a place for feminist mothers to record and pass on their own life-cycle perspectives of feminist mothering and to connect with those of other feminist mothers. Additionally, a motherline ensures that feminist mothers have a connection with a worldview that is centred and draws upon feminist's crucial gender based analysis of the world—including parenting. It also promises a legacy of feminist mothering and motherwork for others. (18)

With Green, I believe that "motherline stories contain invaluable lessons and memories of feminist mothering, as well as support for mothers" (18). Looking back at three plus decades of feminist mothering, I realize that it has been precisely these stories—shared across telephone lines, kitchen tables and more recently keyboards—that have sustained me as a feminist mother. It was the understanding, encouragement, and reassurance from other feminist mothers that helped to restore my confidence and conviction, and enabled me to continue anew the difficult but necessary work of feminist mothering. Building on my work of cultural bearing in African American culture,[2] Green argues that mothers in sharing their stories of feminist mothering are similarly cultural bearers of feminism. I would like to conclude this chapter on feminist mothering with Green's words because for me they best represent the promise of feminist mothering as explored in this chapter: "Through developing a feminist motherline, with feminist mothers being the cultural bearers of feminism in their daily lives, empowerment for mothers and children is sure to follow."

Notes

1. Several books have examined the relationship between Feminism and Motherhood but very little has been published on Feminist Mothering. For two important works on the former topic see Laura Umansky, *Motherhood Reconceived: Feminism and the Legacy of the Sixties*, 1996 and Susan E Chase and Mary F. Rogers, *Mothers & Children: Feminist Analysis and Personal Narratives*.
2. Please see my book on Toni Morrison, noted above.

Chapter Four

Matricentric Feminism and its Relationship to Academic Feminism

The aim of the three previous chapters was to document and detail matricentric feminism as enacted in theory, activism, and practice. The aim of this chapter is to explore matricentric feminism in relation to feminist theory and women's studies, or what may be termed "academic feminism." More specifically, this chapter argues that matricentric feminism has largely been ignored by feminist scholars and has yet to be incorporated into the field of academic feminism. In making this claim, I am not saying no feminist scholarship on motherhood exists—the previous three chapters show that much has been written on motherhood from a feminist perspective—but rather that matricentric feminism remains peripheral to academic feminism. As academic feminism has grown and developed as a scholarly field, it has incorporated various theoretical models and diverse perspectives to represent the specific concerns and experiences of particular groups of women, such as global feminism, queer feminism, third-wave feminism, and womanism. In contrast, academic feminism has not recognized or embraced a feminism developed from and for the specific experiences and concerns of mothers, or what I have termed matricentric feminism. The first section of the chapter considers both the disavowal of motherhood in twentieth-century academic feminism and the disappearance of motherhood in twenty-first-century academic feminism. This section then examines the place of motherhood over the last decade in the following: 1) the syllabi of introduction to women's studies courses; 2) articles and book reviews published in women's studies journals; 3) the content of introduction to women's studies texbooks; and 4) papers presented at the National Women's Studies Association annual conference. The chapter then ruminates on possible reasons for the exclusion of matricentric feminism in academic feminism, including confusing mothering with motherhood, the conflation of matricentric feminism with maternalism and gender essentialism, and the cultural ascendancy of postmaternal thinking. The chapter concludes with a section on mothers in academe and considers the reasons for the low numbers of mothers in the academic profession.

The Disavowal of Motherhood in Twentieth-Century Academic Feminism

In her 1986 book *A Lesser Life*, Sylvia Ann Hewlett writes "Motherhood is the problem that modern feminists cannot face" (184). Hewlett goes on to say: "many contemporary feminists have reviled both mothers and babies. Some feminists rage at babies; others trivialize them. Very few have attempted to integrate them into the fabric of a full and equal life" (184-185). Significantly, Laura Umansky in her book *Motherhood Reconceived* positions her argument as a rebuttal to Hewlett's claim: "Critics who accuse feminists of ignoring mothers or motherhood," Umansky writes, "are not only wrong [but] have completely missed the mark" (2). *Motherhood Reconceived*, as Umanksy explains, "addresses what emerged between the late 1960s and early 1980s as a public, nationwide, written feminist discussion about the meaning of motherhood" (8). She argues that "feminist discussions have subjected the institution of motherhood and the practice of mothering to their most complex, nuanced and multi-focused analysis" (2). Umansky identifies two distinct perspectives in this feminist discussion on motherhood:

> the negative discourse that views motherhood as an oppressive institution and is aligned with birth control and abortion rights alongside a critique of the nuclear family ... [and the] positive force [holding] the potential to bond women to each other, and to nature, to foster a liberating knowledge of self, to release the very creativity and generativity that the institution of motherhood denies to women. (3)

Motherhood Reconceived documents and discusses the movement from a critical stance on motherhood found in liberal and radical-libertarian feminist writings of the late 1960s and early 1970s to the celebratory view of mothering present in Black and cultural feminist writings of the mid-1970s to the early 1980s. Her book concludes with this assertion: "American feminists have long and vigorously debated the many issues that lie at the heart of motherhood. They might disagree over whether the bath is half empty or half full, but they have most decidedly not thrown the baby out with the bathwater" (164).

I read *Motherhood Reconceived* when it was first published in 1996 and have read it several times since. Although I found Umansky's argument persuasive, it did not reflect my own experiences of being a motherhood scholar in the field of academic feminism or the experiences of the hundreds of motherhood scholars I have met over the last two decades plus as a motherhood researcher. Di Brandt opens the prologue to her book *Wild Women Dancing* by discussing how the birth of her first child in 1977 called into question all she had learned—or thought she had learned—in the graduate English literature program that she completed the same year. She writes, "It was like falling into a vacuum narratively speaking. I realized suddenly with a shock, that none of the texts I had read so carefully, none of the literary skills I had acquired so diligently as a student of literature had anything remotely to do with the experience of becoming a mother" (3). Similarly, I entered motherhood the same year that I completed an honours bachelor of arts in English and women's studies. When I became a mother unexpectedly at the age of twenty-three in the final year of my honours degree, I reflected back on the courses I had taken and realized that I never had a single course in which motherhood was discussed in a thorough way—and this was in coursework leading to a degree in women's studies. Numerous and diverse topics were covered, including health, work, education, sexuality, aging, and violence against women—but not the topic of motherhood. Moreover, the few times that motherhood was discussed, it was framed as a "prison of domesticity" —a theme of late-nineteenth-century literature or the "motherhood-as-patriarchal-trap" paradigm of early 1970s feminist thought. With the notable exception of a Canadian women writers course, none of my undergraduate courses included a maternal perspective on the women's issues studied, nor did the professors call attention to the absence of motherhood in the courses or position the subject as a worthy and deserving topic for feminist scholarly inquiry.

Two years later, in 1986, I began my PhD in English and gave birth to my second child in December 1986 and my third child three years after that. At twenty-eight years old with three children born in five years and the only mother in my PhD program, I hungered for stories and theories by and about mothers and wondered, as did Di Brandt, "Where ... were the mothers, symbolic or otherwise, whom I might have turned to in that moment of aloneness and desperation?" (4). In 1990, I designed a third-year women's studies course on motherhood to address and correct the silencing and marginalization of motherhood in academe; it was the first course on this topic in North America. As I note in my chapter on designing and teaching this course in *Rocking the Cradle*, York University did not offer a single course on the subject of motherhood as late as 1991, despite housing two large and successful women's studies programs and a student population of forty thousand. I have taught this course now for twenty-five years, and although the course's inception was important for the development of motherhood scholarship and my own survival as a mother scholar, I still needed and longed for more at that time. I longed for a community to sustain and support the work I was doing as a mother academic and as a scholar of motherhood—a place where I did not have to defend or justify my motherhood scholarship or my identity as a mother academic.

By the mid-nineties as I was completing my PhD, the topic of motherhood increasingly became a significant and central topic in feminist writing, as evidenced by the numerous books and articles published on motherhood and the growing number of university classrooms across the disciplines and academic levels that began teaching this topic. Indeed, for scholars from a multitude of fields, motherhood became their central research area. In the summer of 1996, shortly after completing my PhD in English and while teaching as contract faculty at York University, I was invited by the Centre for Feminist Research at York (cfr) to host an event on motherhood. Initially, we thought of having a small afternoon event to discuss a particular motherhood theme. However, after a handful of meetings and discussions with scholars outside the university, we decided on a day-long conference titled "Mothers and Daughters: Moving into the Next Millennium" to be held in 1997, and sought funding for this through the Social Science and Humanities Council of Canada. The grant required a detailed program, including a list of the presenters and keynote speakers and full abstracts of the papers presented. With just six weeks before the grant deadline, I sent out invitations to established motherhood scholars to be keynote speakers and distributed a call for papers to recruit session presenters. As this was in the early days of the Internet, before there was a plethora of websites and when email was often tediously slow, a great deal of correspondence was still done by fax and phone. I phoned, faxed, and emailed all the leading motherhood scholars on my "wish list"—those that I had read for my dissertation and taught in my women's studies course on motherhood: Christina Looper Baker, Sara Ruddick, Paula Caplan, Maureen Reddy, Patricia Bell-Scott, Marianne Hirsch, Naomi Lowinsky, Valerie Walkerdine, and Suzanna Dunuta Walkers, to name but a few. And to my amazement and delight, most said "yes"! Arriving to the centre each day, I would find the fax machine full, and often jammed with a stack of abstracts, and my desk littered with those now old-fashioned pink phone message slips, most marked urgent. Many of the abstracts were sent with a personal note, often scribbled, saying how much this conference meant to them, how thrilled they were to be able to attend a conference on motherhood, and how much this was needed in their research and lives as motherhood scholars.

I remember one day when I was feeling particularly overwhelmed by the flood of interest and the deluge of calls and emails requesting immediate confirmation of acceptance, the director of the centre stuck her head into my office and said, "Andrea, with this motherhood thing, I think you are onto something." Indeed, in fewer than six weeks, I had received more than 160 abstracts from scholars around the world, who were all eager to be part of this very first international conference on motherhood. I received the grant, and the one-day conference—originally envisioned as an afternoon tea—became a three-day conference in September 1997, which was attended by close to two hundred researchers and activists from more than a dozen countries around the world. Over the three days of this hugely successful conference, it became apparent that a second conference on motherhood was wanted and needed, and so on behalf of the CFR, I organized a second international conference on the topic "Mothers and Sons Today: Challenges and Possibilities" in September 1998. From these two conferences, three books—*Redefining Motherhood: Changing Identities and Patterns* (Sharon Abby and Andrea O'Reilly 1998); *Mothers and Daughters: Connection, Empowerment, Transformation* (Andrea O'Reilly and Sharon

Abby 2000); *Mothers and Sons: Feminism, Masculinity and the Struggle to Raise Our Sons* (Andrea O'Reilly 2001)—were published as well as an issue ("Looking Back, Looking Forward: Mothers, Daughters, and Feminism") in the journal *Canadian Women's Studies/les cahiers de la femme* (vol. 18, nos. 2-3, 1998). All received far more submissions than could be published which, coupled with the overwhelming response to the conferences, revealed that motherhood scholars needed and wanted a space of their own, in which their research would be supported and respected. Indeed, throughout the two conferences, motherhood scholars spoke about the absence of a scholarly association on motherhood as a missing piece in the field of maternal scholarship and called for a scholarly association to meet this need. In response to these requests and in recognition of the reality that a scholarly association on motherhood was long overdue, the Association for Research on Mothering—now The Motherhood Initiative for Research and Community Involvement (MIRCI)—was formed and officially launched at the 1998 conference. In 1999, the *Journal of the Association for Research on Mothering*—now the *Journal of the Motherhood Initiative*—was established, and in 2006, Demeter Press, the first and still only feminist press on mothering, was born.

This year, MIRCI celebrates its twentieth anniversary, and Demeter its tenth. In those years, MIRCI has hosted forty-nine international conferences and has published thirty-eight journal issues and eighty plus books on the topic of mothering and motherhood. However, despite these many conferences hosted by our association and the journal issues and books published by our press, not to mention the many other conferences and books on motherhood that took place over the last two decades, I still hear, as I did twenty years ago at our first motherhood conference, stories from motherhood scholars about how their work has been ignored, dismissed, invalidated, or trivialized by academic feminists. I continue to hear how the women's studies conferences that they attend have few, if any papers, on motherhood; how motherhood is seldom a topic of discussion in women's studies classrooms and rarely included in academic feminist textbooks; and how articles on motherhood or reviews of motherhood books are all but absent in the leading women's studies journals. How can we as mother academics reconcile the exclusion and isolation experienced by mother scholars in academic feminism with Umansky's claim, noted above, that "feminist discussions have subjected the institution of motherhood and the practice of mothering to their most complex, nuanced and multi-focused analysis" (2)?

I think that this disconnect between what Umansky is claiming and what actual mother scholars are experiencing is the result of different historical timeframes and their particular view of mothering as well as the important distinction between feminist writing and the discipline of academic feminism. I agree with Umansky that from the mid-1970s to the early 1980s, mothering was explored and, indeed, celebrated in feminist writings, but the theoretical perspective of this writing was specifically that of cultural-difference feminism—a mode of feminism that by the 1990s, as Samira Kawash notes, "had been eclipsed and was no longer a serious topic of discussion in feminist graduate programs or in the academic feminist press" (970). Thus, in the mid-to-late 1990s when motherhood studies came into being, the mode of feminist theory that would have been receptive to this new scholarship, that of difference -cultural feminism, had fallen out of favour among academic feminists. As well, an important distinction must be made between what has been written by feminists and what is canonized in and by academic feminism. Again, I agree with Umanksy that much was written on motherhood from the mid-1970s to the late 1980s, but did these publications become the key texts in women's studies and were they included in undergraduate courses or on graduate exam reading lists? My experience and those of the many mother scholars I have spoken to over the years, suggest otherwise. Moreover, I contend that liberal feminism's negative stance on motherhood has had a far greater effect on current thinking on motherhood than the celebratory view of mothering present in difference-cultural feminism. Ask any student of women's studies and I would venture that they are more likely to regard motherhood as the cause of women's oppression than as a site of and for women's empowerment. Finally, moving two decades beyond the time period of Umansky's study, I argue that in the twenty-first century, not only is motherhood now viewed negatively, as it was with liberal feminism, but it has all but disappeared as a topic in academic feminism.

The Disappearance of Motherhood in Twenty-First-Century Academic Feminism

Samira Kawash argues that beginning with Rich's *Of Woman Born* and until the late 1990s, there was in her words a "rich feminist tradition of thinking about motherhood ... that was widely reviewed and recognized as groundbreaking" (970), and she highlights, in particular, the books *Motherhood Reconceived* by Laura Umansky (1996) and *Cultural Contradictions of Motherhood* by Sharon Hays (1996). However, she argues that by 2000, "the topic [of motherhood] had drifted to the margins of feminist studies" (970). The leading feminist journal, *Signs*, for example, Kawash notes, published a book review of two books on motherhood and reproductive technology in 2009. Before that, the last time *Signs* reviewed a book on motherhood was 1998 (Forcey). Kawash goes on to argue that "This trickle of attention is in dramatic contrast to the previous decade: in the period 1995-1996 *Signs* published three review essays on motherhood studies, discussing in detail more than 30 titles published between 1993-1994 alone" (970). The sudden disappearance of motherhood did not just occur in *Signs*. In 1999, *Frontiers* published a special issue on "Motherhood and Maternalism"; the next time a feminist journal offered a similarly themed issue was the fall-winter of 2009, when *Women's Studies Quarterly*'s special issue on motherhood appeared (Kawash 970-971). After searching the women's studies international index for the 2000s, Kawash finds "a surprising paucity of critical essays, studies, or book reviews on the topics of mothering-motherhood" (971). In addition, she laments that when she was the director of one PhD program in women and gender studies in the mid-2000s, she could not "recall receiving a single graduate application that proposed a study on mothering-motherhood." Kawash concludes that when mothering did appear, it was "subsumed into discussions of women and work, migration, or reproduction (new reproductive technologies and abortion)" (971).

In the spring and summer 2016, my research assistant and I undertook a study on the representation of motherhood in four women's studies venues: panels presented at the annual conference of the National Women's Studies Association between 2010 and 2015; articles and books reviews in five feminist journals—*Signs, Frontiers, Women's Studies Quarterly, Feminist Studies,* and *Gender and Society*—from 2005 to 2015; the table of contents of ten introduction to gender and women's studies textbooks; and the syllabi of fifty introduction to women's studies courses.

The breakdown of papers at the National Women's Studies Association (NWSA) annual conference (appendix B) is as follows: 2015: 506 papers with 18 on motherhood; 2014: 593 papers with 29 on motherhood; 2013: 767 papers with 24 on motherhood; 2012: 741 papers with 10 on motherhood and 3 on the maternal; and 2011: 757 papers with 19 on motherhood and 2 on the maternal. Overall, 105 papers were presented on motherhood from a total of 3,364 papers, or less than 3 percent. More popular topics included academe (118), activism (193), trans-national (235), race (216), trans and queer issues (156), and gender (70). Thus, more than twice as many papers on transnational issues were presented than on motherhood, and twice as many papers on race than on motherhood. And combining the topics of trans, queer, and gender studies, more than twice as many papers on gender and sexuality were published than on motherhood. Less than three percent, I would suggest, is far too low given that motherhood studies is as least as established an academic field as transnational studies and sexuality studies, yet there were twice as many papers on these topics than there were on motherhood. Moreover, to my knowledge, there has been only one plenary panel (in 2006) on the topic of motherhood at a NWSA conference, and there has never been a motherhood scholar or a motherhood activist as the keynote speaker in the organization's forty-year history.

Similar low percentages are found in the number of articles and book reviews on motherhood in gender and women's studies journals (appendix C). From 1 January, 2006, to 31 December, 2016, the percentages of articles and book reviews on motherhood are as follows: for *Signs*, only 3 percent of their articles and book reviews were on motherhood; for *Frontiers*, 6 percent; for *Feminist Studies*, 1.6 percent; for *Women's Studies Quarterly*, 4 percent; and for *Gender Studies*, 5 percent. In contrast, the percentages for the topic of sex-sexuality are 11 percent, 5 percent, 10 percent, 4 percent, and 11 percent, respectively, and for gender, 17 percent, 8 percent, 9 percent, 6 percent, and 31 percent, respectively. While the combined totals for sex-sexuality and gender are 41 and 71, respectively, the total for motherhood is 19.6. The average percentage was 3.92 percent for motherhood, 8.2 percent for sex-sexuality, and 14.2 percent for gender. Thus, there were more than twice as many reviews or articles on the topic of sex-sexuality and close to four times as many reviews or articles on gender than on motherhood.

The percentage of motherhood content is even lower in introduction to gender and women's studies textbooks (appendix D). None of the reviewed ten textbooks, published between 2001 and 2016, have a section on motherhood. Sample section topics include the following: diversity and difference; theoretical perspectives; representation, language, and culture; socialization; work; families; sexualities; bodies; violence against women; global politics and the state; social politics and feminist movements; constructions of sex and gender; gendered identities; cultural representations and body politics; gendering work; globalization, and activism; transnational feminism; systems of privilege and inequality; learning gender; inscribing gender on the body; sex, power, and intimacy; and health and reproductive justice. This absence is particularly notable in such textbooks as the recent *Everyday Women's and Gender Studies: Introductory Concepts* (2016), which has no section on motherhood but includes the chapter "The Manly Art of Pregnancy," and *Feminist Frontiers* (2011), which likewise has no section on motherhood but includes the chapter "Masculinities and Globalization." As well, *Listen Up: Voices from the Next Feminist Generation* (2001) has no chapters on motherhood but includes the chapters "On the Rag" and "Abortion, Vacuum Cleaners and the Power Within."

Four textbooks have sections on the family—*Feminist Frontiers* (2011), *Women's Voices, Feminist Visions: Classic and Contemporary Readings* (2014), *Reconstructing Gender: A Multicultural Anthology* (2008), *The Gendered Society* (2011)—but only four of the approximately twenty-five chapters in these family sections cover the topic of motherhood. The most discussed topics are heterosexuality and gender, as evidenced in following chapters: "The Premarital Pelvic Exam and Heterosexuality during the Cold War"; "What if Marriage is Bad for Us?"; "Household Labour and the Routine Production of Gender"; "What Is Marriage for?"; "Marriage and Love"; "Situating Home at the Nexus of Public and Private Spheres: Aging, Gender, and Home Support Work in Canada"; and "For Better or Worse: Gender Allures in the Vietnamese Global Marriage." Interestingly, there are as many chapters on fathering as there are on mothering in the family sections, even though it is mothers, not fathers, who overwhelmingly do the carework in families. As well, the topic of motherhood, as opposed to fatherhood, is represented and regarded as an established scholarly field with considerable research. Thus, one would expect to find more scholarship on motherhood than fatherhood in introductory textbooks.

Six of the collections have chapters on motherhood; however, all but one of the chapters were under thirteen pages in length. *Gender and Women's Studies in Canada: Critical Terrain* (2013) includes two chapters on motherhood: "Don't Blame Mother: Then and Now" by Paula Caplan and "The Leaner, Meaner Welfare Machine: The Ontario Conservative Government's Ideological and Material Attack on Single Mothers" by Margaret Hillyard Little. *Reconstructing Gender: A Multicultural Anthology, 5th edition* (2008) includes two chapters, "The New Momism" by Meredith Michaels and Susan Douglas and "Bloodmothers" by Patricia Hill Collins, whereas *Women's Lives: Multicultural Perspectives* (2008) includes three chapters—"Who Is Your Mother? Red Roots of White Feminism" by Paula Gunn Allan; "Mother's Day Proclamation 1870" by Judith Ward Howe; and "The Mommy Tax" by Ann Crittenden. *Feminism Is for Everybody: Passionate Politics* (2000) has one chapter on motherhood, "Feminist Parenting" by bell hooks, as did *Women's Voices, Feminist Visions: Classic and Contemporary Readings* (2014) with "Lullabies Behind Bars" by Beth Schwartzapel. The page count for the above nine chapters is under one hundred pages. These nine chapters along with the four in the family sections make a total of thirteen chapters on motherhood in the introduction to women and gender studies textbooks examined. At approximately a combined page count of 150 pages of the total 5,111 pages of these books, the percentage of motherhood content in the ten introduction to gender and women's textbooks is just under 3 percent.

An even lower percentage of motherhood content is found in the fifty introduction to women and gender studies course syllabi examined. Ten of the fifty courses include at least one reading on the topic of motherhood (Appendix E). The initial count of ten suggests a percentage of 20 percent. However, the perspective of many of these courses is that of reproductive rights and justice, which includes such readings as "Indian Transnational Surrogacy and the Disaggregation of Motherhood Work"; "Asian Communities for Reproductive Justice"; "Reproductive Justice"; "Abortion is a Motherhood Issue" and "Outcast Mothers and Surrogates: Racism and Reproductive Politics in the Nineties". One course includes two readings on childbirth from a reproductive rights perspective. Interestingly, in three of the courses in which motherhood is examined, the subject of the reading is lesbian or

Black motherhood. One course includes the reading "In Search of Australian Women," and the focus of the class discussion is on grandmothers, mothers, and daughters. Another course has an assignment, but not a reading, on interviewing two women from two different generations, with the goal of understanding your mother's perspective on feminism, the women's movement, and women's roles. Another course includes an excerpt from Betty Friedan's *The Feminine Mystique*. Only one of the ten courses has a full unit on motherhood in which motherhood is examined from more than a single perspective and from more than a reproductive rights paradigm. But interestingly, this unit includes an interview with Rebecca Walker, a feminist writer well-known for her mother-blame perspective. In addition to the ten courses that have at least one reading on motherhood, three of the courses have readings on the family. However the themes of the one course are "Gender and the Family", "Family Systems, Family Lives" and "Marriage and Love." While with the second they are "Families: World's Toughest Job", and "Why Women Can't Have it All." In total, these fifty course syllabi contain hundreds of readings, but I would argue that less than ten of these are specifically on the topic of motherhood and from a mother-centred perspective; that is roughly a percentage of less than 1 percent.

The percentages of motherhood content in women's studies conferences, journals, textbooks, and syllabi range from under 1 percent to just under 3 percent. Given that 80 percent of women become mothers in their lifetime, there is an evident disconnect between the minimal representation of motherhood in academic feminism and the actual lives of most women. Indeed, as Eva Feder Kitty emphasizes, most women care for their dependents at some point, and for many women, "this occupies the better part of their lives" (qtd. in Stephens 141). Moreover, these low percentages do not reflect or capture the considerable and significant research done on motherhood over the last twenty years.

The Baby Out With the Bathwater: Reasons for the Exclusion of Motherhood in Academic Feminism

I have attempted to make sense of this disappearance of motherhood in academic feminism in the twenty-first century. The demand for a theory and practice based on a specific identity of women is hardly an innovative or radical claim. Over the last forty plus years, many groups of women have argued that mainstream feminism—largely understood to be liberal feminism—has not adequately represented their perspectives or needs. Women of colour, for example, have advocated that feminism address the intersectionality of their oppression as racialized women, a feminism now known as womanism; women from the global south have called for the development of a theory of global feminism; and queer, lesbian, bi, and trans women have supported growth of queer feminist theory and activism. Likewise, the development of third-wave feminism in the 1990s grew out of young women's sense of alienation from the aims of second-wave feminism. When such women demanded a feminist theory of their own, the larger feminist movement acknowledged, albeit often reluctantly, that such women had been excluded from the larger canon of feminist thought. Feminist theory was subsequently revised to include these different positions and perspectives within feminism. Most introduction to women's studies textbooks or courses now include chapters or units on socialist feminism, global feminism, queer feminism, third-wave feminism, and womanism, and these perspectives and topics are well represented at women's studies conferences and in women's studies journals. Moreover, as documented in the above study, many topics relevant to the experiences of racialized, poor, transnational, queer and young women are examined in women's studies conferences, journals, and textbooks.

However, as mothers began to call for feminism for and about mothers over the last decade or so—what I have defined as matricentric feminism—and to ask for its inclusion in academic feminism, their calls were not met with the same respect or recognition. More often than not, their claims were dismissed, trivialized, disparaged, and ridiculed: why would mothers need such a mother-centred feminist perspective? The question implies that mothers do not have needs or concerns separate from their larger identity of women. It troubles me deeply that feminists are able to understand the intersectionality of gendered oppression when it comes to race, class, sexuality, and geographical location but not so for maternity. But I would argue—and I suspect most mothers would agree—that maternity needs to be likewise understood in terms of intersectional theory. The category of mother is distinct from the category of woman: many of the problems mothers face—social, economic, political, cultural, and psychological—are specific to their work and identity as mothers. Indeed, mothers, arguably more so than women in general, remain disempowered despite forty years of feminism. Mothers, in other words, do not live simply as women but as mother women, just as Black females do not live simply as women but as racialized women. Moreover, mothers' oppression and resistance under patriarchy are shaped by their maternal identity, just as Black women's oppression and resistance are shaped by their racialized identity. Thus, mothers need a feminism of their own—one that positions mothers' concerns as the starting point for a theory and politic of empowerment. For me, this seems self-evident. Why then is maternity not understood to be a subject position and, hence, not theorized as with other subject positions in terms of the intersectionality of gendered oppression and resistance? Why do we not recognize mothers' specific perspectives as we do for other women, whether they are queer, working class, racialized, and so forth? Why do mothers and mothering not count or matter?

Kawash in her review article discussed earlier argues that "the marginalization of motherhood in feminist thought over the last 15 years was a political rejection of maternalist politics constructed as a backlash to feminism and the result of dramatic upheavals in feminist theory" (971). Indeed, Kawash argues that "by the late 1990s difference feminism had been eclipsed and was no longer a serious topic of discussion in feminist graduate programs or in the academic feminist press." "The deconstruction of 'woman' and the post structuralist accounts of gender and power," she continues, "left motherhood to the side, an embarrassing theoretical relic of an earlier naïve view of the essentialist woman, and her shadow, the essential mother" (971). Building on Kawash's argument, I argue that it is more precisely a misreading of maternity and maternalism in matricentric feminism that has resulted in the disappearance of motherhood in and by academic feminism. More specifically, I contend that academic feminism confuses mothering with motherhood and conflates maternalism, and hence gender essentialism, with matricentric feminism. Finally, I discuss Julia Stephens's concept of "postmaternal thinking" as a deliberate and necessary erasure of the maternal in both culture and theory. This line of argument is not to say that these are the only reasons for the disappearance of motherhood documented in the above study. Although I would argue that Ann Snitow likewise misreads the representation of motherhood in matricentric texts, she argues in her 1992 article "Feminism and Motherhood: An American Reading" that it is the pronatalist stance of these writings that alienates feminists from motherhood scholarship. In her 1999 book *The Impossibility of Motherhood*, Patrice DiQuinzio argues that feminism's reliance on a politic and theory of gender-neutral individualism renders motherhood problematic, as discussions of maternity, by necessity, accentuate the gendered and relational dimensions of maternal subjectivity. Building on DiQuinzio's concept of "the dilemma of difference," I consider specifically how academic feminism enacts confusion, conflation, and erasure in its understanding of motherhood, and how in doing so, academic feminism does indeed throw out the baby with the bathwater.

Confusing Mothering with Motherhood

It is my view that the earlier negative stance on motherhood and the current disappearance of motherhood in academic feminism is the result of a larger and pervasive feminist discomfort with all things maternal and more specifically as a result of confusing the institution of motherhood with the experience of mothering. Much of second-wave feminism—in particular that of liberal and radical-libertarian feminism—views motherhood as a significant, if not the determining, cause of women's oppression under patriarchy. As Rosemarie Putnam Tong notes in her second edition of *Feminist Thought*, Betty Friedan's *The Feminine Mystique*, a central liberal feminist text, "advised women to become like men" (31). The now-infamous quote from *The Feminine Mystique*—"the problem that has no name"—quickly became a trope for the dissatisfaction supposedly felt by stay-at-home mothers. Friedan states that "in lieu of more meaningful goals, these women spend too much time cleaning their already tidy homes, improving their already attractive appearances, and indulging their already spoiled children" (69-70). Moreover, Friedan argues that "contemporary women needed to find meaningful work in the full-time, public workforce" (22). Along the same lines, radical-libertarian feminist Shulamith Firestone claims that "the material basis for the sexual/political ideology of female submission and male domination was rooted in the reproductive roles of men and women" (qtd. in Tong 52). Elsewhere, Firestone writes:

No matter how much educational, legal, and political equality women achieve and no matter how many women enter public industry, nothing fundamental will change for women as long as natural reproduction remains the rule and artificial or assisted reproduction the exception. Natural reproduction is neither in women's best interests nor in those of the children so reproduced. The joy of giving birth—invoked so frequently in this society—is a patriarchal myth. In fact, pregnancy is barbaric, and natural childbirth is at best necessary and tolerable and at worst like shorting a pumpkin. (92)

For Friedan and Firestone, motherhood is a patriarchal institution that causes women's oppression, and, thus, for them, the feminist solution is to disavow and denounce motherhood.

However, as motherhood scholars and mothers alike have rightly argued, such reasoning is deeply flawed in its failure to take into account the important difference between the institution of motherhood and women's experiences of mothering. In *Of Woman Born*, as discussed in chapter one, Rich distinguishes between two meanings of motherhood, one superimposed on the other: "the *potential relationship* of any woman to her powers of reproduction and to children"; and "the *institution*—which aims at ensuring that that potential—and all women—shall remain under male control" (13). The term "motherhood" refers to the patriarchal institution of motherhood, which is male defined and controlled and is deeply oppressive to women, whereas the word "mothering" refers to women's experiences of mothering and is female defined and potentially empowering to women. The reality of patriarchal motherhood, thus, must be distinguished from the possibility or potentiality of feminist mothering. To critique the institution of motherhood, therefore, is "not an attack on the family or on mothering *except as defined and restricted under patriarchy*" (Rich 14). In other words, whereas motherhood as an institution is a male-defined site of oppression, women's own experiences of mothering can be a source of power. It has long been recognized among scholars of motherhood that Rich's distinction between mothering and motherhood was what enabled feminists to recognize that motherhood is not naturally, necessarily, or inevitably oppressive. Rather, mothering, freed from motherhood, could be experienced as a site of empowerment and a location of social change if, to use Rich's words, women became "outlaws from the institution of motherhood." However, in much of academic feminism, this crucial difference between the institution and the experience is not recognized or understood. As a result, mothering becomes confused with motherhood, and maternity is regarded solely and exclusively as a patriarchal entity.

Conflating Matricentric Feminism with Maternalism and Gender Essentialism

Rachel V. Kutz-Flamenbaum, as noted in the introduction, argues that "maternalism, like paternalism, is an ideology and philosophy" (712). She continues:

> It [maternalism] asserts that "mother knows best" and that women, as a group, maintain a set of ideas, beliefs or experiences that reflect their motherly knowledge and motherly strengths. Maternalism suggests that women are (and should be) the moral conscience of humanity and asserts women's legitimate investment in political affairs through this emphasis. (712)

However, as I explain in this book's introduction, a matricentric perspective is not to be confused with a maternalist one. Although some perspectives in matricentric feminism may be considered maternalist, they are largely limited to the activism of certain motherhood organizations, as noted in the second chapter. Moreover, again as discussed in chapter two on maternal activism, maternalism in these instances functions more often as a position rather than an identity; it is performed rather than essentially determined and derived. Moreover, matricentric feminism, as evidenced in chapter one, understands motherhood to be socially and historically constructed and positions mothering more as a practice than an identity. Central to matricentric feminism is a critique of the maternalist stance that positions maternity as basic to and the basis of female identity; it challenges the assumption that maternity is natural to women—all women naturally know how to mother—and that the work of mothering is driven by instinct rather than intelligence and developed by habit rather than skill. Although matricentric feminism does hold a matrifocal perspective and insists that mothering does matter, it does not advance a maternalist argument or agenda.

However, matericentric feminism, in its focus on a gendered experience: that of mothering (and the related ones of pregnancy, childbirth and breastfeeding), does force us to address the thorny issue of gender difference. As noted above, feminist theory, with the notable exception of difference-cultural feminism, positions gender difference as central to, if not the cause of, women's oppression. Liberal feminists advocate what has been called "sameness feminism," wherein women become more like men; radical-libertarian feminists promote androgyny; and poststructuralist feminists seek to destabilize and deconstruct gender difference all together. Indeed, as Niamh Moore notes, "challenging biological determinism and other essentialisms has been a crucial policy strategy for feminists" (qtd. in Stephens 141). Thus, because feminists are uncomfortable with anything that underscores gender difference and suggests essentialism (i.e., men are naturally this way, and women are naturally that way), motherhood becomes problematic, as it more than anything else is what marks gender difference: only biological females can biologically become mothers. And because gender difference is seen as structuring and maintaining male dominance, many feminists seek to downplay and disavow anything that marks this difference—the main one, of course, being motherhood. For many feminists, to call attention to women's specific gendered subjectivity as a mother is to subscribe to an essentialist viewpoint: acknowledging and affirming what is seen as marking and maintaining gender difference and, hence, the oppression of women. Indeed, as Julie Stephens writes in *Confronting Postmaternal Thinking*: "the primary focus of the second-wave feminist movement has been one long struggle against essentialism, whether this be biological, cultural or ideological. This makes any discussion linking women and care, or mothering and nurture, particularly troubling" (10). Consequently, as Stephens goes on to argue, "any activism done in the name of the maternal will be unsettling, particularly for those who perceive feminism as primarily a struggle against essentialism" (141).

I agree that gender is constructed—sex does not equal gender or as Simone de Beauvoir said "one is not born a woman but made one"—and thus people cannot define themselves or limit their lives to that which is socially constructed by gender. However, I likewise believe that feminists should not disavow motherhood to facilitate this destabilizing of gender. I believe it is possible to simultaneously argue that gender is constructed and that motherhood matters and that maternity is integral to a mother's sense of self and her experience of the world. In my view, the apprehension over gender difference is the elephant in the room of academic feminism; it has shut down necessary and needed conver-sations about important—and yes gendered—dimensions of women's lives: menstruation, pregnancy, childbirth, breastfeeding, and mothering. Mothers can no longer talk about their reproductive identities and experiences without being called essentialist. But maternal scholars do not reduce women's sense of self to motherhood, nor do they say that this is what makes her a woman or that motherhood is more important than other variables that constitute self. They say only that motherhood matters and that it is central and integral to understanding the lives of women as mothers. Thus, mothers need a feminism, in both theory and practice, for and about their identities and experiences as mothers.

Postmaternal Thinking

Julie Stephens in *Confronting Postmaternal Thinking* argues that there exists today "a cultural anxiety around nurture, human dependency, caregiving and emotion (1). This anxiety is what she calls "postmaternal thinking." Importantly, Stephens's concept of the maternal refers *not* to a belief in innate gender difference but to a concept of what she describes as a relational, dependent, connected maternal subjectivity— "a selfhood that is the antithesis of the abstract, gender-neutral, individual, [who is] self-sufficient, free-floating ... [and] favoured by the neoliberal market" (33, 35). As Stephens writes:

> Repeated expressions of anxiety around the naming of certain values as maternal, go far beyond individual instances of maternal ambivalence. The point here is a cultural one. It is not about mothering but about the way the maternal is constituted in policy debates, popular culture, personal narratives, and conceptions of desirable selfhood. (41)

Thus, according to Stephens, "the current cultural devaluation of the principles of nurturance and care are akin to an umothering of society as whole" (132). She warns that "failing to remember the relational, connected maternal self, is to risk joining hands with neoliberalism in masking human dependency" (35). Her book *Post-*

maternal Thinking, in Stephens's words, "strives toward an active practice of remembering the maternal (and maternalism) as a paradigm of nurture and care applicable to other social relations [and] [it] also remembers maternal care as an impetus for social activism" (14).

Significantly, Stephens argues that postmaternal thinking emerges in and through what she terms "cultural forgetting" and that this has been pronounced in academic feminism:

> In the popular imagination, second-wave feminism is still linked with the glorification of market work and the devaluing of family work. This memory of feminism relies on a particular kind of cultural forgetting. More specifically, it is a forgetting that renders invisible forms of feminism that have always challenged an assumed alliance between economic participation and emancipation. (26)

The question that must be asked, according to Stephens, is not why feminism has failed motherhood but why "feminism is *remembered* as having forgotten motherhood and whether the dominance of this cultural memory has contributed to the emergence of post-maternal thinking" (41). Feminism must forget what Stephens terms "the nurturing mother," for to remember her is to remember dependency, which is in Stephens's words "the anathema to a particular kind of feminist selfhood" (53). As Stephens explains: "Familiar, public renderings of feminism's history often depict the women's movement as an inexorable march towards modernity. If women were to become modern, emancipated subjects, certain things would have to be left behind. The so-called ancient maternal ties were seen to be the first to go" (94). "While this celebratory narrative of feminist modernity," Stephens continues, "may capture significant dimensions of the women's movement, it reinforces postmaternal thinking: the widespread cultural anxiety around nurture and care ... and naturalizes an opposition between feminism and maternal forms of subjectivity and strengthens neoliberal policy agendas" (94). This telling enacts one version of feminism's history as orthodoxy and serves to reinforce and legitimate a "farewell to maternalism," in which "care is viewed as a constraint and dependency a burden for the free-floating autonomous individual" (29).

Though not emphasized by Stephens, the cultural ascendancy of postmaternal thinking in feminism and the general culture has paralleled the rise of neoliberalism; both began in the 1900s and gained momentum in the first two decades of the twenty-first century. Yet neoliberalism is what gave rise to postmaternal thinking, and postmaternal thinking, in turn, secures and sustains neoliberalism. It is important to note that the emergence of both neoliberalism and postmaternal thinking corresponds to the disappearance of motherhood in academic feminism. Moreover, this disavowal of the maternal in twenty-first-century academic feminism is deliberate and necessary, and it is enacted in order to protect and promote the illusion of the autonomous subject favoured by neoliberalism and celebrated in much of feminist theory. Just as the maternal was actively forgotten in the telling of feminism, today, it is actively ignored. I argue that the erasure of the maternal in feminist theory is less about concerns over gender essentialism than about the need to mask and deny the maternal—nurturance, human dependency, caregiving, and emotion—in in our lives. To acknowledge the maternal is to remember that human beings are not self-sufficient, free-floating, and unencumbered subjects—the kind who are championed by neoliberalism and celebrated in feminist modernity. Finally, postmaternal thinking facilitates and justifies the confusion of motherhood with mothering and the conflation of the maternal with gender essentialism, which is accomplished, as discussed earlier, by positioning the maternal as both obsolete and aberrant: the very antithesis of modern and emancipated feminist subjectivity.

Mothers in Academe

In the final section of this chapter, I consider another possible reason for the disavowal, if not disappearance, of motherhood in academic feminism: the low number of mothers in academe, particularly in positions of power and influence. In making this argument and devoting a full section of this chapter to this topic, I am not suggesting that people's personal identities should inform the scholarship or teaching that they do or that nonmothers should not do maternal scholarship—many nonmothers do motherhood research and do it well. But I do believe that if there were more mothers in academe, there would be more academic research and teaching on the subject of motherhood.

I have included in this chapter an extended section on the topic of academic motherhood—which is drawn from the introduction to

Academic Motherhood in the Post Second-Wave Context, edited by Lynn O'Brien Hallstein and me—because few scholars in the larger field of matricentric feminism are familiar with this topic, as it tends to be read and taught in the context of women and work rather than from the perspective of matricentric feminism. However, it is my belief that the topic of academic motherhood must inform matricentric feminist theory, as it provides much needed insight on the discrimination faced by mothers in the paid labour force and how it may be challenged and changed. As well, many who are engaged in maternal scholarship work in an academic context. Finally, as I noted above, I believe that there is a direct causation between the low numbers of mothers in academe and the dearth of motherhood research and teaching therein.

Recent studies of both academic women and mothers (Mason and Goulden, "Do Babies Matter?"; Mason and Goulden, "Do Babies Matter [Part II]?"; Wolfinger et al.) reveal that gender discrimination against academic mothers continues to be widespread in academe, primarily because of women's ongoing caregiving responsibilities. Indeed, even though more and more women are completing PhDs and are entering the academic "pipeline," academic mothers do not have gender equity with male academics, including male academics who also have children. Mary Ann Mason and Marc Goulden, for example, argue that "Even though women make up nearly half of the PhD population, they are not advancing at the same rate as men to the upper ranks of the professoriate; many are dropping out of the race" ("Do Babies [Part II]" 11). The primary reason women are dropping out or "leaking out of the pipeline" is because having children penalizes academic mothers far more than it does academic fathers; indeed, sometimes having children even benefits academic fathers. Mason and Goulden wryly argue that "'Married with children' is the success formula for men, but the opposite is true for women, for whom there is a serious 'baby gap'" ("Do Babies [Part II]" 11). More pointedly, in their earlier essay, Mason and Goulden also note that "there is a consistent and large gap in achieving tenure between women who have early babies and men who have early babies [having a baby prior to five years after a parent completes his or her PhD], and this gap is surprisingly uniform across the disciplines and across types of institutions" ("Do Babies Matter?" 24). They also note that "surprisingly, having early babies seems to help men; men who have early babies achieve tenure at slightly higher rates than people who do not have early babies" (24).

The opposite is the case for women who have early babies. Consequently, Mason and Goulden find that women with early babies often "do not get as far as ladder-rank jobs," and they often make family-work choices that "force them to leave the academy or put them into the second tier of faculty: the lecturers, adjuncts, and part-time faculty" ("Do Babies Matter" 24).

Moreover, Mason and Goulden's general findings are also confirmed by The American Association of University Professors (aaup). In their "Statement of Principles on Family Responsibility and Academic Work" from 2001, the aaup reveals the following:

> although increasing numbers of women have entered academia, their academic status has been slow to improve: women remain disproportionately represented within instructor, lecturer, unranked positions; more than 57 percent of those holding such positions are women while among full professors only 26 percent are women; likewise among full-time faculty women, only 48 percent are tenured whereas 68 percent of men are. (55)

Even though more women are earning their doctorates, Alice Fothergill and Kathryn Felty also note that "the structure of tenure-track jobs has not changed in any real way to accommodate them" (17). Perhaps this is why "the number of women in tenure track jobs has declined: from 46 percent in 1977 to 32 percent in 1995" (Fothergill and Felty 17). Angela Simeone argues that this research on motherhood in academe shows the following:

> marriage and family, while having a positive effect on the [academic] careers of men, has a negative effect on the progress of women's careers. Married women, particularly with children are more likely to have dropped out of graduate school, have interrupted or abandoned their careers, be unemployed or employed in a job unrelated to their training, or to hold lower academic rank. (12)

Thus, the research is clear: academic norms have harmful effects on academic women's careers once they become mothers.

Academic mothers also face the same "maternal wall" that other professional women face. Joan Williams's groundbreaking work in *Unbending Gender*, for example, explores how the ideal-worker theory shapes professional and managerial workplaces, including academe. Williams argues that the ideal worker is the unencumbered worker—unencumbered by family responsibilities—and that this idea is based on a traditional, heterosexual, married-couple model, in which men go to work to earn a salary and women stay at home to tend to children and other family-life issues. Based on this theory, professional institutions assume and expect the ideal worker to work uninterrupted across their career with no time off for family responsibilities, to prioritize career success, and to change work hours and even geographic location as needed to advance a career. Even though this theory is based on traditional gender norms, it still applies across professional institutions, including academe.

Because women, including academic women, still have more responsibility for childcare and family-life management, Williams concludes that mothers face a "maternal wall" because they are unable to meet these ideal-worker norms. In fact, Williams defines the maternal wall as "bias and stereotyping that affect mothers in particular as opposed to women in general" (97). The maternal wall manifests itself in both obvious and subtle ways, including the following: negative competence assumptions (once mothers, women are regarded as less committed to their careers); negative prescriptive stereotyping, both benevolent and hostile (it is assumed that mothers should be more feminine and devoted to family, lest they be viewed as too masculine); and attribution bias (the assumption that if mothers are away from or late to work, then, it is because of their children) (97). The maternal wall, Williams continues, is made up of three interconnected practices that compel mothers out of the workforce: "the executive schedule (extensive overtime), the marginalization of part-time workers, and the expectation that workers who are 'executive material' will relocate their families to take a better job" (70).

When comparing professions, it is important to remember that all professional women have been largely unsuccessful in their attempts to wed motherhood with a career. A study cited by Crittenden, for example, shows that less than 20 percent of college-educated baby boomer women have managed to achieve both motherhood and a career by their late thirties or forties; another study shows "that baby boomer women without children have been twice as successful in achieving a career as the women with children" (32). Sylvia Hewlett's study, reported in her bestselling book *Creating a Life*, shows that "across a range of professions, high achieving women continue to have an exceedingly hard time combining career and family: 33 percent of high-achieving woman and 49 percent of ultra-achieving women are childless at age 40. (This compares to 25 percent of high-achieving men and 19 percent for ultra-achieving men" [86]). Hewlett concludes: "the more successful the woman, the less likely it is she will find a husband or bear a child. For men the reverse is true. The more successful the man, the more likely he is to be married with children" (42). Investigating professions as diverse as medicine, law, business and government service, Crittenden concludes that while women were entering these professions in record numbers, few women were represented at the senior levels of the profession and most of these women were childless.

Even though all professional women face barriers wedding motherhood and professional life, academic mothers actually seem to face more challenges than women in other professions, particularly in law and medicine. A significant, and to many a surprising, finding of Hewlett's research, for example, is the fact that female academics have the highest rate of childlessness (43 percent) (97). Likewise, a 1988 Canadian Association of University Teachers report states that "of all the professions, that of university teaching is the one in which women have the least number of children" (qtd. in Dagg and Thompson 84). Teresa M. Cooney and Peter Uhlenberg in their 1989 article "Family-Building Patterns of Professional Women," developed from a study of the 1980 United States census, similarly finds that lawyers and professors are more likely to be childless than are physicians and that physicians tend to have more children than lawyers or teachers do (752). After ten years of marriage, the rate of childlessness among lawyers and professors is approximately 25 to 30 percent greater than that among physicians. And among those aged between thirty-five and thirty-nine, professors are far more likely than both physicians and lawyers to be childless. And postsecondary teachers in this age group have fewer children than both lawyers and physicians: the mean number of children for women with children is for physicians, 2.18; for lawyers, 1.93; and for post-secondary teachers, 1.80.

Significantly, in their 2008 article "Alone in the Ivory Tower," Nicholas Wolfinger and his colleagues show that these statistics have remained largely unchanged over the last two decades. Their review of the 2000 census PUMS (Public Use Micro Sample) illustrates that "physicians have the highest rate of birth events followed by attorneys and academics" (i). Moreover, their study also reveals the following:

Male physicians and lawyers are the most likely to have babies in the household, whereas women faculty are the least likely. Female physicians, male faculty and female lawyers are in the middle. Although female physicians and lawyers have a higher rate of birth events than male faculty from ages 30-39, male faculty from ages 25-29 and from ages 40-44 have more babies in the household. Nevertheless, both male and female faculty have fewer babies than do members of other professions. Finally, all groups except faculty family have the most birth events in their early thirties. For female faculty the peak years are the late thirties. Note also that these patterns of birth events diverge substantially for those of the male and female population in general. (8)

Furthermore, the authors also highlight that although "faculty overall are less likely than physicians to have a baby in the household, the disparity is larger for women than men, with female faculty 41% less likely than female physicians to have had a recent birth event." They conclude that "Female lawyers are also less likely than female physicians to have a baby in the household, with 23% lower odds" (11). In other words, professional men have more babies than professional women and women professors have fewer children than women attorneys and doctors.

The above studies analyze the data to determine the reasons for this disparity in birth events among female professionals. The key variables appear to be marriage, income, and the training required for each profession. The study by Wolfinger and his colleagues shows that "female faculty are less likely to be married than female physicians: 61 percent of female faculty and 59% of female lawyers are partnered, compared to 70% of physicians [and] female faculty is the most likely (13%) of the three professions to be separated, divorced or widowed" (12). However, another pertinent question remains: why do female faculty members have lower rates of marriage and higher rates of separation and divorce?

The first variable is related to income differences among the three professions. In relation to income, female professors earn less than both lawyers and physicians. The starting salaries for each vary: USD

$120,000 for a physician, $60,000 for a lawyer, and $51,000 for a professor (Wolfinger et al. 5). This higher income, as Wolfinger et al. explain, enables female physicians "to pay for childcare or provide their partners with the opportunity to be stay-at-home fathers" (Wolfinger et al. 12). Similarly, Teresa Cooney and Peter Uhlenberg find that "for women aged 35-39, marriage is associated with a 17% increase in income for female physicians while it relates to a 19% and 15% loss in income for lawyers and teachers respectively" (736). Moreover, "for female physicians aged thirty-five to fifty who live alone with children, they earn 17% less, whereas teachers and lawyers earn 27% and 31% less respectively" (756). In other words, and as Cooney and Uhlenberg explain, "not only does it appear that women physicians experience relatively small losses in their human capital investments and relatively large net gains when they marry and/or have children, but also women physicians who follow these family paths earn higher incomes, on average, than women lawyers and teachers who completely forgo such family roles" (756). Again, what needs to be asked and what will be considered below is why does the profession of medicine, as compared to those of law and postsecondary teaching, allow for not only higher numbers of children for women but also higher incomes when married and less of a salary decrease when single.

Another variable or piece of the puzzle is the training required for professions, or as Cooney and Uhlenberg describe it, the different structured career paths among academic, legal, and medical professions. As Cooney and Uhlenberg observe: "lawyers who enter in law firms and teachers who accept university appointments typically work in a position for five to seven years before being considered for partnership or tenure respectively. In contrast, after their training, physicians move almost immediately into a group or private practice, or gain hospital privileges" (757). Moreover, as Cooney and Uhlenberg go on to explain, "Women lawyers and teachers may delay marriage, remarriage or childbearing until they have passed their major career hurdles" (757). A similar explanation is offered by Wolfinger et al.:

> The unique career structure of academia offers no good opportunity to take time out to have children. After four to eight years in graduate school, assistant professors have about six years to publish or perish. Only after tenure and promotion from assistant to associate professor are faculty assured of job security.

> The median doctorate recipient is already 33 or 34 years of age; after a probationary assistant professorship, close to 40. In terms of career development this would be an ideal time for female professors to start their families, but biologically they are already past prime childbearing age. (4)

Indeed, as Mary Ann Mason elaborates further in a 2003 interview, "Academic women are expected to work hardest during their tenure-track years, precisely when their biological clocks are ticking the loudest ... these busy-career-building years are also the most likely the reproductive years" (qtd. in Wilson 3).

Academic women's fertility is also affected by the kinds of jobs available in academe. There is a paucity of well-paid part-time professional options that allow an academic mother to keep her professional status while also mothering (Wolfinger et al. 4). As Wolfinger and his colleagues describe the issue:

> Academics who want to work less than full-time generally must resort to the reduced pay and status of adjunct professorships. In contrast, both medicine and law presumably offer more opportunities for part-time employment.... Not all lawyers [for example] aspire to have high-powered corporate careers. Also the failure to make partner is not as catastrophic as failing to get tenure: one can simply move to another law firm. Faculty usually has to relocate if they do not get tenure but wish to remain in academia. (4)

Finally, the highly specialized training of academe makes it nearly impossible for a professor in the humanities or liberal arts to find employment outside of the university upon graduation; a physician or lawyer would likely be able to find well-paying work outside of their profession—in government, the no-profit sector, consulting, and so forth. In contrast, a PhD graduate in medieval history has only a university to turn to for employment. Indeed, as it is often joked in liberal arts PhD programs across North America, it is either a spot in a university or one in the welfare line. In academe, there are few if any "off ramps" to well-paid part-time academic work or to full-time work outside of university teaching. Indeed, as Kathleen Christensen, director of the Workplace, Workforce, and Working Families organization at the Alfred P. Sloan Foundation comments: "There is only one genuinely legitimate career path in the academy. It's very rigid, up or out, and you have to get on and stay on or you're penalized if you deviate" (qtd. in Wilson 3). The literature reviewed above reveals that the relatively low wages of professors, the lower rates of marriage for academics, and the lengthy and highly specialized career path of postsecondary teaching all support the contention that the structure of academe and concurrent norms make academe, in several key ways, more challenging for mothers, in general and specifically in comparison to law and medicine.

However, it is important to clarify a key area that academe is actually less demanding than law and medicine: the number of hours worked each week. In the articles noted above, the authors argue that hours worked—in addition to income, marriage, career path—is a key variable in determining the likelihood of women having children in the legal, medical, and academic professions. Wolfinger et al. report that "in contrast to their male counterparts, working long hours is associated with decreased fertility among professionals. Most notably, putting in 40-49 hours a week lowers the odds of women fast-track professionals having a baby by 37%; working 50-59 hours a week decreases the odds by 54% and working 60 or more hours deceases them by 63%" (11). However, they go on to say that "among female profess-ionals, faculty work the least, with a median 40 hours per week; physicians work the most, with a median workload of 50 hours; and lawyers are in the middle, at 45 hours" (11). Significantly, although overall increased hours are associated with decreased fertility, female professors with the fewest work hours have the lowest rate of fertility.

Cooney and Uhlenberg's study reveals a similar inconsistency: "physicians, on average, work 5 to 10 more hours per week than lawyers. Teachers are working the fewest hours" (754). However, "although physicians and their husbands," Cooney and Uhlenberg write, "work more hours than other professional women and their husbands, they are still more likely to have children, and more of them, than these other couples" (754). These numbers suggest that it is not the hours worked that determine fertility but the nature of the work done and whether such work is compatible with motherhood. Given these numbers, it is the specific culture of "unboundedness" of academic work and not the hours undertaken to perform this work that also makes academe particularly incompatible with motherwork. Indeed, the work of academe, more so than law and medicine, lacks clear boundaries and, rather than make "juggling it all"—career, children, and family—easier, this lack of boundaries actually makes it more challenging. In a 2001 bulletin, for example, the American Association of University Professors notes "The lack of a clear boundary in academic lives between work and family has, at least historically, meant that work has been all pervasive, often to the detriment of the family" (qtd. in Ward and Wolf-Wendel 233).

Moreover, in their 2004 article "Managing Complex Roles in Research Universities," Kelly Ward and Lisa Wolf-Wendel consider three theoretical models—role conflict, ideal worker, and male clockwork—to examine what has been termed the "unboundedness" of academic culture, which makes university work particularly incompatible with motherhood. The first, role conflict, they explain, "posits that individuals have limited time and energy, and adding extra roles and responsibilities necessarily creates tensions between competing demand and a sense of overload." The second theoretical framework, ideal worker, is particularly prevalent in academe, as it requires, in their words, "a singleness of purpose that parenthood does not always allow" (3). The third explanation, male clockwork, as discussed above, assumes "an idealized trajectory of a faculty career (i.e. from graduate school, to assistant, associate, full professor, in direct succession) may not describe the actual or expected career of an academic woman. For some women, the balance between work and family disrupts the standard timetable for the ideal career trajectory" (3). Although the word "unboundedness" is not used by Ward and Wolf-Wendel, the concepts and terms of their three-explanation model—singleness of purpose, overload, standard timetables—speak to and further confirm the unboundedness of academic work.

When most professors do their work, unlike many other professions, much of that work is not done at the workplace or office. Professors do not normally work set hours in an office as most professionals do: their work is done in the evenings, on weekends, and is often undertaken at home. As well, university teaching is less task driven than other careers. Unlike law or medicine, in which the work and its completion are clearly defined and marked as when a court case or a surgery is concluded, academic work has less clearly defined boundaries of completion: there are always more articles to read and more students waiting to discuss their assignments. Moreover, university teaching, unlike most careers, is composed of three very distinct jobs—teaching, including graduate supervision, research, and university service—and all are tasks that are not only never ending but require different, and often conflicting, skills and scheduling. As well, the reflection and writing needed for scholarly research, which is the foremost demand of university teachers on the tenure track, require large and uninterrupted blocks of time for it to be undertaken and completed successfully.

Finally, in academe there are less definable measures of achievement: a professor dedicated to teaching will still have students who fail, and a professor committed to scholarly excellence and who is awarded research funding is always aware that there other, more prestigious grants to be applied for. Indeed, the academic career, as Lotte Bailyn of the Massachusetts Institute of Technology acutely observes is "paradoxical." She goes to explain:

> Despite its advantages of independence and flexibility, it is psychologically difficult. The lack of ability to limit work, the tendency to compare oneself primarily to the exceptional giants in one's field, and the high incidence of overload make it particularly difficult for academics to find satisfactory integration of work with private life.... It is the unbounded nature of the academic career that is at the heart of the problem. Time is critical for professors, because there is not enough of it to do all the things their jobs require: teaching, research, and institutional and professional service. It is therefore impossible for faculty to protect other aspects of their lives. (220)

It is the unboundedness of academic work that is incompatible with motherhood because the lack of clear boundaries between work and family makes it difficult for academic mothers to manage it all. The unboundedness of academe is compounded, however, by the requirement of being disembodied—that the body and its functions, particularly reproductive functions and the lifecycles associated with it (pregnancy, birthing, nursing, and providing ongoing sustenance to self and others) are to be kept separate from intellectual life for career-path success. As discussed above, because of the ideal-worker norms, the length of training, which coincides with women's reproductive timeline, and the limitless nature of the work of academe, ideal academic workers must be disembodied to be successful. These requirements have worked for men because of the traditional gendered division of labour in homes and society: normative men have had women to do the necessary home, family, and body work that all people require. Without children, women are able to function as disembodied and unencumbered workers more or less like men if they are not mothers. (However, it is crucial to note that all women still do more community and family work.) But once they become mothers, such unencumbered and disembodied work is impossible because mothers are embodied through pregnancy, childbirth, nursing, and the physical care that is required of children, especially young children. Moreover, because mothering requires embodiment not just to be a good mother but to ensure the welfare of children when meeting these demands, it is especially hard for academic mothers to continue do the disembodied cerebral job of the mind: the reading, thinking, and writing that are required for the life of an academic.

Of course, academic mothers can try to fake an unnumbered or disembodied self by passing as a nonmother (i.e., being in the "motherhood closet"), or if a mother is economically privileged, then she can "download" such work to others by buying reproductive caregiving, usually from other less privileged women. Of course, only privileged women are financially able to "download" carework to others. Many intensive mothers, however, are reluctant to do so, as it fundamentally violates the norms of intensive mothering.

Thus, ironically, there is an unbounded culture at the heart of academe that is similar to the unbounded demands at the heart of the intensive mothering ideology, such that the norms of academic life become incompatible with the norms of intensive mothering. In short, academic mothers have two contradictory and impossible demands to be unbounded. On one hand, the unbounded nature of academe demands and requires unencumberedness from family life and child-rearing responsibilities and disembodiment at its core for professional and career success. And, on the other hand, ironically, mothering stipulates that "good" mothers must be without boundaries when it comes to their maternal thinking and practice, which demands and requires at its core that good mothers are unencumbered by professional work, or at least that mothers act as if they are when they are mothering their children. To put it another way, mothering suggests that good mothers act as if they are unencumbered by work demands, even when they are encumbered by professional life, whereas academe suggests good academics act as if they are unencumbered by motherwork, even when they are encumbered by those demands.

Before concluding this section, I would like to briefly share my story of being an academic mother because I think that making the abstract personal shows in a concrete way how discrimination plays out in the lived lives of academic mothers. As well, as I discuss later, my personal story points to real and practical ways to make the needed changes in academe for academic mothers. I began my PhD six months pregnant, with a son who had just turned two. Looking back now, I am amazed at both my defiance and naïveté. I firmly believed that if I continued to work hard, all would be fine. My daughter was born 30 December, 1986; I was back in class on January 4, with my hospital bracelet still on. There was no maternity leave for graduate students then, although I did receive a six-week paid maternity leave from teaching. In December, when our daughter was born, my partner and I lost our daycare subsidy, and we had to remove our son from daycare. Child Services reasoned that my spouse's contract teaching did not constitute full-time employment, as they counted only in-class teaching hours. We fought, and our eventual victory resulted in a change in municipal policy. However, for nine months, I was a full-time graduate student and a teaching assistant, with a two-year-old, an infant, and no childcare. To make matters worse, my daughter refused to take a bottle until she was nine months old, which meant that I could not leave her for more than three hours at a time. That winter, my spouse finished teaching a class at 1:00 p.m., and my graduate course also started then but on the other side of campus. I would nurse my newborn daughter at 12:00 p.m., bundle her and her brother up in their winter apparel, dash to my spouse's classroom (as much as this is possible with a stroller and a toddler in tow), hand them off to him, and then I would literally run to class. During this time, I managed to attend classes, do my readings, present my seminars, and begin the research for my course papers; the lack of childcare, however, prevented me from completing the papers on time. Because of the December birth of my daughter, I had enrolled in one full course and one half course, which ended in December, putting me half a course behind schedule. I hoped to complete my outstanding course work in the summer. The department, however, argued that since I was a half course behind, I should take a course in the summer to get back on schedule. So here I was, taking a full graduate course in four months, again with no childcare, and, of course, not completing the outstanding papers. In September, though ahead of schedule by a half course, I was put under informal probation because of my incomplete course work. That year, I finished my courses and got caught up on some of the earlier incomplete work. Most of the time, I felt as if my life was spiraling out of control; as one assignment was finished, another came due, and the whole time my progress was under constant surveillance. Such stress triggered what is euphemistically termed "writer's block": weeks went by, and I could not write a sentence. I was undergoing a crisis of confidence and faith, and struggling through exhaustion. In the fall of 1988, my status was assessed again, and it was determined that I was to sit my minor field comprehensive exams (an eight-hour exam) in May; by that time all course work would be completed. Failing to honour these commitments would result in my status being changed to part-time. Part-time study is frequently championed as the option of choice for mother students. (Though, of course, it is never asked of father students.) For me, it would mean the end of my academic career; as a part-time student, I would lose my scholarship and no longer be entitled to a teaching assistantship. As well, I would be ineligible for daycare subsidy, student loans, and even student housing.

Although my children were still quite young (one and four), I was determined to honour my commitments. And then I found myself pregnant again in the fall of 1988. (All three pregnancies were the result of birth control failures.) I hid my pregnancy all winter because I knew that if my pregnancy had been discovered, my full-time status would have been jeopardized. Reflecting back on this, I feel shame, guilt, fear, and disbelief. It was 1989, and a straight-A student studying women's studies and recipient of an Ontario graduate scholarship was compelled to hide her pregnancy. I felt like one of those Victorian fallen women whom I had been studying. The day of my minor field exam, my pregnancy was discovered; I could hardly hide my protruding belly on that hot day in the middle of May. The department chair, after learning that two of my remaining three course papers were still incomplete, phoned the Department of Graduate Studies and changed my status to part-time. So as I wrote the exam seven months pregnant on a sweltering hot day trying to explain the complexities of deconstruction theory (which, ironically, disavowed the gendered reality of my pregnant state) and rushing madly to the bathroom for much needed pee breaks (I was not given additional time for such breaks, despite being seven months pregnant), my career as an academic came to an end. Although I hope that my graduate director did not mean to end my academic career by changing my status to part time, that would have been the result. As a part-time student, I would have lost my scholarship, my daycare subsidy, my teaching position, my student housing, and would have become ineligible for student loans. In just over two and half years (September 1986 to May 1989), I had completed the four full courses of my PhD program, wrote my minor field exam, and although I had two course papers outstanding, my professors supported extending these assignments. As well, during this time, I held a prestigious scholarship. I have since learned that there were other students in my department who were at the same stage, or further behind, as I was, but none of them were put under probation or had their status reduced to part time. Fortunately, when my professors learned that my status was changed to part time, they lobbied on my behalf, struck a committee that resulted in maternity leave for graduate students, and I was awarded two retroactive maternity leaves (four months each), which, appropriately enough, put me well ahead of schedule. I finally completed my PhD in June 1996. In 1993, I withdrew from my studies and wrote my dissertation as I worked full time as a "part time" professor, another one of the ironies of university life. As I look back at my graduate career, I am less bitter than I was a few years ago, although I still mourn for that young woman whose stress, guilt, and anxiety I can still feel today.

Despite the outright discrimination I experienced as an academic mother, I successfully completed my PhD. This was made possible by the factors identified as necessary in the scholarship on academic motherhood; onsite, high quality, and affordable childcare, and (eventual) maternity leave from my studies (or in the instance of faculty, stopping the tenure clock). But my story also illustrates other key variables for academic mothers to succeed, ones rarely highlighted in the scholarly literature on academic motherhood: advocacy and mentoring. When my professors learned that my status had been changed to part time, they acted: they contacted the graduate director to express their outrage; they set up a committee to demand maternity leave for graduate students, which was eventually implemented. Earlier in this chapter, I shared the story about being invited by the director of the Centre of Feminist Research to host an event on motherhood, which eventually led to a conference, a grant, and four book publications. The director of the centre worked with me at each stage and showed me how to successfully run a conference, write a grant, and how to get my work published. And not surprisingly, these grants and book publications helped me secure a tenure-track position. Today, as a full professor, I try to do the same: I include graduate students and junior faculty on my grant projects, journal editorial boards, and conference committees and invite them to co-edit or edit Demeter Press publications. This is not to say, however, that advocacy and mentoring are enough: all of us must continue to fight for institutional change. And, indeed, at York University, some progress has been made for graduate students, though less so for faculty. Whereas I eventually received a four-month maternity leave, students today receive a full year and by the late 1990s, the six-week paid leave that I received from my tutorial teaching had been increased to four months. But it was advocacy that brought about these changes. Moreover, given how formidable the challenge is to bring about real institutional change and how slow and incremental this progress is, I believe that we must mentor and advocate for academic mothers. I do believe that in this instance, the master's tools refashioned as maternal mentoring and advocacy may indeed bring down the master's house or, at the very least, help to make academe a more just and equitable place for mothers. And in doing this, a place for motherhood studies in the discipline of academic feminism can be secured.

Conclusion

"Motherhood studies as an area of scholarship," Kawash writes in her review article, "is on precarious grounds: ignored by mainstream academic feminism, fragmented and discontinuous in the academic margins" (986). In making this argument, Kawash uses as her example York university's refusal to provide institutional funding for *The Association for Research on Mothering* (ARM) and the resulting closure of the association in 2010. Kawash writes that "The fact that neither the university system nor the institution of academic feminism appears willing to support a scholarly community and research program that explicitly foregrounds mothering is discouraging" (986). However, as Kawash goes on to argue, "but the fact is, even before York pulled the plug, the established academic community completely ignored the work of *ARM*. Neither O'Reilly's work nor the Demeter volumes were reviewed in any significant feminist journals, and *JARM* had few institutional subscribers" (986). Thus, "while motherhood has been an energizing topic in the past decade," Kawash argues, "there has been little of boundary-crossing movement between academic and popular discussion, and the movement between feminist studies and motherhood studies has been only in one direction" (986). But as Kawash, concludes:

> Feminist theorists, scholars, and writers, as well as feminist mother activists, have a lot to say to each other, and a lot to learn from each other, about motherhood. Motherhood studies needs the perspectives and commitments of feminism as well as the institutional resources that feminism and women's studies have accumulated over the past four decades. At the same time, feminism cannot possibly hope to remain relevant without acknowledging motherhood in all its contradictions and complexities. (986-987)

Indeed, in the words of maternal theorist Patrice DiQuinzio. "to the extent that mothering in all its diverse forms, remains an important aspect of women's lives and that decisions about whether, when, and how to mother continue to face almost all women, feminism cannot claim to give an adequate account of women's lives and to represent women's needs and interests if it ignores the issue of mothering" ("Mothering and Feminism" 545).

In this chapter, I have discussed the disavowal of motherhood in twentieth-century academic feminism and documented its disappearance in twenty-first-century academic feminism. As well, I have suggested possible explanations for this disappearance: the confusion of mothering with motherhood, the conflation of matricentric feminism with maternalism and gender essentialism, amd the cultural ascendancy of postmaternal thinking along with the inadequate representation of mothers in academe.

However, despite the disavowal and disappearance of motherhood in academic feminism, we do have a feminist theory and movement of our own as evidenced in the previous three chapters. But matricentric feminism must be more than acknowledged as a legitimate, viable, independent school of feminist thought; it must be integrated into mainstream academic feminism. But how do we accomplish this? We need more women doing motherhood scholarship and more mother professors in academe. We demand that matricentric feminism have a chapter of its own as do other schools of feminism theory—queer, global, womanist, third wave—in our feminist theory readers, that introduction to women's studies courses and textbooks include sections on motherhood, that women's journals and conferences include more papers on motherhood, and that more books on motherhood are reviewed. We must continuously challenge the conflation of mothering with motherhood within academic feminism as well as counter the association of matricentric feminism with gender essentialism. And decisively and urgently, we must interrupt the received narrative of academic feminism, in particular its normalization of the genderless and autonomous subject, in order to foreground the centrality of women's reproductive identities and lives and the importance of care in our larger culture. Indeed, as Ann Marie Slaughter comments, "The bottom-line message is that we are never going to get gender equality between men and women unless we value the work of care as much as we value paid work. That's the unfinished business" (qtd. in McCarthy). Finally and most importantly, we must demand that matricentric feminists be recognized and respected as the feminists that they are and that their feminism, that of matricentric feminism, have a room of its own in the larger home of academic feminism.

Works Cited

Abbey Sharon, and Andrea O'Reilly editors. *Redefining Motherhood: Changing Identities and Patterns*, Second Story Press, 1998.

Almond, Barbara. *The Monster Within: The Hidden Side of Motherhood*. University of California Press, 2010.

Anderson, Kim. "Giving Life to the People: An Indigenous Ideology of Motherhood." *Maternal Theory: Essential Readings*, edited by Andrea O'Reilly, Demeter Press, 2007, pp. 761-781.

Arcana, Judith. *Our Mothers' Daughters*. Shameless Hussy Press, 1979.

Backes, Nancy. "'Beyond the World of Guilt and Sorrow': Separation, Attachment and Creativity in Literary Mothers and Sons." *The Journal of the Association for Research on Mothering*, vol. 2, no. 1, spring-summer 2000, pp. 28-45.

Badinter, Elizabeth. *Mother Love: Myth and Reality*. Macmillan, 1981.

Bell-Scott, Patricia, et al. editors. *Double Stitch: Black Women Write about Mothers and Daughters*. Beacon, 1991.

Benjamin, Jessica. "The Omnipotent Mother: A Psychoanalytic Study of Fantasy and Reality." *Representations of Motherhood*, edited by Donna Basin et al. Yale University Press, 1999, pp. 129-146.

Bernard, Jesse. "Letter to Her Daughter." *Between Ourselves: Letters between Mothers and Daughters*, edited by Karen Payne, Houghton Mifflin Company, 1983, pp. 271-272.

Bernard, Wanda Thomas, and Candace Bernard. "Passing the Torch: A Mother and Daughter Reflect on Their Experiences across Generations." *Canadian Women's Studies Journal/cahier de la femme*, vol. 18, no. 2&3, summer-fall 1998, pp. 46-50.

Berry, Cecelie S. "Home Is Where the Revolution Is." *Salon*, Salon Media Group, 1999, http://www.salon.com/1999/09/29/ moms_at_home/. Accessed 10 Sept. 2016.

Blades, Joan, and Kristin Rowe-Finkbeiner. *The Motherhood Manifesto: What America's Moms Want and What To Do About It.* Nation Books, 2006.

Blakely, Mary Kay. *American Mom Motherhood Politics and Humble Pie.* Pocket Books, 1994.

Blakey, Mary Kay. "Who Are We This Time?" *Mothers and Sons: Feminism, Masculinity and the Struggle to Raise Our Sons*, edited by Andrea O'Reilly. Routledge, 2001, pp. 25-44.

Bort, Julie, et al. *Mommy Guilt: Learn to Worry Less, Focus on What Matters Most, and Raise Happier Kids.* Amacom, 2005.

Braedly, Susan. and Meg Luxton. "Competing Philosophies: Neoliberalism and Challenges of Everyday Life." *Neoliberalism and Everyday Life*, edited by Susan Braedly and Meg Luxton, McGill-Queens University Press, 2010, pp. 3-21.

Brandt, Di. *Wild Mother Dancing: Maternal Narrative in Canadian Literature.* University of Manitoba Press, 1993.

Braithwaite, Ann, and Catherine M. Orr, *Everyday Women's and Gender Studies: Introductory Concepts.* Routledge, 2016.

Buchanan, Andrea. *Mother Shock: Tales from the First Year and Beyond—Loving Every (Other) Minute of It.* Seal Press, 2003.

Bueskens, Petra. "The Impossibility of 'Natural Parenting' for Modern Mothers: On Social Structure and the Formation of Habit." *Journal of the Association for Research on Mothering*, vol. 3, no. 1, 2001, pp. 75-86.

Bueskens, Petra. *Modern Motherhood and Women's Dual Identities: Rewriting the Sexual Contract.* Routledge, 2017.

Butler, Judith. *Bodies That Matter: On the Discursive Limits of "Sex."* Routledge, 1993.

Butterfield, Elizabeth. "Maternal Authenticity." *Encyclopedia of Motherhood*, edited by Andrea O'Reilly, Sage Press, 2010, pp. 700-701.

Caplan, Paula. *Don't Blame Mother: Mending the Mother-Daughter Relationship.* Harper and Row, 1989.

Chandler, Mielle. "Emancipated Subjectivities and the Subjugation of Motherhood Practices." *Redefining Motherhood: Changing Patterns and Identities*, edited by Sharon Abbey and Andrea O'Reilly, Second Story Press, 1998, pp. 270-286.

Chase, Susan E., and Mary F. Rogers. *Mothers & Children: Feminist Analysis and Personal Narratives.* Rutgers University Press, 2001.

Collins, Patricia Hill. "Shifting the Center: Race, Class, and Feminist Theorizing About Motherhood." *Mothering: Ideology, Experience, and*

Agency, edited by Evelyn Nakano Glenn et al., Routledge, 1994, pp. 45-65.

Collins, Patricia Hill. "The Meaning of Motherhood in Black Culture and Black Mother-Daughter Relationships." *Double Stitch: Black Women Write About Mothers and Daughters.* Eds. Patricia Bell-Scott, et al. New York: Harper Perennial, 1993. 42-60.

Collins, Patricia Hill. *Black Feminist Thought: Knowledge, Consciousness and the Politics of Empowerment.* Routledge, 1991.

Coulter, Myrl. "Feminism and Motherhood. Jane Urquhart, Carol Shields, Margaret Laurence and Me." Dissertation, University of Regina, 2007.

Copper, Baba. "The Radical Potential in Lesbian Mothering of Daughters." *Politics of the Heart: A Lesbian Parenting Anthology*, edited by Sandra Pollack and Jeanne Vaughn, Irebrand Books, 1987, pp. 186-193.

Cooney, Teresa M., and Peter Uhlenberg. "Family Building Patterns of Professional Women: A Comparison of Lawyers, Physicians, and Post Secondary Teachers." *Journal of Marriage and Family*, vol. 51, no. 3, 1989, pp. 749-758.

Chodorow, Nancy. "Family Structures and Feminine Personality." *Women, Culture, and Society*, edited by Michelle Zimbalist Rosaldo and Louise Lamphere, Stanford University Press, 1974, pp. 43-65.

Chodorow, Nancy. *The Reproduction of Mothering.* University of California Press, 1999.

Craddock, Karen, editor. *Black Motherhood(s): Contours, Contexts and Considerations.* Demeter Press, 2015.

Crittenden, Ann. *The Price of Motherhood: Why the Most Important Job in the World Is Still the Least Valued.* Henry Holt and Company, 2001.

Dagg, Anne Innis, and Patricia J. Thompson. *MisEducation: Women & Canadian Universities.* Ontario Institute for Studies in Education Press, 1988.

Dally, Ann. *Inventing Motherhood.* Schocken, 1987.

Daly, Brenda O., and Maureen T. Reddy. Editors. *Narrating Mothers: Theorizing Maternal Subjectivities.* University of Tennessee Press, 1991.

Debold, Elizabeth, et al. *The Mother Daughter Revolution.* Addison-Wesley, 1993.

de Marneffe, Daphne. *Maternal Desire: On Children, Love, and the Inner Life.* Brown and Company, 2004.

DiQuinzio, Patrice. "Mothering and Feminism: Essential Mothering and the Dilemma of Difference." *Maternal Theory*, edited by Andrea O'Reilly, Demeter, 2007, pp. 542-555.

DiQunizio, Patrice. *The Impossibility of Motherhood: Feminism, Individualism and the Problem of Mothering.* Routledge, 1999.

DiQuinzio, Patrice. "The Politics of the Mothers' Movement in the United States: Possibilities and Pitfalls." *Journal of the Association for Research on Mothering*, vol. 8, no. 1-2, 2006, pp. 55-71.

Disch, E. *Reconstructing Gender: A Multicultural Anthology*, 5th ed., McGraw-Hill, 2008.

Dixon, Penelope. *Mothers and Mothering: An Annotated Bibliography.* Garland Publishing, 1991.

Doucet, Andrea. *Do Men Mother?* University of Toronto Press, 2006.

Douglas, Susan J., and Meredith Michaels. *The Mommy Myth: The Idealization of Motherhood and How It Has Undermined Women.* Free Press, 2004.

Dworkin, Shari L., and Faye Linda Wachs. *Body Panic: Gender, Health, and the Selling of Fitness.* New York University Press, 2009.

Edelman, Hope. *Motherless Daughters: The Legacy of Loss.* Delta, 1994.

Edmonds-Cady, Cynthia. "Mobilizing Motherhood: Race, Class and the Uses of Maternalism in the Welfare Rights Movement." *Women's Studies Quarterly*, vol. 37, no. 3-4, 2009, pp. 206-222.

Edwards, Arlene. "Community Mothering: The Relationship Between Mothering and the Community Work of Black Women." *Journal of The Association for Research on Mothering*, vol. 2, no. 2, 2000, pp. 66-84.

Ennis, Linda Rose. "Intensive Mothering: Revisiting the Issue Today." *Intensive Mothering: The Cultural Contradictions of Modern Motherhood*, edited by Linda Rose Ennis, Demeter Press, 2014, pp. 1-23.

Evans, Elrena, and Caroline Grant. *Mama PhD: Women Write about Motherhood and Academic Life.* Rutgers University Press, 2009. Findlen, Barbara. *Listen Up: Voices From the Next Feminist Generation.* Seal Press, 2001.

Firestone, Shulamith. *The Dialectic of Sex.* Bantam Books, 1970. Forcey, Linda. *Mothers of Sons. Toward an Understanding of Responsibility.* Praeger, 1987.

Fothergill, Alice, and Kathryn Felty. "'I've Worked Very Hard and Slept Very Little:' Mothers on the Tenure Track in Academia." *Journal of the Association for Research on Mothering*, vol. 5, no. 2, 2003, pp. 7-19.

Fox, Bonnie. "Motherhood as a Class Act: The Many Ways in Which 'Intensive Mothering' is Entangled with Social Class." *Social Reproduction: Feminist Political Economy Challenges Neo-Liberalism*, edited by

Kate Bezanson and Meg Luxton, McGill-Queens University Press, 2006, pp. 231-262.

Fox, Faulkner. *Dispatches from a Not-So-Perfect Life or How I Learned to Love the House, the Man, the Child.* Harmony Books, 2003.

Friedan Betty. *The Feminine Mystique.* 1963. Dell, 1974.

Gatrell, Caroline. "Motherhood Movement." *Encyclopedia of Motherhood,* edited by Andrea O'Reilly, Sage Press, 2010, pp. 821-823.

Gibbons. Meghan. "Political Motherhood in the United States and Argentina." *Mothers Who Deliver: Feminist Interventions in Public and Interpersonal Discourse,* edited by Joceyln Fenton-Stitt and Pageen Reichert Powell, SUNY Press, 2010, pp. 253-278.

Gibson, Margaret. "Queer Mothering and the Question of Normalcy." *Mothers, Mothering and Motherhood across Cultural Difference: A Reader,* edited by Andrea O'Reilly, Demeter Press, 2014, pp. 347-366.

Gibson, Margaret, editor. *Queering Motherhood: Narrative and Theoretical Perspectives.* Demeter Press, 2014.

Gibson, Priscilla. "Developmental Mothering in an African American Community: From Grandmothers to New Mothers Again" *Journal of the Association for Research on Mothering,* vol. 2, no. 2, 2000, pp. 31-41.

Gilligan, Carol. *In a Different Voice: Psychological Theory and Women's Development.* Harvard University Press, 1982.

Glickman, Rose L. *Daughters of Feminists: Young Women with Feminist Mothers Talk about Their Lives.* St. Martin's Press, 1993.

Golden, Marita. *Saving our Sons: Raising Black Children in a Turbulent World.* Doubleday, 1995.

Gordon, Tuula. *Feminist Mothers.* New York University Press, 1990.

Gore, Ariel, and Bee Lavender, editors. *Breeder: Real Life Stories from the New Generation of Mothers.* Seal Press, 2001.

Green, Fiona J. *Feminist Mothering in Theory and Practice, 1985-1995: A Study in Transformative Politics.* The Edwin Mellen Press, 2009.

Green, Fiona, J. "Feminist Mothers: Successfully Negotiating the Tensions Between Motherhood and Mothering." *Mother Outlaws: Theories and Practices of Empowered Mothering,* edited by Andrea O'Reilly, Women's Press, 2004, pp. 31-42.

Green, Fiona J. "Developing a Feminist Motherline: Reflections on a Decade of Feminist Parenting." *Journal of the Association for Research on Mothering,* vol. 8, no. 1-2, 2006, pp. 7-20.

Green, Fiona J. "Matroreform: Feminist Mothers and Their Daughters Creating Feminist Motherlines." *Journal of the Association for Research on Mothering*, vol. 20, no. 2, 2008, pp. 1-11.

Green, Fiona J., and Deborah Byrd, editors. *Maternal Pedagogies: In and Outside the Classroom*. Demeter Press, 2011.

Green, Fiona J., and Gary Lee Pelletier, editors. *Essential Breakthroughs: Conversations about Men, Mothers and Mothering*. Demeter Press, 2015.

Hall, Pamela Courtenay. "Mothering Mythology in the Late Twentieth Century: Science, Gender Lore, and Celebratory Narrative." *Canadian Woman Studies*, vol. 18, no. 1-2, 1998, pp. 59-63.

Hansen, Elaine Tuttle. *Mother without Child: Contemporary Fiction and the Crisis of Motherhood*. University of California Press, 1997.

Hayden, Sara, and D. Lynn O'Brien Hallstein. *Contemplating Maternity in an Era of Choice: Explorations into Discourses of Reproduction*. Lexington Press, 2010.

Hays, Sharon. *The Cultural Contradictions of Motherhood*. Yale University Press, 1996.

Hewett, Heather. "Talkin' Bout a Revolution: Building a Mothers' Movement in the Third Wave." *Journal of the Association for Research on Mothering*, vol. 8, no. 1-2, 2006, pp. 34-54.

Hewlett, Sylvia A. *Creating a Life: What Every Woman Needs to Know about Having a Baby and a Career*. Miramax Books, 2003.

Hewlett, Sylvia Ann. *A Lesser Life: The Myth of Women's Liberation in America*. Warner, 1986.

Hirsch, Marianne. *The Mother/Daughter Plot: Narrative, Psychoanalysis, Feminism*. Indiana University Press, 1989.

Hirshman, Linda R. *Get to Work: A Manifesto for Women of the World*. Viking, 2006.

Hobbs, Margaret, and Carla Rice. *Gender and Women's Studies in Canada: Critical Terrain*. Women's Press, 2012.

hooks, bell. *Talking Feminist, Talking Black*. South End Press, 1989.

hooks, bell. *Yearning: Race, Gender, and Cultural Politics*. South End Press, 1990.

hooks, bell. *Feminism is For Everybody: Passionate Politics*. South End Press, 2000.

hooks, bell. "Revolutionary Parenting." *Maternal Theory: Essential Readings*, edited by Andrea O'Reilly, Demeter Press, 2007, pp. 145-156.

Horwitz, Erika. "Mothers' Resistance to the Western Dominant Discourse on Mothering." Dissertation, Simon Fraser University, 2003.

Horwitz, Erika. "Resistance as a Site of Empowerment: The Journey Away From Maternal Sacrifice." *Mother Outlaws: Theories and Practices of Empowered Mothering*, edited by Andrea O'Reilly, Women's Press, 2004, pp. 43-58.

Jackson, Marni. *The Motherzone: Love, Sex, and Laundry in the Modern Family*. MacFarlane, Walter, Ross, 1992.

James, Stanlie M. "Mothering: A Possible Black Feminist Link to Social Transformation." *Theorizing Black Feminism: The Visionary Pragmatism of Black Women*, edited by Stanlie James and A.P. Busia, Routledge, 1999, pp. 44-54.

Jenkins Nina, "Black Women and the Meaning of Motherhood." *Redefining Motherhood: Changing Patterns and Identities*, edited by Sharon Abbey and Andrea O'Reilly, Second Story Press, 1998, pp. 201-213.

Jeremiah, Emily. "Troublesome Practices: Mothering, Literature, and Ethics." *Mother Matters: Motherhood as Discourse and Practice*, edited by Andrea O'Reilly, Demeter Press, 2004, pp. 231-41.

Johnson, Miriam. *Strong Mothers, Weak Wives: The Search for Gender Equality*. University of California Press, 1988.

Kawash, Samira. "New Directions in Motherhood Studies." *Signs*, vol. 36, no. 4, 2011, pp. 969-1003.

Kilburn, Michael. "Spivak, Gayatri Chakravorty." *Scholar Blogs Postcolonial Studies @ Emory, Emory*, 2012, scholarblogs.emory.edu/postcolonialstudies/2014/06/19/spiv-ak-gayatri-chakravorty/. Accessed 12 Sept. 2016.

Kimmel, Michael and Jacqueline Holler. *The Gendered Society, Canadian Edition*. Oxford University Press, 2011.

Kinser, Amber E, editor. *Mothering in the Third Wave*. Demeter Press, 2008.

Kirk, Gwyn and Margo Okazawa-Rey. *Women's Lives: Multicultural Perspectives*. 6th ed., McGraw-Hill Higher Education, 2012.

Kutz-Flamebaum, Rachel V. "Maternalism." *Encyclopedia of Motherhood*, edited by Andrea O'Reilly. Sage Press, 2010, pp. 712-716.

Kuwabong, Dannabang. "Reading the Gospel of Bakes: Daughters' Representations of Mothers in the Poetry of Claire Harrise and Lorna Goodison." *Canadian Woman Studies/les cahiers de la femme*, vol. 19, no. 2-3, 1998, pp. 132-138.

LaChance, Sarah Adam. "Maternal Thinking." *The Encyclopedia of Motherhood*, edited by Andrea O'Reilly, Sage Press, 2010, pp. 726-727.

Ladner, Joyce. *Tomorrow's Tomorrow: The Black Woman*. Doubleday, 1971.

Launius, Christie, and Holly Hassel. *Threshold Concepts in Women's and Gender Studies: Ways of Seeing, Thinking, and Knowing*. Routledge, 2015.

Lavell-Harvard, Dawn Memee, and Jeanette Corbiere Lavell, editors. *Until Our Hearts Are On the Ground: Aboriginal Mothering, Oppression, Resistance and Rebirth*. Demeter Press, 2006.

Lawson, Erica. "Black Women's Mothering in a Historical and Contemporary Perspective: Understanding the Past, Forging the Future." *Journal of the Association for Research on Mothering*, vol. 2, no. 2, 2000, pp. 21-30.

Logsdon-Conradsen, Susan. "Harnessing the Radicalizing Experience of Motherhood to Create Anti-Violence Activists." NWSA Conference, November 2010, Lecture.

Lorde, Audre. *Sister Outsider*. The Crossing, 1984.

Lowinsky, Naomi Ruth. *Stories from the Motherline: Reclaiming the Mother-Daughter Bond, Finding Our Feminine Souls*. Jeremy P. Tarcher, 1992.

Lowinsky, Naomi Ruth. *The Motherline: Every Woman's Journey to Find Her Female Roots* (Formerly titled, *Stories from the Motherline: Reclaiming the Mother-Daughter Bond, Finding Our Feminine Souls*). Jeremy P. Tarcher, 1992.

Lucas, Sheri. "Mamazons." *Encyclopedia of Motherhood*, edited by Andrea O'Reilly. Sage Press, 2010, pp. 682-683.

Malin, Jo. *The Voice of the Mother: Embedded Maternal Narratives in Twentieth-Century Women's Autobiographies*. Southern Illinois University Press, 2000.

Martinez, Elizabeth, and Arnoldo Garcia. "What is Neoliberalism?" *Corpwatch: Holding Corporations Accountable*, Corpwatch, n.d., www.corpwatch.org/article.php?id=376. Accessed 11 Sept. 2016.

Mason, Mary Ann. "Men and Mothering." *Chronicle of Higher Education*, 2009, www.chronicle.com/article/MenMothering/44863. Accessed 11 Sept. 2016.

Mason, Mary Ann and Marc Goulden. "Do Babies Matter (Part II)?: Closing the Baby Gap." *Academe*, vol. 90, no. 6, 2004, pp. 10-15.

Mason, Mary Ann and Marc Goulden. "Do Babies Matter?: The Effect of Family Formation on the Lifelong Careers of Academic Men and Women" *Academe*, vol. 88, no. 6, 2002, pp. 21-27.

Maushart, Susan. *The Mask of Motherhood: How Becoming a Mother Changes Everything and Why We Pretend It Doesn't*. Penguin Books, 2000.

McCarthy, Ellen. "Why Neither Men Nor Women Can 'Have It All.'" *The Toronto Star*, Toronto Star Newspapers, Ltd, 30 Aug. 2016, http://torontostar.newspaperdirect.com/epaper/viewer.aspx. Accessed 11 Sept. 2016.

Mellor, Christine. *The Three-Martini Playdate: A Practical Guide to Happy Parenting*. Chronicle Books, 2004.

Middleton, Amy. "Mothering under Duress: Examining the Inclusiveness of Feminist Theory of Inquiry." *Journal of the Association for Research on Mothering*, vol. 8, no. 1-2, 2006, pp. 72-82.

Milkie, Melissa A., and Catherine H. Warner. "Status Safeguarding: Mothers' Work to Secure Children's Place in the Social Hierarchy." *Intensive Mothering: The Cultural Contradictions of Modern Motherhood*, edited by Linda Rose Ennis, Demeter Press, 2014, pp. 66-85.

Moravec, Michelle. "Another Mother for Peace: Reconsidering Maternalist Peace Politics from the Historical Perspective 1967- 2007." *Journal of the Motherhood Initiative*, vol. 1, no. 1, 2010, pp. 9-29.

Morgan, Robin. "Every Mother's Son." *Lesbians Raising Sons*, edited by Jess Wells. Ayson Books, 1997, pp. 38-50.

Morrison Toni. "A Conversation with Bill Moyers" (1989). *Conversations with Toni Morrison*, edited byDanielle Taylor-Guthrie, University of Mississippi Press, 1994, pp. 262-274.

Nathanson, Janice. "Maternal Activism: How Feminist Is It?" *Feminist Mothering*, edited by Andrea O'Reilly, SUNY Press, 2008, pp. 243-256.

Nathanson, Jessica, and Laura Camille Tuley, editors. *Mother Knows Best: Talking Back to the "Experts."* Demeter Press, 2009.

Nelson, Margaret K. *Parenting out of Control: Anxious Parents in Uncertain Times*. New York University Press, 2010.

O'Brien, Mary. *The Politics of Reproduction*. Harper Collins, 1981.

O'Brien Hallstein, D. Lynn. "Second Wave Silences and Third Wave Intensive Mothering." *Mothering and Feminism in the Third Wave*, edited by Amber E. Kinser, Demeter Press, 2008, pp. 107-116.

O'Brien Hallstein, D. Lynn. "Second Wave Successes and Third Wave Struggles." *Women's Studies in Communication*, vol. 31, no. 2, 2008, pp. 143-150.

O'Brien Hallstein, D. Lynn. "Maternal Agency." *Encyclopedia of Motherhood*, edited by Andrea O'Reilly, Sage Press, 2010, pp. 697-699.

O'Brien Hallstein, D. Lynn. "Public Choices, Private Control: How Mediated Mom Labels Work Rhetorically to Dismantle the Politics of Choice and White Second Wave Feminism." *Contemplating Maternity in an Era of Choice: Explorations into Discourses of Reproduction*, edited by Sara Hayden and D. Lynn O'Brien Hallstein. Lexington Books, 2010, pp. 5-27.

O'Brien Hallstein, D. Lynn. *White Feminists and Contemporary Maternity: Purging Matrophobia*. Palgrave, 2010.

O'Brien-Hallstein, D. Lynn. "She Gives Birth, She's Wearing a Bikini: Mobilizing the Postpregnant Celebrity Mom Body to Manage the Post-Second Wave Crisis in Femininity." *Women's Studies in Communication*, vol. 34, no. 2, 2011, pp. 111–138.

O'Brien Hallstein, D. Lynn, and Andrea O'Reilly, editors. *Academic Motherhood in a Post-Second Wave Context: Challenges, Strategies and Possibilities*. Demeter Press, 2012.

O'Brien, Hallstein, D. Lynn, and Andrea O'Reilly. "Introduction," *Academic Motherhood in a Post-Second Wave Context: Challenges, Strategies and Possibilities*, edited by D. Lynn O'Brien Hallstein and Andrea O'Reilly, Demeter Press, 2012, pp. 1-46.

O'Reilly, Andrea. "A Mom and her Son: Thoughts on Feminist Mothering." *Journal of the Association for Research on Mothering*, vol. 2, no. 1, spring-summer, 2000, pp. 179-193.

O'Reilly, Andrea. editor. *Mothers and Sons: Feminism, Masculinity and the Struggle to Raise our Sons*. Routledge, 2000.

O'Reilly, Andrea, editor. *Mother Matters: Motherhood as Discourse and Practice*. Association for Research on Mothering, 2004.

O'Reilly, Andrea, editor. *From Motherhood to Mothering: The Legacy of Adrienne Rich's "Of Woman Born"*. SUNY Press, 2004.

O'Reilly, Andrea, editor. *Mother Outlaws: Theories and Practices of Empowered Mothering*. Women's Press, 2004.

O'Reilly, Andrea. *Toni Morrison and Motherhood: A Politics of the Heart*. SUNY Press, 2004.

O'Reilly, Andrea. "We Were Conspirators, Outlaws from the Institution of Motherhood." Mothering against Motherhood and the Possibility of Empowered Maternity for Mothers and Their Children." *From Motherhood to Mothering: The Legacy of Adrienne Rich's "Of Woman Born"*, edited by Andrea O'Reilly, SUNY Press, 2004, pp. 159-174

O'Reilly, Andrea. "Between the Baby and the Bathwater: Some Thoughts on a Mother Centered Theory and Practice of Feminist Mothering."

Journal of the Association for Research on Mothering, vol. 8, no. 1-2, 2006, pp. 323-330.

O'Reilly, Andrea. *Rocking the Cradle: Thoughts on Motherhood, Feminism, and the Possibility of Empowered Mothering*. Demeter Press, 2006.

O'Reilly, Andrea, editor. *Maternal Theory: Essential Readings*. Demeter Press, 2007.

O'Reilly, Andrea, editor. *Feminist Mothering*. SUNY Press, 2008.

O'Reilly, Andrea, editor. *Maternal Thinking: Philosophy, Politics, Practice*. Demeter Press, 2009.

O'Reilly, Andrea, editor. *Encyclopedia of Mothering*. Sage Press, 2010.

O'Reilly, Andrea, editor. *Twenty-First-Century Motherhood: Experience, Identity, Policy, Agency*. Columbia University Press, 2010.

O'Reilly, Andrea, editor. *The Twenty-First-Century Motherhood Movement: Mothers Speak Out on Why We Need to Change the World and How to Do It*. Demeter Press, 2011.

O'Reilly, Andrea. "I Should Have Married Another Man: Heterosexual Partnerships and their Impact on Mothers' Success in Academe." *Academic Motherhood in a Post-Second Wave Context: Challenges, Strategies and Possibilities*, edited by D. Lynn O'Brien Hallstein and Andrea O'Reilly, 2012, pp. 197-213.

O'Reilly, Andrea. "Introduction." *Mothers, Mothering and Motherhood across Cultural Difference*, edited by Andrea O'Reilly, Demeter Press, 2014, pp. 1-6.

O'Reilly, Andrea, editor. *Mothers, Mothering and Motherhood across Culture Difference: A Reader*. Demeter Press, 2014.

O'Reilly, Andrea, and Sara Ruddick. "A Conversation about Maternal Thinking." *Maternal Thinking: Philosophy, Politics and Practice*, edited by Andrea O'Reilly, Demeter Press, 2009, pp. 14-38.

Orenstein, Peggy. *Flux: Women on Sex, Work, Kids, Love, and Life in a Half-Changed World*. Double Day, 2000.

Pappano, M, Aziza, and Dana Olwan, editors. *Muslim Mothering: Local and Global Histories, Theories, and Practices*. Demeter Press, 2016.

Parker, Roszika. *Mother Love/Mother Hate*. Basic Books, 1995.

Pearson, Allison. *I Don't Know How She Does It: The Life of Kate Reddy, Working Mother*. Anchor, 2002.

Peskowitz, Miriam. *The Truth Behind the Mommy Wars: Who Decides what Makes a Good Mother?* Seal Press, 2005.

Pipher, Mary. *Reviving Ophelia: Saving the Selves of Adolescent Girls*. G.P. Putman's Sons, 1994.

Rainwater, Lee, and William L. Yancey, editors. *The Moynihan Report and the Politics of Controversy*. mit Press, 1967.

Reddy, Maureen, et al., editors. *Mother Journeys: Feminists Write about Mothering*. Spinsters Ink, 1994.

Reddy, Maureen T. *Every Day Acts against Racism: Raising Children in a Multiracial World*. Seal Press, 1996.

Rich, Adrienne. *Of Woman Born: Motherhood as Experience and Institution*. 2nd ed., W.W. Norton, 1986.

Roberts, Dorothy. *Killing the Black Body: Race, Reproduction, and the Meaning of Liberty*. Pantheon Books, 1997.

Ruddick, Sara. *Maternal Thinking: Toward a Politics of Peace*. Beacon Press, 1989.

Rutter, Virginia Beanne. *Celebrating Girls*. Conari Press, 1996.

Sangha, Jasjit Kaur, editor. *South Asian Mothering: Negotiating Culture, Family and Selfhood*. Demeter Press, 2012.

Shaw, Rhonda and Alison Bartlett, editors. *Giving Breastmilk: Body Ethics and Contemporary Breastfeeding Practice*. Demeter Press, 2010.

Shaw, Susan M. and Janet Lee, Oregon State University. *Women's Voices, Feminist Visions: Classic and Contemporary Readings*. 6th ed., McGraw-Hill, 2015.

Shields, Julie. *How to Avoid the Mommy Trap: A Roadmap for Sharing Parenting and Making it Work*. Capital Books, 2002.

Showalter, Elaine. *A Literature of Their Own: British Women Novelists from Brontë to Lessing*. Princeton University Press, 1999.

Showalter, Elaine. "Toward a Feminist Poetics." *The New Feminist Criticism: Essays on Women, Literature and Theory*, edited by Elaine Showalter. 1986, pp. 125-143.

Simeone, Angela. *Academic Women Working Towards Equality*. Bergin and Garvey Publishers, 1987.

Simpson, Bria. *The Balanced Mom: Raising Your Kids without Losing Your Self*. New Harbinger Publications, 2006.

Smith, Babette. *Mothers and Sons: The Truth about Mother-Son Relationships*. Allen and Unwin, 1995.

Smith, Janna Malamud. *A Potent Spell: Mother Love and the Power of Fear*. Houghton Mifflin Company, 2003.

Smith Silva, Dorsia and Janine Santiago, editors. *Latina/Chicana Mothering*. Demeter Press, 2011.

Snitow, Ann. "Feminism and Motherhood: An American Reading." *Maternal Theory: Essential Readings*, edited by Andrea O'Reilly, Demeter Press, 2007, pp. 290-310.

Spivak, Gayatri. *In Other Worlds: Essays in Cultural Politics*. Routledge, 1987.

Stack, Carol B. *All Our Kin: Strategies for Survival in a Black Community*. Harper & Row, 1974.

"Statement on Principles on Family Responsibility and Academic Work," *The American Association of University Professors*, aaup, n.d., www.aaup.org/report/statement-principles-family-responsibilities-and-academic-work. Accessed 11 Sept. 2016.

Stephens, Julie. *Confronting Postmaternal Thinking: Feminism, Memory, and Care*. Columbia University Press, 2011.

Stone, Pamela. *Opting Out? Why Women Really Quit Careers and Head Home*. Berkeley: University of California Press, 2007.

Taylor, Verta, et al. *Feminist Frontiers*. 9th ed., McGraw-Hill, 2012.

"Theory." *Oxford Canadian Dictionary*, 2nd edition, Oxford University Press, 2006.

Thurer, Shari. *The Myths of Motherhood: How Culture Reinvents the Good Mother*. Penguin, 1994.

Tiemann, Amy. *Mojo Mom: Nurturing Your Self While Raising a Family*. Avery, 2009.

Tong, Rosemarie. *Feminist Thought: A More Comprehensive Introduction*. 4th ed., Westview Press, 2014.

Trebilcot, Joyce, editor. *Mothering: Essays in Feminist Theory*. Rowman and Littlefield, 1984.

Tucker, Judith Stadtman. "The Motherhood Papers: Morality or Equality? Maternal Thinking and the Social Agenda." *The Mothers Movement Online*, The Mothers Movement Online, 2003, www.mothersmovement.org/features/mhoodpapers/maternalism/morality_equality.htm. Accessed 11 Sept. 2016.

Tucker, Judith Stadtman. "Motherhood and its Discontents: The Political and Ideological Grounding of the 21st Century Mothers' Movement." *"Motherhood and Feminism" Conference, Association for Research on Mothering*, Toronto, Ontario, 2004.

Tucker, Judith Stadtman. "The Motherhood Papers: The New Future of Motherhood: Mothers Don't 'Choose' Their Way Into the Motherhood

Problem, and We Can't Choose Our Way Out of it. So Where Do we go From Here." *The Mothers Movement Online*. The Mothers Movement Online, 2005, www.mother-smovement.org/features/mhoodpapers/new_future/0505_1.htm. Accessed 11 Sept. 2016.

Tucker, Judith Stadtman. "Rocking the Boat: Feminism and the Ideological Grounding to the Twenty-First Mothers' Movement." *Feminist Mothering*, edited by Andrea O'Reilly, SUNY Press, 2008, pp. 205-218.

Tucker, Judith Stadtman. "From Choice to Change: Rewriting the Script of Motherhood as Maternal Activism." *Twenty-First-Century Motherhood Movement: Experience, Identity, Policy, Agency*, edited by Andrea O'Reilly. Columbia University Press, pp. 293-309.

Turnage, Barbara. "The Global Self-Esteem of an African-American Adolescent Female and Her Relationship with Her Mother." *Mothers and Daughters: Connection, Empowerment and Transformation*, edited by Andrea O'Reilly and Sharon Abbey. Rowman and Littlefield, 2001, pp. 175-187.

Umansky, Lauri. *Motherhood Reconceived: Feminism and the Legacies of the Sixties*. New York University Press, 1996.

Vandenbeld Giles, Melinda. "Introduction: An Alternative Mother-Centered Economic Paradigm." *Mothering in the Age of Neo-Liberalism*, edited by Melinda Vandenbeld Giles, Demeter Press, 2014, pp. 1-30.

Walker, Alice. *In Search of Our Mothers' Gardens*. Harcourt Brace Jovanovich, 1983.

Walker, Rebecca. "Becoming the Third Wave." *Ms. Magazine*, Jan. 1992, pp. 39-43.

Wane, Njoki Nathani. "Reflections on the Mutuality of Mothering: Women, Children and Othermothering." *Journal of the Association for Research on Mothering*, vol. 2, no. 2, fall-winter 2000, pp. 105-116.

Waring, Marilyn. *If Women Counted: A New Feminist Economics*. Harper and Row, 1988.

Warner, Judith. *Perfect Madness: Motherhood in the Age of Anxiety*. Riverhead Books, 2005.

Ward, Kelly, and Lisa Wolf-Wendel. "Academic Motherhood: Managing Complex Roles in Research Universities." *The Review of Higher Education*, vol. 27, no. 3, 2004, pp. 233-257.

Wells, Jess. "Lesbians Raising Sons." *Mothers and Sons: Feminism, Masculinity and the Struggle to Raise Our Sons*. Routledge, 2001, pp. 157-162.

Westkott, Marcia. "Mothers and Daughters in the World of the Father." *Frontiers*, vol.3, no. 2, 1978, pp. 16-21.

Wilkinson, Stephanie. "Say You Want A Revolution? Why the Mothers' Revolution Hasn't Happened ... Yet." *Brain, Child Magazine*. Brain, Child. 2005, www.brainchildmag.com/essays/ fall2005_wilkinson.html. Accessed 11 Sept. 2016.

Williams, Joan. *Unbending Gender: Why Family and Work Conflict and What To Do About It*. Oxford University Press, 2000.

Wilson, Natalie. "From Gestation to Delivery: The Embodied Activist Mothering of Cindy Sheehan and Jennifer Schumaker." *Mothers Who Deliver: Feminist Interventions in Public and Interpersonal Discourse*, edited by Joceyln Fenton-Stitt and Pageen Reichert Powell, SUNY Press, 2010, pp. 231-252.

Wilson, Robin. "How Babies Alter Careers for Academics: Having Children often Bumps Women off the Tenure Track a New Study Shows." *The Chronicle of Higher Education*, December 5, 2003: 1-7.

Wolf, Naomi. *The Beauty Myth*. Anchor Books, 1991.

Wolf, Naomi. *Misconceptions: Truth, Lies, and the Unexpected on the Journey to Motherhood*. Anchor Books, 2003.

Wong, Gina. "Images and Echoes in Matroreform: A Cultural Feminist Perspective." *Journal of the Association for Research on Mothering*, vol. 8, no. 1-2, 2006, pp. 135-146.

Woolf, Virginia. *A Room of One's Own*. Oxford, 1929.

Wolfinger, Nicholas, et al. "Alone in the Ivory Tower: How Birth Events Vary among Fast-Track Professionals." Paper presented at the *2008 Annual Meeting of the Population Association of America*, New Orleans, LA., 2008.

Wood, Julia T. *Gendered Lives: Communication, Gender, and Culture*. 7th ed., Wadsworth, 2007.

Appendices

Appendix A

GWST 2513
Mothering and Motherhood
Fall-Winter 2015-2016, York University

Course Description:

This course explores mothering-motherhood as it is examined in contemporary maternal theory. Students will read most of the key theorists on motherhood across a wide range of perspectives and disciplines. As well, students will take up various issues and perspectives from the theories and examine them in fiction. Class, cultural, and racial differences of mothering and motherhood will be emphasized.

Course Learning Objectives:

The purpose of this course is to assist students in developing a critical overview of the issues mothers face in contemporary societies, locally and globally. Students will be able to identify the myths of motherhood and the social, political, and economic inequalities influencing maternal-child welfare. At the end of this course, students will have a broad familiarity with feminist theoretical, fictional, and empirical literature about mothers, mothering, and motherhood.

The specific objectives of the course are that students will be able to:

- Understand the difference between motherhood as institution and mothering as experience
- Understand how and why motherhood functions as a patriarchal institution that is culturally produced and how and why such an institution oppresses women

- Critically engage with various feminist theories on patriarchal motherhood
- Apply such theories to mothering narratives
- Understand how mothering as experience may be a place or position of empowerment and agency for women
- Critically engage with key interdisciplinary readings about mothering and motherhood relevant for students in women's studies, humanities, social science, social work, sociology, and political science

Required Texts: Available In Bookstore

Laurence Margaret, *Fire Dwellers*. 1969. McClelland and Stewart, 1991.

O'Reilly, Andrea. editor. *Mothers, Mothering, Motherhood Across Cultural Difference: A Reader*. Demeter Press, 2014.

O'Reilly, Andrea, editor. *Maternal Theory: Essential Readings*. Demeter Press, 2007.

Pearson, Allison. *I Don't Know How She Does It*. Random House, 2002.

Rich, Adrienne. *Of Woman Born*. W. W. Norton, 2006.

Shriver, Lionel. *We Need to Talk about Kevin*. HarperCollins, 2003.

Toews, Miriam. *Summer of My Amazing Luck*. Random House, 2006.

Course Schedule

First Term

Week One: Introduction

Week Two: Mothering versus motherhood; overview of the history of motherhood: Rich *Of Woman Born* and Thurer (page 331 of *Maternal Theory*); Film *The Goddess Remembered*

Motherhood

Week Three: As above.

Week Four: Intensive mothering, sensitive mothering, natural mothering, new momism, motherhood religion: Hays (page 408); Bobel (page 782); Wakerdine and Lucy (page 224); Warner (page 705); and Micheals and Douglas (page 617) in *Maternal Theory*; Film: *Rosie the Riveter*.

Week Five: Continue with above readings.

Week Six: Maternal Thinking, Wife Role, and Mask of Motherhood: Ruddick (page 96), Maushart (page 460) in *Maternal Theory*, and Johnson (emailed).

Week Seven: As above. Mother Blame and Bad Mothers: Caplan (page 592) and Ladd-Taylor (page 660) in *Maternal Theory*.

Week Eight: As above: Laurence, *Fire Dwellers*.

Week Nine: Pearson, *I Don't Know How She Does It*.

Week Ten: Shriver, *We Need to Talk about Kevin*; **ESSAY DUE.**

Week Eleven: Continue with Shriver. Introduction to *Reader* and Introduction to *Mother Outlaws* (emailed); Working Mothers and Stay at Home Mothers; Guerrina (page 467) and Bode/ Letherby (page 429) in *Reader*; and Crittenden (page 601) in *Maternal Theory*.

Week Twelve: As above; Film: *The Motherload*; **JOURNALS DUE.**

Second Term

Mothering

Week Thirteen: *African American Mothering*: Hill-Collins (page 274 and 311), hooks (page 266), in *Maternal Theory* and O'Reilly (page 93) in *Reader*.

Week Fourteen: As above.

Week Fifteen: Aboriginal Mothering: Anderson (page 761) in *Maternal Theory* and Brant (page 7) in *Reader*.

Week Sixteen: As above.

Week Seventeen: Young Mothers: Byrd (page 487) in *Reader* and *Summer of My Amazing Luck*.

Week Eighteen: As above.

Week Nineteen: Queer Mothering: Lorde (page 157), Cooper (page 186), Lewin (page 370) and Polikoff (page 194) in *Maternal Theory*; Gibson (page 347) in *Reader*; Film: *Politics of the Heart*.

Week Twenty: As above.

Week Twenty-One: Feminist/Empowered Mothering: Gore (page 756) and O'Reilly (page 792) in *Maternal Theory*.

Week Twenty-Two: As above.

Week Twenty-Three: Matricentric Feminism/Maternal Activism: "Maternal Activism: The 21st Century Motherhood Movement" (emailed): Film: *Every Mother's Son*.
ESSAY DUE.

Week Twenty-Four: As above and Wrap Up:
JOURNAL DUE.

Assignments

Attendance-Participation: **10%**

First Essay (5-7 pages): **20%**

Two journals (For each term the student is to submit **six (for a total of 12)** 2-3 page analyses of class readings): **40%**

Final Essay (8-10 pages): **30%**

Appendix B

National Women Studies Association (NWSA) Data: 2011-2015

Methods: This data was collected through a search of the *All Academic Convention* website: https://convention2.allacademic. com/one/nwsa/nwsa15/. This website includes NWSA papers, sessions, panels, and workshops (including topics and themes). The website, however, is not very user friendly: searches come back with panels and individual papers listed. True counts were, thus, difficult to determine. Below are searches for panels that are based on research area. Each panel has approximately three or four presenters. Workshops are listed separately.

NWSA: Data from the past five years (online data only available for this time period) lists approximately 3,364 papers. Aside from motherhood-mothering, top panels or themes are listed below; the total number of papers is listed in parenthesis after the name of the conference, followed by a list of thematic panels and the number of papers presented on each. Of the total number of papers presented during this period, only three percent were on motherhood-mothering.

NWSA 2015 Conference, Milwaukee, Wisconsin (506): motherhood (18), race (27), transnational (40), feminisms (43), intersectionality (48), activism (54), and academe (57).

NWSA 2014 San Juan, Puerto Rico (593): motherhood (29), African American (46), pedagogy (49), feminisms (52), transnational (53), academe (61), social justice (86), and activism (110).

NWSA 2013 Cincinnati, Ohio (767): maternal (4), transnational (23), motherhood (24), race (25), activism (29), work (31), politics (44), queer (47), feminism (49), and trans (67).

NWSA 2012 Oakland, California (741): maternal (3), motherhood (10), Indigenous (17), transnational (33), work (45), race (68), gender (70), and feminisms (164).

NWSA 2011 Atlanta, Georgia (757): maternal (2), motherhood (19), queer (45), work (46), race (50), transnational (86), and feminisms (184).

Appendix C

Top Five Academic Journals
January 2006 to December 2016

Methods: We obtained this data by conducting an extensive online search of the top five women, gender, and feminist studies academic journals. Based on those results, we looked up the table of contents for *Signs, Frontiers, Feminist Studies, Women's Studies Quarterly,* and *Gender & Society,* and inputted them into a spreadsheet. From there, we searched for keywords using the *countif* function. Chapters covered a very broad range of topics.

Below are the figures for the following topics: mothers, maternal, and mothering; gender; and sexuality, sexualize,* and sex.

Please note that we used the wildcard * to come up with different variations of words. The journal *Gender & Society* has a very searchable database, so we were able to input keywords directly.

Signs: 899 articles

motherhood-maternal: 3%
sex: 11%
gender: 17%

Frontiers: 300 articles

motherhood-maternal: 6%
gender: 8%
sexuality-sexualize*-sex: 5%

Feminist Studies: 491 articles

motherhood-maternal: 1.6%
gender: 9%
sexuality-sexualize*-sex: 10%

Women's Studies Quarterly: 733 articles

motherhood-maternal: 4%
gender: 6%
sexuality-sexualize*-sex: 4%

***Gender & Society*:** 844 articles

motherhood-maternal: 5%
gender: 31%
sexuality-sexualize*-sex: 11%

Appendix D

Introduction to Women's Studies Textbooks

Methods: Once we searched through the introductory to women's studies syllabi, we looked for trends in introductory textbooks. Below are the top ten textbooks that we examined. During our investigation, we briefly looked up the table of contents for each book and checked for motherhood content. If there was no motherhood content, we looked for material related to families and family systems.

Braithwaite, Ann, and Catherine M. Orr. *Everyday Women's and Gender Studies: Introductory Concepts.* Routledge, 2016.

- No motherhood content

Launius, Christie, and Holly Hassel. *Threshold Concepts in Women's and Gender Studies: Ways of Seeing, Thinking, and Knowing.* Routledge, 2015.

- No motherhood content

Shaw, Susan M., and Janet Lee. *Women's Voices, Feminist Visions: Classic and Contemporary Readings.* 6th edition, McGraw-Hill, 2014.

Family topics covered in the "Family Systems, Family Lives" include the following:

- Definitions of Family
- Institutional Connections
- Power and Family Relationships
- Mothering
- Marriage and Love
- Who Wants to Marry a Feminist?
- Don't Give Up Your Day Job: Leslie Bennetts on the Feminine Mistake
- Partners as Parents: Challenges Faced by Gays Denied Marriage
- Hardscrabble Salvation

Motherhood readings include:

- Beth Schwartzapfel, "Lullabies Behind Bars."
- Maya Angelou, "Our Grandmothers."

Hobbs, Margaret, and Carla Rice. *Gender and Women's Studies in Canada: Critical Terrain.* Toronto: Women's Press, 2013. Print.

Motherhood readings include:

- Paula Caplan, "Don't Blame Mother: Then and Now."
- Margaret Hillyard Little, "The Leaner, Meaner Welfare Machine: The Ontario Conservative Government's Ideological and Material Attack on Single Mothers."

Kirk, Gwyn and Margo Okazawa-Rey. *Women's Lives: Multicultural Perspectives.* 6th ed., McGraw-Hill, 2012.

Motherhood readings include:

- Paula Gunn Allen, "Who Is Your Mother? Red Roots of White Feminism."
- Julia Ward Howe, "Mother's Day Proclamation–1870."
- Ann Crittenden, "The Mommy Tax."

Taylor, Verta, Nancy Whittier, and Leila Rupp. *Feminist Frontiers.* 9th ed., McGraw-Hill, 2011.

Chapters on the family include the following:

- Carolyn Herbst Lewis, "Waking Sleeping Beauty: The Premarital Pelvic Exam and Heterosexuality During the Cold War."
- Laurie Essig and Lynn Owens, "What if Marriage is Bad for Us?"
- Kathleen Gerson, "Moral Dilemmas, Moral Strategies, and the Transformation of Gender: Lessons from Two Generations of Work and Family Change."
- Hung Cam Thai, "For Better or Worse: Gender Allures in the Vietnamese Global Marriage Market."

Kimmel Michael, and Jacqueline Holler. *The Gendered Society.* Oxford University Press, 2011. Print.

The book includes the section "The Gendered Family: Gender at the Heart of the Home" with the following chapters listed:

- Gillian Ranson, "No Longer 'One of the Boys': Negotiations with Motherhood, as Prospect or Reality, among Women in Engineering."

- Lena Dominelli, Susan Strega, Chris Walmsley, Marilyn Callahan, and Leslie Brown, "'Here's My Story': Fathers of 'Looked After' Children Recount Their Experiences in the Canadian Child Welfare System."
- Anne Martin-Matthews, "Situating 'Home' at the Nexus of Public and Private Spheres: Aging, Gender, and Home Support Work in Canada."
- Scott Coltrane, "Household Labour and the Routine Production of Gender."

Disch, E. *Reconstructing Gender: A Multicultural Anthology.* 5th ed., McGraw-Hill, 2008.

A section on families includes the following chapters:

- Jeanne Flavin, "Contemporary Challenges to Black Women's Reproductive Rights."
- Patricia Hill Collins, "Bloodmothers, Othermothers, and Women-Centered Networks."
- Kathleen Gerson, "Dilemmas of Involved Fatherhood."
- Audre Lorde, "Man Child: A Black Lesbian Feminist's Response."
- Raul E. Ybarra, "I Am a Man."
- E.J. Graff, "What Is Marriage For?"
- Pat Gozemba and Karen Kahn, "Free to Marry, At Last—May 17, 2004."

The book contains one chapter on motherhood:

– Susan Douglas and Meredith Michaels, "The New Momism."

Findlen, Barbara. *Listen Up: Voices From the Next Feminist Generation.* Seal Press 2001.

– No motherhood content

hooks, bell. *Feminism Is for Everybody: Passionate Politics.* South End Press, 2000.

– Chapter on feminist parenting by bell hooks

Appendix E

Introduction to Women's Studies Syllabi

Methods: Data collection for course syllabi included a call-out through our networks (via our constant contact email database) and social networking sites (Facebook and Twitter). This call-out produced twenty-one course syllabi. The rest were either taken directly from university websites or through email requests to departmental administrators and course instructors. We received course syllabi from different sections of the same university as well. These syllabi greatly differed in content and topics. In addition, some course instructors were extremely resistant and refused to give copies of their syllabus because of intellectual property rights concerns.

Fifty Course Syllabi

*different professors and sections listed for the same university

Keene State College #1*: IIWGS 101: Introduction to Women's and Gender Studies

Keene State College #2*: IIWGS 101: Introduction to Women's and Gender Studies

Texas Christian University #1*: WOST 20003: Introduction to Women's Studies: Sex, Gender, and the Disciplines

Texas Christian University #2*: WOST 20003: Introduction to Women's Studies: Sex, Gender, and the Disciplines

Roosevelt University: WGS 110-02: Introduction to Women's and Gender Studies

Cottey College #1*: WST 105: Introduction to Women's Studies

Cottey College #2*: WST 105: Introduction to Women's Studies

Gettysburg College: WGS 120: Introduction to Women, Gender, & Sexuality Studies

University of South Florida #1*: WST 3015: Introduction to Women's (and Gender) Studies

University of South Florida #2*: WSS 3015: Introduction to Women's Studies

Sonoma State University: WGS 280.2: Women's Bodies: Health and Image

University of New Brunswick: GWS 1003: Intro to Gender & Women's Studies

The George Washington University: Women's Studies 2120: Introduction to Women's Studies

SUNY Genseo #1*: WMGST 100: Introduction to Women's & Gender Studies

SUNY Genseo #2*: WMGST 100: Introduction to Women's Studies

Rhode Island College: GEND 200-01: Gender and Society

Mount Royal University: Sociology 2233: Sociology of Gender

Virginia Tech: WGS 1824: Introduction to Women's and Gender Studies

University of Wisconsin: WST 150: Introduction to Women's and Gender Studies

Concordia University: WSDB 290/4 Introduction to Historical Perspectives in Women's Studies

University of Lethbridge #1*: WGST 1000Y: Knowing Bodies: An Introduction to Women and Gender Studies

University of Lethbridge #2*: WGST 1000Y: Knowing Bodies: An Introduction to Women and Gender Studies

University of Alberta: WGS 101: Representations of Girls and Women

University of Alberta: WGS 220: Women in Canadian Society

Saint Mary's University: WMST 1200.1 Introduction to Women and Gender Studies

Brock University: WGST 1F90: Introduction to Women's and Gender Studies

Acadia University: WGST 1413: Introduction to Women's and Gender Studies

University of Waterloo: WS 101: Introduction to Women's Studies

University of Western Ontario: Women's Studies 1020E: Introduction to Women's Studies

University of Wisconsin: WS 102: Gender, Women and Society.

University of Maryland: WMST250: Introduction to Women's Studies: Women, Art, and Culture

University of Calgary: Women's Studies 201: Introduction to Women's Studies

University of Saskatchewan: WGST 112.3: Introduction to Women's and Gender Studies

Columbia University, Barnard College: WMST V1001, Introduction to Women's and Gender Studies

Brandon University #1*: GWS 36:161: Introduction to Women's Studies: Issues in Feminism

Brandon University #2*: GWS 36:161: Introduction to Women's Studies: Issues in Feminism.

University of Victoria: GWS 36:162: Introduction to Women's Studies: Contemporary Issues in Gender

Massachusetts Institute of Technology: WGS.101: Introduction to Women's and Gender Studies

McGill University: WMST 200: Introduction to Women's Studies

Wilfred Laurier University: WS1000: Introduction to Women and Gender Studies

Maryland University: WMST 200: Introduction to Women's Studies

Pittsburgh University: GSWS 0100: Introduction to Gender, Sexuality, and Women's Studies

Seneca College: SOC211: Women's Studies Introduction

Yukon College: WGST 100: Introduction to Women's Studies I

Nipissing University: GEND 1006: Introduction to Gender, Power, and Justice

Lakehead University: Women's Studies 1100: Women's and Gender Studies

University of Hawaii: WS 151: Introduction to Women's Studies

University of Ottawa: FEM1100: Women, Gender, Feminism: An Introduction

University of Massachusetts: WS 201: Critical Perspectives in Women's Studies

Washington State University: Women's Studies 101.1: Gender and Power: Introduction to Women's Studies

Chapters and Sections on Motherhood

Virginia Tech: Introduction to Women's and Gender Studies

Kalindi Vora, "Indian Transnational Surrogacy and the Disaggregation of Motherhood Work."

Laura Briggs, "Why Feminists Should Care about the Baby Veronica Case."

The George Washington University: Introduction to Women's Studies

Diane Bell, "In Search of Australian Women," edited by Diane Bell and Ponch Hawkes, *Generations: Grandmothers, Mothers, and Daughters*, Spinifex, 1987, pp. 257-268.

University of Wisconsin: Introduction to Women's and Gender Studies

Documentary viewing: "The Business of Being Born"

Joy Harjo, "Three Generations of Native American Women's Birth Experience"

Judith Arcana, "Abortion is a Motherhood Issue"

American Congress of Obstetrics & Gynecologists, "Statement on Home Births"

Rahina Reiko Rizzuto, "What My Mother Never Told Me, or How I Was Blindsided by Childbirth and Survived"

Naomi Wolf, "Giving Birth" Childbirth Panel

Acadia: Introduction to Women's and Gender Studies

Patricia Hill Collins, "Shifting the Center: Race, Class and Feminist Theorizing about Motherhood." *Mothering: Ideology, Experience and Agency*, edited by E. Nakano Glenn et al., Routledge, 1994, pp. 45-65.

University of Lethbridge: Knowing Bodies: An Introduction to Women and Gender Studies

Women and the Family: Nicholas D Kristof and Sheryl Wu Dunn, *Half the Sky: Turning Oppression into Opportunity for Women Worldwide*. Vintage Books, 2010, pp. 61-92;

Betty Friedan, "The Problem That Has No Name." *The Feminine Mystique*, W.W. Norton & Company, 1963, pp. 57-78.

University of Saskatchewan: Introduction to Women's and Gender Studies

Fiona Nelson, "Becoming a Lesbian Mother"

University of Hawaii: Introduction to Women's Studies

Patricia Hill Collins, "The Meaning of Motherhood in Black Culture and Black Mother-Daughter Relationships"

Gettysburg College: Introduction to Women's Studies

Interview Project worth 15% of grade. This assignment requires you to interview two women from two different generations from your own family (for example, mother and grandmother), to report the findings, and to write a reflective response. Goals include: gaining an understanding of your mother's perspective on feminism, the women's movement, and women's roles. The student should then reflect on her or his mother's responses. Are there any surprises? Are there similarities with your own views? Most importantly, how do you feel your mother's perspectives have affected you and the choices you have made in life? For male students, how do you feel your mother's perspectives have influenced your perceptions of women? Offer critical analysis and connect your research observations with relevant theory from the class—make connections. Do not assume that you "already know" your mother's or interviewee's answers—respectfully ask her these questions as a professional researcher and record her responses as exactly as you can.

University of Windsor: Introduction to Women's and Gender Studies

Penni Mitchell, "Mommies Yes, Women No"

Nadra Kareem, "All in the Family: A Q&A with Author Rebecca Walker" Bree Kessler, "VW's High-Concept(ion) Advertising"

Deesha Philyawm, "Ain't I A Mommy?"

Veronica I. Arreola, "Mommy and Me: Looking for Missing Voices in the Burgeoning World of Mom Blogs"

University of Alberta: WGS 220: Women in Canadian Society

Angela Y. Davis, "Outcast Mothers and Surrogates: Racism and Reproductive Politics in the Nineties"

Chapters and Sections on the Family

Wilfrid Laurier: Introduction to Women and Gender Studies
- Gender and the Family
- Family Systems
- Family Lives
- Marriage and Love Partnership Laws

University of New Brunswick: Introduction to Gender and Women's Studies
- World's Toughest Job
- Why Women Can't Have it All

Saint Mary's University: Introduction to Women and Gender Studies
- Four classes on families

About the Author

Andrea O'Reilly, PhD, is full professor in the School of Gender, Sexuality and Women's Studies at York University, founder and director of *The Motherhood Initiative* (1998-2019), founder/editor-in-chief of the *Journal of the Motherhood Initiative* and publisher of Demeter Press. She is the founder and creator of the Mothers and Covid-19 Facebook Group. She is co-editor/editor of twenty-five books including *Mothers, Mothering, and COVID-19: Dispatches from a Pandemic* (2021), *Feminist Parenting: Perspectives from Africa and Beyond* (2020) and *Feminist Perspectives on Young Mothers and Mothering* (2019). She is editor of the *Encyclopedia on Motherhood* (2010) and co-editor of the *Routledge Companion to Motherhood* (2019). Her forthcoming edited collections include: *Monstrous Mothers: Troubling Tropes* (2021), and *Maternal Regret: Resistances, Renunciations, and Reflections* (2022). She is author of *Toni Morrison and Motherhood: A Politics of the Heart* (2004); *Rocking the Cradle: Thoughts on Motherhood, Feminism, and the Possibility of Empowered Mothering* (2006); and *Matricentric Feminism: Theory, Activism, and Practice* (2016). She is currently writing the monograph *Matricritics: Reading the Maternal in Post-2010 Women's Fiction* and conducting a SSHRC funded research project on Mothers and Covid-19. She has presented her research at over one hundred conferences, has authored eighty articles/chapters and has received more than a million dollars in grant funding for her research projects. She is twice the recipient of York University's "Professor of the Year Award" for teaching excellence and is the 2019 recipient of the Status of Women and Equity Award of Distinction from OCUFA (Ontario Confederation of University Faculty Associations).

About the Cover Artist

Stephanie Jonsson is a PhD. Candidate in the School of Gender, Feminist, and Women's Studies at York University. In February 2020, Stephanie began experimenting with painting to cope with stress, anxiety, and imposter syndrome. Her favorite technique is acrylic paint pouring which she uses to make abstract art. *Sundays are for crafting* is a motto Stephanie now lives by to remind herself about the importance of stepping back from our work lives so we can find our passion in life.

Stephanie's art can be found on Instagram at Femdemic_Creations.

Deepest appreciation to
Demeter's monthly Donors

DEMETER

Daughters
Rebecca Bromwich
Summer Cunningham
Tatjana Takseva
Debbie Byrd
Fiona Green
Tanya Cassidy
Vicki Noble
Bridget Boland
Naomi McPherson
Myrel Chernick

Sisters
Kirsten Goa
Amber Kinser
Nicole Willey
Christine Peets